MOTHER JOURNEYS

Feminists Write about Mothering

MOTHER
JOURNEYS

Feminists Write about Mothering

Edited by

Maureen T. Reddy, Martha Roth, and Amy Sheldon

spinsters ink
minneapolis

10 9 8 7 6 5 4 3 2

Spinsters Ink
P.O. Box 300170
Minneapolis, MN 55403-5170

Cover Art and Design
Tara Christopherson, Fruitful Results Design

Production

Melanie Cockrell	Cynthia Fogard	Lou Ann Matossian
Lynette D'Amico	Kelly Kager	Liz Tufte
Patty Delaney	Carolyn Law	Susan Vaughan
Helen Dooley	Lori Loughney	Nancy Walker
Joan Drury	Rhonda Lundquist	

Library of Congress Cataloging-in-Publication Data
Mother journeys: feminists write about mothering / edited by Maureen Reddy, Martha Roth, Amy Sheldon.
    p.   cm.
  ISBN 1-883523-04-4 : $29.95. — ISBN 1-883523-03-6 (pbk.) : $15.95
  1. Mother and child—Literary collections. 2. American literature—Women authors.
  3. Motherhood—Literary collections. 4. Feminism—Literary collections.
  I. Reddy, Maureen T. II. Roth, Martha. III. Sheldon, Amy, 1942–
PS509.M6M57   1994
810.8'03520431—dc20
94–18338
CIP

Printed on recycled paper with soy ink

Dedication

_____

For our mothers and our daughters:
Belle
Jennifer
Joann
Molly
Nicole
Siobhan
Sylvia
Talia

Acknowledgments

(This page is an extension of the copyright page.)

"Statement to the Court" by Martha Boesing is reprinted from *Hurricane Alice: A Feminist Quarterly,* Vol. 1, No. 2, Fall/Winter 1983-84. Reprinted by permission of the author.

"Untitled" photo and text by Judith Lermer Crawley is excerpted from *Giving Birth Is Just the Beginning: Women Speak about Mothering,* Judith Lermer Crawley. Montreal: Book Project, 1987. The book may be ordered ($20.00 U.S., $25.00 Canadian) from Montreal: Book Project, Box 275, Station NDG, Montreal, Quebec, Canada H4A 3P6.

"Missing" by Rita Dove first appeared in *Ploughshares,* Vol. 15, No. 4, Winter 1989. "Persephone Falling" and "Persephone Underground" by Rita Dove first appeared in *Sequoia,* Vol. 32, No. 1, Spring/Summer 1988. Reprinted by permission of the author.

"Three Sonnets for Iva" by Marilyn Hacker first appeared in *Taking Notice,* Alfred A. Knopf, 1980. Copyright © 1990 by Marilyn Hacker. Reprinted by permission of the author.

"Mother Underground" by Molly Hite is reprinted in part from *Feminist Studies,* Volume 20, No. 1 (Spring 1994): pp. 59-66, by permission of the publisher, Feminist Studies, Inc. c/o Women's Studies Program, University of Maryland, College Park, MD 20742.

"Overzealous Superheroes" and "Syl, Are There Summer Camps for Pre-Borns?" copyright © 1990 by Nicole Hollander. "When Moms Get Their Own Fairy Godmother" copyright © 1991 by Nicole Hollander. Reprinted by permission of Sylvia Syndicates and Nicole Hollander.

"Counting Cost" from *Healing Heart* Copyright © 1989 by Gloria T. Hull. Used by permission of the author and of Kitchen Table: Women of Color Press, P.O. Box 908, Latham, NY 12110.

"Blood Chant" by Linnea Johnson was first published in *Women's Review of Books,* 1988. Reprinted by permission of the author.

"Beginning with Gussie" by Maxine Kumin is from *Women, Animals and Vegetables: Essays and Stories,* and is reprinted with the permission of W.W. Norton & Company, Inc. Originally from *The American Voice,* 1991. Copyright © 1991 by Maxine Kumin.

"The Mother Journey" by Molly Layton first appeared in the *The Family Therapy Networker,* 1989. Reprinted by permission of the author.

"Black and Blue" by Jane Lazarre is from *Worlds Beyond My Control,* by Jane Lazarre, Dutton (an imprint of New American Library, a division of Penguin U.S.A.), 1991. pp. 87-102. Reprinted by permission of The Wendy Weil Agency, Inc. Copyright © 1991 by Jane Lazarre.

"On Weaning in America" is from *Winter Place,* by Genny Lim, Kearney Street Workshop Press, © 1989. Reprinted by permission of the author.

"Mother and Child: The Erotic Bond" by Lynda Marín first appeared in *Sub/versions.* Feminist Studies, working paper No. 11. University of California, Santa Cruz. Winter 1992.

"Reflections on Motherhood" by Greta Hofmann Nemiroff was first published in *Giving Birth Is Just the Beginning: Women Speak about Mothering,* by Judith Lermer Crawley. Montreal: Book Project, 1987. The book may be ordered ($20.00 U.S., $25.00 Canadian) from Montreal: Book Project, Box 275, Station NDG, Montreal, Quebec, Canada H4A 3P6.

"The Moment the Two Worlds Meet" by Sharon Olds is from *The Gold Cell* by Sharon Olds. Copyright © 1987 by Sharon Olds. Reprinted by permission of Alfred A. Knopf, Inc.

"Cambodia" by Alicia Ostriker was previously published in The *Mother/Child Papers,* Santa Monica: Momentum Press, 1980. Reprinted by Beacon Press, 1986. Reprinted by permission of the author.

"Once More Out of Darkness" by Alicia Ostriker was originally published in *Once More Out of Darkness and Other Poems,* by Alicia Ostriker, Berkeley Poets Co-op and Press, 1974. Reprinted by permission of the author.

"All the Women Caught in Flaring Light," by Minnie Bruce Pratt originally appeared in *Crime Against Nature* by Minnie Bruce Pratt, Firebrand Books, Ithaca, New York. Copyright © 1990 by Minnie Bruce Pratt. Reprinted by permission of the author.

"The Reconstruction" by Judy Remington first appeared in *Hurricane Alice: A Feminist Quarterly,* Vol. 7, No. 4, 1990. Reprinted by permission of the author.

"Kings Are Royaler Than Queens" by Amy Sheldon first appeared in *Young Children* Vol. 45, No.2, pp.4-9. National Association for the Education of Young Children: Washington, DC. Copyright © 1990 by Amy Sheldon. Reprinted by permission of the author.

"Jessica's Poems" by Madelon Sprengnether first appeared in slightly different form in *Hurricane Alice: A Feminist Quarterly,* Vol. 4, No. 3, 1987. Reprinted by permission of the author.

Table of Contents

Section II
Discoveries Through Our Children

Section III
The Politics of Mothering

Section IV
Continuity with Our Own Mothers

Prologue:

What is "Feminist Mothering"?

From the beginning of the contemporary feminist movement, mothers and motherhood have been important topics of discussion; oddly, though, in reviewing the literature of feminism, readers seldom discover the voices of feminist mothers themselves speaking *as mothers*. Usually mothers are objects of analysis, with feminists often replicating the nonfeminist interest in mothers chiefly as objects of their children's demands. Feminism has been largely the daughter's critique.

When we editors thought about it, we found some likely reasons for this relegation of mothers to, at best, a secondary position: women are all daughters first. If daughters become mothers, it is only after years of relating to mother figures from whom daughters must in many cases struggle to differentiate ourselves. For many feminists, self-definition has come in opposing their mothers' values, viewpoints, and voices. At best, feminists have been able to "understand" their thoughts and actions in the context of their lives at a particular historical moment; feminists may also "reconcile" themselves with mothers. Specific honoring of the mother in each woman—relinquishing or re-thinking the privilege of the daughter who questions and reinvents the family— can feel dangerous. Fear of this dangerous identity may masquerade as boredom: "Nobody wants to hear from their *mother.*"

This collection seeks to shift the focus of attention from daughters to mothers. As editors, we asked feminist mothers to tell us what the experience of mothering means to them: how it affects their lives and their work, how it relates to their politics, what it is like to mother. Our intention is to honor the voice of the feminist mother, the mother who criticizes the status quo and who does not want to turn her children into new little patriarchal replicants.

What does it mean to be a feminist mother in the 1990s? This collection offers multiple, complicated, sometimes contradictory answers to that question. The essays, stories, poems, and art in *Mother Journeys* testify to feminists' varying experiences of motherhood, including struggling single mothers, lesbian adoptive mothers, professional women wounded in their attempts to bear children, and middle-aged mothers muddling through their children's adolescence. African-American, Asian-American, European-American, Latina, Jewish-American, and Native American women speak from unique experiences of coming to feminist consciousness.

These pieces are grouped into sections reflecting a sense of their generational continuity: "Discovering Ourselves," "Discoveries through Our Children," "The Politics of Mothering," and "Continuity with Our Own Mothers." Each section opens with one of Nancy Spero's wonderful drawings, which look at the violence in mothering, vividly showing how images of nurture and creation can be turned back on themselves—how phallic bomb imagery can be united with misogynist violence. A number of themes run through and across these sections: violence; conflict with majority values, especially as represented by children's schools; sadness at children's inevitable contact with racist, misogynist culture; and pride in self and family for doing things in feminist ways.

Some of the contributors to this volume have faced terrible difficulties; some continue in hardship and many in uncertainty. The writers range in age from their twenties to their sixties. Some are wives, some are single, some live in lesbian or heterosexual relationships. Our contributors include well-known writers and several who have never before written for publication. Here, feminist mothers write about abortions, infertility, miscarriages, the death of children. They also write about joy: the sensual joys of mothering, the intellectual joy of discovering another person's growth, and ultimately the joy of claiming identities as women with choices.

With this book, the editors and contributors seek nothing less than to change the popular myths about mothering by giving voice to feminist mothers' real experiences and real wisdom. We see this collection as contributing to the feminist project of redefining motherhood, along with such recent books as Sara Ruddick's *Maternal Thinking,* Marianne Hirsch's *The Mother/Daughter Plot,* and Brenda Daly and Maureen Reddy's *Narrating Mothers: Theorizing Maternal Subjectivities.* Unlike these other works on the theme of feminism and motherhood, however, this collection is not academic, nor is it focused on a particular issue, such as peace or literary theory. We are aiming this collection at a wide audience, thinking of our readers as feminist mothers, feminists who are not mothers, mothers who are not feminists, and people who are neither feminists nor mothers, but interested in the topic: in life, in growth, in choice, and in change.

Nancy Spero

Section I

Discovering

Ourselves

Section I

Discovering Ourselves

Feminism began for many women with understanding the sources of oppression and liberation in our lives as women. Early in the process of political awakening, nascent feminists realized that female biology is one of the most important sources of oppression. The writers in this section have chosen to use and to value their capacity for mothering out of their feminist understanding that the female body is also a source of celebration and power.

They are adoptive mothers as well as biological ones; the masculinist assumption that women are "naturally" maternal affects us all. Weaving the crimson fiber of motherhood into the texture of feminist lives is a source of anguish as well as fulfillment, because it engages feelings about mothers—love for them, rivalry with them, sometimes anger at them and sometimes denial of any conflict with them—and forces a recognition of how even feminists collaborate in devaluing motherhood.

These writers became mothers with their whole selves, bodies, minds, and spirits. The voices in this section speak—often comically, sometimes ruefully—of ambivalence, of flux, of the process of change. All of the writers report on discoveries, welcome and unwelcome, that follow on becoming a mother. Their realities changed when they had children, yet they often found mothering powerfully congenial and even liberating.

Lynda Marín discovers a disturbing intensity in her feelings for her young son, which she describes lyrically in "Mother and Child: The Erotic Bond." In "Once More Out of Darkness," Alicia Ostriker clothes ferocious ambivalence and political anger in formal delicacy and wit when she compares birthing a baby to violent masculine pursuits like football and war. Nicole Hollander's Sylvia cartoon provides a humorous view of what feminist mothers might really want.

In "Two Moms, Two Kids, and a Dog," Sarah Bruckner describes how her pleasure in mothering is complicated by society's homophobia and heterosexism. For most of her career, Sharon Olds's precise, wrenching lyric poetry has reported on her family life. "The Moment the Two Worlds Meet" explores some of the multiple meanings motherhood has for her. Martha Roth, in "Beneath the Skin," describes her journey toward acceptance of femininity through the changes her children have rung in her life. In Kimiko Hahn's deceptively simple prose poems, the writer places her feelings about her children and family in a social context. Shirley Nelson Garner writes of the territorial struggles her children wage over the geography of her body in "Maternal Boundaries; or, Who Gets 'the Lap'?"

Discovering ourselves has meant reconciling feminist theoretical convictions with the soft, smelly, infinitely grueling and rewarding experience of bearing and raising children—an ordinary miracle. Akasha (Gloria T.) Hull's poem, "Counting Cost," counts up some of the costs of the "woman-thing / that mother bind."

Mother and Child:
The Erotic Bond

Lynda Marín

N o one is prepared for becoming a mother even though the world is full of discourse on the subject. I became a mother at thirty-eight and by then I thought I knew a few things. I knew for a fact that I would never be adequately prepared, for instance, and that I would just do it the way every other woman probably had, the best way I could. Right from the beginning of the pregnancy I felt myself initiated into the realm of the best-kept secrets. No one had ever mentioned, for instance, the tingly little cramps just over the pubic bone that set in almost immediately with a first pregnancy and raise the fear that just when you'll need those very muscles to be strong they seem to be giving out. Many months after the birth of my son, a mother of three told me they're called round ligament pains. Nor did anyone ever mention the invisible belt of hivelike itching that often occurs in the second through fourth months of pregnancy. And although I had heard plenty of warnings about menstrual spotting in the the first four months, no one ever told me about the incontinence that might accompany the entire pregnancy and beyond. "Incontinence?" my friend Katherine laughed when I mentioned it a few years later. "Oh, yeah, forget about running, jumping, or sneezing!"

The best-kept secrets pile up around the subject of childbirth, post-partum "depression," and the first twelve months. My son was born prematurely and so I encountered a whole other set of secrets no one thinks she'll need to know until she does. I remember, though, being determined, as I had heard other women say they had been, to not forget a thing, to document every private discovery, every hidden event. But denial, displacement, and cultural mandates for self-effacing motherhood aside, there are compelling logistical reasons why new mothers keep the secrets. They are too exhausted, disoriented, and busy for the most part to be recording them all, and by the time they aren't (do I really believe such a time arrives?) the vagaries of memory commit those secrets yet again to the farthest outposts, the silent margins that delimit the discourses of mothering. And so I have failed, like so many other mothers, to resist the inevitable. Most of the best-kept secrets of pregnancy and early motherhood lie buried safely within me shimmering just out of reach in some vast and timeless collective.

But that is not that. Other secrets replace them, take up the present moment, carry thornier implications. A secret that compels me now, that has increasingly gained complexity in the last two years, has to do with the erotic bond between my son and me. That the bond is an erotic one is not in itself a secret. This is the secret upon which Freud founded psychoanalysis as we know it—that the child has drives that are sexual and that the first objects of those drives are its parents, most initially its mother('s body). But what we do with that bit of psycho-analytic insight is what we seem so bent on keeping hidden.

Alexander likes to say he is "four-and-three-quarters." I got plenty of warning about this age, about the intensity of the little boy's attach-ment to the mother and his Oedipal struggle to possess her entirely for himself. Numbers of women friends with boys assured me that their preschool age sons really do propose marriage to them, intercept their affectionate gestures intended for spouses or lovers, and lavish them with tender phrases and caresses. How dear, I thought. And how poignant the necessity of redirecting these most passionate expressions of desire. Nevertheless, that is exactly what our culture requires, however mediated by our various ethnicities and classes, in order that the boy child identify finally with the other, the father, the law, to take up his place in culture as a man. And while I am ceaselessly rewriting culture's script for men, I recognize my limited power in this arena. I have one son whom I would wish to become an unusual man, a man who resists his gender identity enough to grapple always with the rigors of self-reflection and the complexities of social construction. But seeing no other alternative (how many androgynes do I actually know?), I would wish him still to identify as a man. So it was with a sense of forewarning and purposefulness that I imagined myself meeting Alexander's first dramatic displays of Oedipal conflict. This sense was nurtured by not only the content but the tone of all those conversations I had had with mothers, the books I had read, the films I had seen. My position always seemed clear. I was the figure who must nurture and assist my son through this difficult attachment/detachment maneuver to/from myself.

But no one had really ever told me, in a way I could hear at least, what it might feel like to be the mother in the Oedipal conflict. Indeed of the three key characters in the Greek myth of Oedipus, Jocasta's experience is least described. Upon discovering that she has had four children with her son Oedipus, we are told, she hangs herself. That, of course, is the best way to keep a secret forever. Still, it seems mothers do something equally silencing in the day-to-day way we do not speak of our erotic feelings toward those most desirable of objects, our children. We say our kids are cute, of course, or beautiful or remarkable, and we endlessly detail their behaviors and idiosyncrasies, but rarely do we acknowledge the erotic component of our own feelings in these observations of them. I say "rarely" because just today, when I was trying to explain the topic of this essay to a friend with a six-month-old daughter, she said simply, "It's the most erotic thing *I've* ever felt. You know it's no joke about pretending to eat her right up. I really do want to. It's just uncontainable, this desire. But what can I do? I can't have sex with her. Although nursing takes care of that." That's right, I thought. The physical intimacy of early infancy does mediate those drives in the parent, does "take care of" the uncontainable desire in a way that can't occur at the Oedipal stage. Now that my son is nearly five, I do not have access to his body in the same ways I did when he was younger, nor does he have the same access to mine. I have to ask permission now to clean out his ears, help blow his nose, or make one last wipe after he gets off the toilet (could I ever have imagined such a thing in the midst of all those diaper changes?). And he knows better now than to try and "pinch" my breasts—"fondle" is, of course, much more like it, but language allows him the same diversionary tactics I use.

In fact, language is the very intervention in our children's developmental process that requires us to come to terms with the erotic energy that infuses our love for them (the developmental process I am referring to is here marked by the Oedipal stage—a crucial step in attaining gender identity that boy and girl children experience quite differently but whose name suggests its emphasis on the boy child's experience). But it is also language that foils our expression of that eroticism. When my son wraps his arms around my legs, sighs, and says, "Mommy, I want to have a baby with you," a number of things inevitably occur in me. The impossible tenderness of the moment is followed by the need to say something. "You do?" I say, stalling for the right response (and noting that last year he wanted to *be* me). I could extend the fantasy toward the realm of the practical and avoid the more problematic implications by asking what he'd do with a baby. Would he like to dress it and feed it and change diapers, etc. But I know that has nothing to do with what he wants. I could redirect the fantasy to include his father, and suggest that what he might like is a sister or brother, but that, I am sure, is not what he is talking about in this moment. I could "reality adjust" him in the service of heterosexuality by assuring him that one day he will marry someone he loves and have a baby with her. But now, far from being a comfort, this assurance will not alleviate the anxiety he must be feeling. After all it was just a short time ago that, lying next to me one morning, staring blankly at the ceiling, he sang a wandering little song that went, "Oh, mommy, I love you so much I don't know what to do." *Good grief, Charlie Brown*, I thought to myself in a voice I use when we're playing sometimes, *I feel the same way about you.* The truth is just that simple and just that complex, too.

I remember a specific moment, a "where-it-all-began" moment when I glimpsed the enormity of language's intervention in the continuum of desire that contained us both. We were in the kitchen and he was two. He had been saying lots of words for a long time, so I had passed beyond the wonder of yet another new one but was enjoying tremendously his pleasure in stringing them all together, his various forays into meaning. "Mommy!" he said, "you want a cookie." And as if my brain were wired through his, I indeed felt hunger for a cookie, as if he had only "read my mind." In the time it took to hand him the cookie, a lot happened. I realized that we had been operating like this for a long time, that the boundarylessness between mothers and preverbal children did not simply shore up with the onset of language but rather found ways to persist inside it. This was the first time I had ever noticed in nearly a year of his acquiring language that he had never used the word *I*. I had been hearing *I* for all those *you*s, and not just by mentally exchanging pronouns but actually registering his desire in my body (what power in a pronoun!), feeling it come up against my often different desire, and finally assigning the conflicting desire to him. Not surprisingly, it was around this time that I noticed other people in the family helping him to make the distinction between *I* and *you*, something that is actually very difficult to explain due to the nature of pronouns themselves, i.e. "Oh, you mean *I* when you say *you*. No, I know you don't mean me, you mean you, but you need to say *I* when you mean you," etc. I left it to the others. I was in no hurry to give up what might be the last vestiges of some of the most compelling commingling I have ever felt.

But the leaving it to others felt like a secret I ought to keep. No one likes the idea that a mother enjoys the boundarylessness of relation with her child. That pleasure suggests too intimately her own regressive, infantile underpinnings. More than anything, we need a mother to be an adult. We want to believe that all her own early polymorphous pleasure has now been securely organized around her genitals and directed toward her adult sexual partner. We like to think of a mother's delight in the softness of her child's skin, the firmness of its body, the familiarity of its smell, the singularity of its voice, the sweetness of its breathing as something quite separate from a woman's delight in the body of her lover. We like to make a clear distinction between motherly affection and female passion. If there were not a clear distinction, what would stop mothers from engulfing their children forever in their own hedonistic designs? What hope would culture have?

But what if one of the best-kept secrets is that there is no distinction, really, between motherly affection and female passion? Or rather, that we practice this same love, this erotic energy continuous with our early attachment to our own mother's (or her substitute's) body, in tirelessly deliberate and mediated ways. And we do this exactly because of the lack of boundary between ourselves and our children, exactly because our children are never entirely other. This is the positive side of the narcissistic attachment to children for which mothers are so often criticized. Never is it more clear than with our own children that what we do unto them, we do unto ourselves. If we support their independence and self-reliance, we inevitably gain more freedom and time for ourselves. If we honor their individual expression and spirit, we usually get respected in return. And if we burden them with guilt and shame, we can count on being plagued with those same feelings about ourselves and our parenting. Since the feedback loop is almost immediate, we learn early how to mediate the merging of desire (ours, theirs, and whatever overlaps), how to negotiate the tangle of erotic drives that constitutes the bond between a mother and a child. The other thing we learn is not to talk about it.

Alexander likes to cuddle a lot. A *lot*. I remember hoping before he was born that he would be an affectionate child because I like to cuddle, too. An astrologer friend assured me in the hospital that his early birth in the sign of Cancer would predispose him to strong emotions and an affectionate nature. For the first year, of course, there's no telling. Five months of colic, followed by teething and developmental anxieties, made it almost impossible to discern what sort of little person he would become. I only know I seemed always to be holding him and always on the lookout for another pair of willing arms. By the second year, though, the astrological prediction seemed to be bearing itself out. And what really confirmed it was the language that began to accompany his affectionate gestures. I can rarely turn down invitations like "I need to cuddle with my soft sweet mommy."

By now Alexander's cuddling is a highly developed art. It begins early in the morning when he appears in my room holding Orker the seal, slips into bed beside me, and coaxes one of my sleepy arms around his middle. This is complicated. On the one hand, I resist. I am never ready to be awake. On the other, I am endlessly grateful that here he is whole in body and spirit, in all his morning good cheer, and almost calm enough to let me pretend to myself that I am resting a little while longer. It's a count-my-blessings kind of moment, and then some. "Mommy," he says, after about ten or fifteen minutes, "let's be animals." This has been going on for as long as I can remember (perhaps this is what replaced nursing so long ago). He is the baby elephant, bird, snake, fish, seal, horse, dog, or kitty, and I am the mommy of the same species. We go looking for food, we have adventures, we don't get caught, we return home where we cuddle, of course. Sometimes he just collapses against me, his face pressing down on mine, and I breathe him in, breathe him out. Sometimes in these moments he says how much he loves me, but most of the time he is talking to himself, or singing, or just staring off. If his dad tries to enter in, Alexander always pushes him away, even though at other times he is quite loving with him. Then suddenly he will disappear under the covers all the way to the foot of the bed. After a lot of tossing and giggling he reappears, naked, having left his pajamas somewhere down at my feet. He presents himself with noisy fanfare, giddy with his own power. He is delighted by his nakedness and, I sense, by something like defying an assumed prohibition. For although nudity is commonplace in our family, he seems to sense that he's on some kind of an edge. He turns his skinny backside to my front and we lie like spoons, half-moaning half-humming an exaggerated "Yummmmmm." The sensuality of this moment that we have constructed almost takes my breath away. For the short time that we snuggle like this, I feel as close to perfectly happy as I imagine possible.

Most of the time I'm the one to say we've got to get up, to eat, to dress, to go to school, etc. But when I can't marshall the forces, or when I am lulled into overtime by the pleasure of our play, I sometimes begin to feel uncomfortable. "OK, I'll be the mommy bird and you be the baby and you cry and I'll feed you. Here, nurse the mommy," he says, pointing to his tummy. And although I'm tempted to kiss that spot as a way of playing along (I can't even imagine pretending to nurse him— here a taboo is in full force), I often hear myself responding with things like, "No, I'm sleeping now," or "Yikes, I fell in the river." Nevertheless I let the game go on. I am, of course, partly curious to see how he plays out being the mommy (she's always good at finding food and fighting off hunters). Now suddenly he's the baby and wants to nurse. I laugh him away, but he insists and pretends to grab for my breast. "Cut it out!" I say partly laughing because he's laughing, but partly serious, too, and in this moment thinking quite concertedly about where the boundaries ought to be. "OK, OK," he says, seems to stop, and then dives towards my chest, kissing me on the clavicle. That he kisses me takes me aback. I see that he does the same thing I do—that he doesn't really pretend to nurse either, that he opts for that more adult vestigial gesture of nursing, the kiss. And, like someone who suddenly realizes she is witnessing an historical event in the making, I think IT IS HAPPENING RIGHT NOW. In this moment, unlike any other that I have known, I am actually the mother and the woman, the original object and its displacement. This is the impossible conjoining that patriarchal and heterosexual culture so labors to veil, to mystify, to interdict, which I can hardly hang on to long enough to mark before it passes imperceptively like water into air.

What, I wonder in moments like these, would I do if he were a girl (or if I had a second child and no time for this sort of play)? Would a daughter his age and I even be playing these games? Or would our games be more informed by the kinds of power struggles that ordinarily accompany a girl child's efforts to separate out who is who in the selfsameness of mother-daughter gender? But just say that we did play mother-and-baby games as part of our morning ritual, would I feel the same ambivalence at the same turns? Would I wonder for a moment about our nakedness together? Or about the appropriateness of the game? My sister-in-law has been saying tactfully for a long time now that "most mothers curtail access to their body to their boy children at this age." She is a psychotherapist and a sensible woman/mother, so I take her advice to heart. But she is also, I always tell her, a white, middle-class American. Many people of other cultures and classes don't operate with these same taboos, and anyway I don't want my body to become distant, mysterious, and only, therefore, an object of frustrated desire. I want a woman's body to be a real thing to him, with its various characterizing features and quirks, cycles and stages. She reminds me, though, and I acknowledge also, that Alexander is growing up in this culture in a predominantly white, middle-class family. But, I ask her obliquely, what woman in her right mind wouldn't want to resist that institution and remold its membership? And how better to do it than with our bodies, the most split-off and thereby suppressed/oppressed instruments culture has at its disposal? And that brings me back to erotic love and its power in the mother-child relationship, because all those normative steps to desexualizing the child's attachment to his/her mother's body are predicated on a split between mother and woman that is culturally required but personally mutilating for both mothers and children, a category that finally includes everyone.

I see that what I am holding out for, in these borderline experiments in erotic love with my son (the wording is so sensitive here, and nothing that I can think to say is quite what I mean), is a rewriting of sexuality as I know it. It is not a free-for-all kind of sexuality that powered the imagination of the "sexual revolution" of the '60s and '70s but left us, men and women, just as split in ourselves as ever. It is an inclusive kind of sexuality that recognizes itself basically everywhere. It is not so scary in its infantility because it's just as much a part of adulthood, too. And if we were to recognize that kind of sexuality much more intimately in ourselves all the time (since it's operating there all the time anyway), we would have to pay it close attention, to be careful and caring with it. I imagine our having to add lots of new words to our language to describe it in its multiple manifestations in any interaction, fantasy, work of art, etc., in much the same way we have thought Inuit peoples to have so many words for snow. But I recognize that as innocently as I try to cast it, it's a sexuality that would not support life on the planet as we know it, that is, would not support social hierarchies, multinational corporations, a free market economy, racism, colonization, or any other of the problematic realities that depend on our ability to split off what's safe and good (mother) from what's desirable (woman).

Last year Valorie (a dear friend and second mother-figure to Alexander) and I took him to the Women's Music Festival. It is an all-women's event, four days of music and sun, hikes and swimming, workshops and food. Boy children ten years of age and under are also allowed. When we got inside the festival grounds, I was amused by the first truckload of women passing by laughing and waving, their bare breasts jouncing to the bumps in the road. They were acting out, I thought, taking every opportunity to do what is everywhere else forbidden. But I didn't blame them. By the next day I didn't blame myself either. In the afternoons the large swimming pool filled up with bodies of every imaginable size, shape, and texture. Mothers, children, lovers, friends towel-to-towel along the steamy concrete deck, dipping in and out of the brisk water. All those naked bodies so happily commingling in the security of our shared gender. Was it erotic to be there? Of course it was. It was magnificently, luxuriously, ubiquitously so. And yet we were as orderly as any other crowd, waited in long lines for dinner and almost as long ones for showers, had regular conversations, and helped each other out in small, immediate ways. I don't remember ever seeing any overtly genital sex acts between women there, although the atmosphere was clearly sexually charged. In fact I felt more comfortable and secure in this crowd than in any other I'd been in.

No surprise, much of that comfort had to do with Alexander, that he was in as safe a place as he could possibly be, all those women/mothers with an eye and an arm out, just in case. I wasn't surprised either that the other children there seemed less competitive, more trusting, and, interestingly, more independent than many kids I've had occasion to know. But I was surprised at my sense of relief when, dropping Alexander off at the festival daycare center, I felt unambivalent pleasure at his fingers tracing my cheekbone and his "Goodbye, my dearest mommy lover." How often I have marked those kinds of good-byes at his regular preschool with a vague anxiety about their possibly problematic implications. How often I have listened furtively to the way other children say goodbye to their mothers hoping to hear equally "excessive" endearments. And how often has the sensible mother within had to remind me that what really should be noted is how happily he says goodbye and lets me go. But what would it mean to never feel one moment of that ambivalence, to trust that this love I feel for my son is as good as it ever gets? What would it mean if I could openly and directly model all my other loves on this, my finest? When it was time to leave the festival, none of us wanted to go home. Alexander made us promise we would bring him back next year. Both Valorie and I got ready for reentry trauma, and we didn't have to wait long. Just twenty minutes down the highway we stopped for gas, minded our business, and, predictably, got harrassed by two drunk men until the tank was filled up.

"How would you feel if Alexander grew up to be gay?" a lesbian friend doesn't quite ask as we speak recently of things erotic and motherly. Or, I think to myself, sexually ambivalent or a cross-dresser or a fetishist, or—? These questions have crossed my mind before. I would be kidding myself to say it wouldn't matter, that whatever his sexuality I would accept it without reservation, remorse, guilt, or judg-ment. "It would be hard," his father says when I ask him the same ques-tions. And I agree. Life is hard enough, and being "different" is that much harder. I'm already feeling sorry that he's having to deal with being left-handed. (I was left-handed, too, but the kindergarten teacher would have none of that.) On the other hand (the right one), to consciously guide him into the heterosexual model of masculinity feels abusive. Yet again, to *not* deliberately guide him in that direction seems at times equally injurious. Example: Alexander at his gymnastics lesson begs me for a leotard like the other kids have (the girls, that is). Here's one of those moments where I watch my conditioning vie with my resistance to it. I think "No," plain and simple, but I try out "Yes" for a fleeting second just to really test myself. After all, I might have been able to say yes just a year ago, but kids say things now to each other about haircuts and clothes and so I know a leotard is sure to bring him immediate censure, probably even from his teacher. Nevertheless, as I am feeling the absurdity of my own explanation to him, that boys and girls usually wear different kinds of uniforms for most kinds of sports (though I am hard pressed to answer his outraged "Why?"), I grind to a halt between what I know and what I want. "If you really want a leotard, you can have one," I tell him, "but you just have to know that someone might make fun of you because you will be different." "Never mind," he says. A week later after co-oping at Alexander's preschool, his dad reports that in the fantasy room Alexander got himself dressed up as a cowboy and then with equal enthusiasm donned an elaborate bride's costume and went through a double wedding ceremony with his friend Evin and another "couple." "How was that?" I ask his dad. "He made a beautiful bride," he says. And we both laugh and remember the evening before when Alexander had said to me at the dinner table, "OK, I'm the bride and you're the broom." "Groom," his dad said, "the man is the groom." "Oh," Alexander says, a little abashed, and then, "No, I want you to be the broom." "OK," I agree. A bride and broom seem likely enough in a domestic sort of way, but then again, if the broom can fly....

On my desk sits a small photo of myself *circa* four "and-three-quar-ters." I retrieved it from my stepfather after my mother died thirteen years ago. It had been taken in Iowa where I lived with a foster parent who must have sent it on to my mother in California. I have often wondered at the self-possessed expression on that child's face, her legs crossed and her hands clasped squarely in her lap. It is one of the few photos I have of my childhood and it has become, by now, one of my most familiar images of myself. Recently, though, while late-night working on some translation at my desk, I saw that photo/myself anew. Who knows what triggered it. Perhaps it was *La Amortajada*, the text I was so feverishly unravelling, about a dead woman's dialogue with her split-off selves, or perhaps it was the residue of a drawn-out, difficult "good night" with Alexander, who that evening thought his bedroom too lonely to fall asleep in. Perhaps it was everything and nothing I could point to, but in any case it happened. I looked at the little girl in the photo and I felt such a surge of desire I must have stopped breath-ing. I wanted her entirely, to embrace her until she melted into me, to infuse her with all of myself, to enjoy the delicious intimacy of her little body as a day-to-day, minute-to-minute commonplace—her skin, her hair, her smell, her sound. I could almost reproduce her right then and there, a tangible, palpable child.

In a trying-to-make-sense-of-this effort I reminded myself that these were actually feelings I have for Alexander. And it did make sense that on account of family resemblance and age correspondence I had, at that moment, mapped the feelings I have for my actual child onto the photographic image that represents for me my internalized child. But the unmediated desire I felt for that small girl in the photo made me at least suspect that it might be the other way around. What I mean to say is what if, for a reason I can't presume to know, for a split second some of my psycho-social infrastructure slipped just enough to reveal another of the best-kept secrets: that all love whether it be for our children, our lovers, our work, our ideas, is fundamentally the same love, is first and last, coming and going, not even erotic but autoerotic? For isn't erotic love just a further development, a successful splitting off, redirecting, and renaming of that first continuous unbounded connection/pleasure we feel with our mother's body?

Of course, autoeroticism is not such a secret since we can find it strategically positioned, just as I'm suggesting now, in psychoanalytic discourse. The real secret, though, is how "ardorously" culture struggles to forget what eroticism actually is, where it comes from, and why it is absolutely everywhere all the time, especially and necessarily in a mother's love for her child. When we successfully forget that fact, as we require ourselves to do in the name of becoming adults, we severely limit the ways we can experience the connection/pleasure which originally nurtured us into life and which sustains our desire for life forever after. It seems evident that one of the reasons, for instance, that Western culture has so little regard, by and large, for what's left of natural life—for plants and animals and earth and atmosphere—is its successful endeavor to see itself as separate from all that life, to forget the connection/pleasure that informs our very being here.

So what *is* a mother to do? If I had never had a child, my task would be the same. I would still have that little girl internalized and her picture on my desk. I would still need to be parenting her, the child she is, the woman I am, the best way I know how. It's just that having Alexander confronts me more urgently to uncover the secret of what that best way is.

"Do you love me so much that you just have to close your eyes?" he asked me the other day when we were hugging. "Yes!" I said, surprised at his accuracy. "Me, too," he said matter-of-factly and patted my hand. But for whatever permission I am learning to give myself in honoring the erotic bond between us, I wonder still if it makes any difference. One morning recently he sits at the table eating cereal and crooning a love song to mother. Something about how wonderful and sweet I am and how much much much he loves loves loves me. "Goodbye," I interrupt him on my way out the door. "Can I have a hug?" The goodbye hug is a ritual. But this morning he doesn't even hear me. His eyes are so far off in his song that I hesitate to ask again, though I suppose that later on he'll think I didn't say goodbye. So I try once more. But it's no use. "I just love her so much my mommy," I hear as I leave the house. Tossing his car pillow into the backseat to make room next to me for my books and papers, I marvel at that other "mommy," that symbolic creature who, seemingly overnight, has exceeded and displaced me, and who, this morning, has him in thrall. I only hope, for all our sakes, she loves him as undividedly as she can.

Once More Out of Darkness

Alicia Ostriker

———————————

Adventure on the box
 these
  photographers swaying in a balloon over
the tundra saw the infant wildebeest dropped, wet, and his
mother lick him clean, and his efforts to stand, skinny and
uncertain, on pin legs, two minutes old, he was up, up and
skipping about the smooth grassed plain, three minutes old,
his mother among the herd at a little distance was galloping
thrusting her head backward anxious as the hyenas advanced;
the newborn understood and fled, but too slowly, and could
not catch the herd; the gap between him and his massed
brothers, running, expanded, five minutes old and the hyenas
in due course, noiselessly, quickly, circle, spring and
rend him.

For everything that lives is holy. Life delights in life.

i

Once more out of darkness
Come the great green hills.
Wind plunges and lifts,
Jays plunge and scream overhead.
Slowly erupts up
Again the risen red.

ii

The supposed virgins sitting in a circle
Under old portraits of Margaret Sanger
Are here to receive their first, new, innocent diaphragms.
I, however, am their fabled goddess.
I am conducted to the sanctuary, I submit to indignities,
Skirt up, feet in stirrups, one look, one rotating poke—
Examination of the entrails? Quite right, due process,
My cow. "Five weeks," the voice intones. "Hooray,"
I say, and pay (the dogfaced nurses cheerful)
And get to a phone fast, pretending to be
(In the shabby drugstore) Western Union, a singing telegram,
"Love, oh love, oh careless love," it sings, "you see
What love has done to me," and hang up giggling.

Consequence: Join the world, which is full
Of ballooning mamas and baffled but willing papas for future
Communion. We join it. We toss
Off quarts of milk, we invent spinach recipes
To rectify the diet, we observe the tenderness
Of my breasts, and that I pee more and sleep more
And weep more, by which signs alone is made known
The invisible change, the silent grafting-on
Or addition of an infinity, the implausible, actual
Shift of the peopled universe, for which we are
Responsible. Nevertheless, my fœtus, I cannot picture
You yet. Are you thumb-length? A fish? Have you a tail?

Are you hairy? Will I be good to you?
Archangel Spock, Guttmacher, Grantley Dick-Read,
Pray for us now, we follow your lead.

iii

A pregnant lady
Yes a pregnant lady
A pregnant lady
Is tastier than pie.
You think it is an egg
You think it is a beachball
You think it is a mushroom
Or a melon strolling by.
For she is satisfied
The flagrant lady
She is gratified
She is highly fattified
She is the sunshine, the middle of the sky.
So beasties love the lady
Love the fragrant lady
Fructified girlie
They hold her in their eye.
For she blows like a rose in the prose
Of the nose
And she blooms in the eardrum like a cry.

iv

What I have said and
What I will say is
Female not feminine
        Yes I said yes
Not analytical not romantic

But the book of practical facts
     I draw you down
What is it save obscene?
Example:
Cynicism of female magazines,
Miss Narcissus, to inspect the pores
And bung them with beauty:
Or serious gossip: or park bench surgery:
Or beheaded fowl: its butchery and cookery:
For everything that lives is holy
Star and stone, princess and whore's face
Exists by grace
Aware of the horror
Aware of the mortality
Aware of the excremental perfume
The fact
The fact blasts in the mind's cavern
Like the yet unborn who one day shall be born.

V

Therefore a swollen freighter
Moving without will
Pursues its nature still.
          The waves go by,
          What freight have I?
          It is daylight,
          It is even,
          It is the world's night
               Travel forward
               Insensible barrow, pilgrim

   Laden:

vi

And I saw Jerusalem descending, a city yet a woman
Twelve gates, and the brightness
From everlasting to everlasting. Now:
For her outsides, car-dumps, motel strips.
For her inside, sewer slums, brain of phone wires,
       edifices of municipal troglodyte, the greased
       slide of paste restaurant, urine movie, puke dancehall,
       meths subway sleep, pus alley . . . rat hunger . . .
Over an empty road you drove
To the brim of a town
Where shone in the darkness four signs: FOOD. BEAUTY.
       GAS. DRUGS.
Her eyes are the suburbs
       Decent
       I want to be decent

In the bath, sweet hills and valleys
Afloat, suspended, miraculous
Mountain land, grazing land, building land, planting land
       Wander here with me
       In a dream on that ancient sea
       That large lump, there the life lies. But:
Doctor, I have one breast pointing down and one breast pointing up.
Doctor, my veins are like hoses.
Give me something. I cannot sleep for the kicking.
I worry. I think there will be pain. What then.
What to do. I grow old even as I tell you this.
       Ugly
       You cannot deny it is ugly

vii

For each day as I wait
The papers making hate
The dope box bleating

Bombs mute, the movie
Screen removing its clothes
Turn me weary, weary
Of time, gyrating
I follow my groove
Washing teaspoons, picking
Up old chicken bones, dragging
My sheets flat, netted, assailed,
Do your dainties have that soiled
Look, it bubbles, it flows.
Let him who is pure
Descend his mire.
Let the official coward
Move nations backward and forward.
      I am making this child for you:
Brown pot of my body
Golden spear of his body
And vowed minds, damned all
From love's beginning either
To be "unfaithful" or to be "faithful,"
That is to rot by
The gaudy wicked lie or the mean inhibited lie,
Came once together
As in the promise.
From the sweat of this,
Male and female bodies
Whirling cracked on the wheel:
      For you:
Of the dripping wound
Of the walls of insanity
Of proud man's contumely, of law's delay
Of fire, famine, age,
Ague, tyranny,
(Did any, on the way,
Spew a babe, on the way to the chambers?
What did the soldiers say?)
Old men that pray in the oven's mouth
Ancestral grief of woman
All shrieks to heaven from the battered down,
      Whoever has died, I make this child for you.

MOTHER JOURNEYS

viii

One black cloud rode down to the sea

The waters are flowing

The dark lilies have knotted the sky
The dark lilies have twisted their fingers

There was a fountain filled with blood
And out of the river the horses are pacing
Out of the river the animals are coming

Down to the sea, down to the sea

ix

He' s got the ball, he's off, he's going down the field. Will
they get him? Look at him run! Look at him run! Arabesque,
plié, glissade. Arabesque, plié, glissade. Arm over arm through the
smooth water. Sever the water arm over arm. Shoulder and
muscled chest surge sundering the resisting fluid. Lashing our
sides to the cliff of an icefall, hanging blind inches beaten by
blizzards, grapes of lungs bursting. With joy! With joy!
I cannot! I cannot!
        One more time now.

He' s got the ball, he' s running, he' s going, the cheering is
tremendous, look at him go! Pull, and. Pull, and. Arabesque,
plié, glissade. Gathering, gathering, straining and pushing.
It' s neck and neck now down the straight, the piston-armed
jockeys horizontal, the flashing whips, thundering horses,
onward to garlands, onward to glory, one to the chest, a left and
a right to the ribs, up the next hill we went like a pestilence
        Breathe, and. Gas, and.

Stumbling on granite we swarmed like turtles, cannon to right,

cannon to left, cannon creating a silence, mortar creating a silence,
horror creating a hollow of painless flowers, lilies, dark rushing
waters, enemy, friend, lover, father, shape whom I meet to murder,
to kiss (O boulder, burden, impossible stone, never to lift, arrive,
never to expel, attain the crest, never again freedom) I struck, now!
ripped cotton and skin, sank soft in the stomach

        Breathe
And bathed like a blessing in blood

≈≈

Like when drunk I like
To wake up next morn
ing and for it to be
Spring! and I come out
Of the pouring glacier with a nice
Heavy happy head in a bed
By blue and branchy window into
Singbirds
        And I float
In the sunny weather
And all day I do
Nothing
And all day I do not get dressed
And my work goes to hell

I see you
Pathos monkey face
I hold and unfold
The wrappings of yowl until
It is a human baby breathing
With its mouth full of my breast and milk
With all perfect fat palpitating
Belly, lovely fingernail
And toenail moons
Most precious, and where my finger feels
Fontanel throb:
Under bone, to make the tongue suck,

Is beating, to puppet the eyelids,
Is boiling, to make a green
Child dance erect,
Behind the temples,
A shy brain dwelling.

Three things are in waiting.
My cave of dreams
To be filled waits
For the shuddering tube and thrust
That drives the seed home
That quiets the womb—
And the mouth of
Our demon in a cloud
Of utter hunger and despair
Until it seizes the nipple
And the milk comes
That full fills it
That quiets it—
And at last the hollow
Of the open earth that waits
For the lowered form that rests
And fills it, breeding to birth
Live things, worms, soft slugs,
Insects, myriad creepers, tremulous
Quivering and quick—
That quiets the earth.

SYLVIA

Nicole Hollander

Two Moms, Two Kids, and a Dog

Sarah Bruckner

B eing a mother has entailed a continuous dismantling of my privacy. My daughters push me to erupt into the sort of gestures of public self-advertisement my own mother brought me up carefully to avoid. Before motherhood got me in its tenacious grip, I did not lose my temper in grocery store checkout lines, sing "The Belly Button Song" at top volume in defiance of startled passersby, say "give me that right now" through clenched teeth. My clothing was not festooned with dinosaur stickers, papers in my briefcase bore no marks of custom-emblazoning in orange crayon. I never undressed other people in airport departure lounges or peered discreetly into their undergarments. I did not, even occasionally, have yogurt in my hair.

Mothering, in short, is frequently a performance art: mothers are judged by whether their children's hair is brushed, socks are matched, noses are wiped. Strangers in malls feel empowered, and apparently compelled, to applaud ("Your daughters are so well-behaved!") or hiss ("You shouldn't let them have lollipops, you know"). And in the case of my family, other questions cry out for retorts that are never satisfying: "Which one of you is the mother?" "How did you get them?" "Are they sisters?" "Do you know anything about their *real* mother?" or "Are you the babysitter?"

Motherhood taps so deeply into raw nerve, is so barefaced a condition and so manifestly in the public domain, that it is ironic as well as painful that I fear writing about it without using a pseudonym. Because my partner is a woman, some managerial maneuvering was required for us to adopt children. While we read daily of mistreated and abused children, children left unattended, given cocaine, starved and locked in rooms by people whose decision to parent never had to pass through the layers of bureaucratic approval, fingerprinting and paperwork we have faced, I was required to convince half a dozen state agencies, the governments of three countries, and the Family Court of a large city, that my home is a fit place to raise a child. I needed letters and affidavits certifying my moral character, my financial assets, and my ability to love a child.

And, in fact, my partner and I agree that the endless clearance procedures are necessary; were we to have in our charge children to be placed with adoptive or foster families, we too would investigate the people we considered entrusting with such precious goods. This complex process took several years and, in our case, still failed to locate the most basic fact of our family life. Just as well, since several recent court cases have exposed the naked prejudice that fuels rigid adherence to right-wing definitions of "family" values, and that denies me, my partner, and our children the right to call ourselves a family.

We did not undertake lightly either parenthood or, for us, its attendant concealments and revelations. We worried, as all couples do, about the impact of demanding young people on our careers, on our social lives, and above all on our bond with each other. We worried about the response of our families, immediate and extended, and of our network of friends and neighbors. We worried about how to present this decision to our colleagues at work. Above all, we worried about the impact on our children of being raised in an alternative, transracial family. Or, I should confess, *I* worried. I have always been the family worrier. My partner, trusting the larger issues to find resolutions for themselves, knew that the small questions would be more relentless: how would we orchestrate child care? what humane measures can be taken to mobilize small people who will not be hurried so that we could get to work in the morning? would we still have time for each other? when, if ever, would we get enough sleep?

The response of our older daughter to her family's differences was quickly to develop a preternaturally acute sense concerning the shockability of those around her. When barely two, Rosa devised her strategy: she waited for brief moments of silence—in crowded elevators, say, or in a restaurant with two of my especially religious and conservative cousins—then announced "I have two moms" in a thrilled voice. Shoe salesmen, dental hygienists, and gas station attendants have been among the audiences for this announcement. Her younger sister Gabriela simply believes it odd and rather sad that many of her friends have only one mother.

Rosa was 17½ months old when we first saw her, brought to us by an entourage of adoption workers in a hotel room in Guatemala City. She was dressed in a frilly pink jumper with lace piping and a matching pink hairbow, and wore black patent leather maryjanes that would remain her only shoes until we returned to the United States and outfitted her with more appropriate footwear for our rowdy and informal lives: sneakers.

Rosa had been living with a doting foster family for five months, and her attachments were fierce. Cheerful and outgoing with us from the first, as befits her naturally affectionate personality, Rosa protested with a screamed "no—no—no" when told I was her mama. The agency people did not handle this transition well, and it was difficult for me not to take the rejections personally. Happily, my partner Alice, not labeled in any threatening way, did not have to bear the same emotional cargo and was able to take over when our toddler was feeling particularly bereft. Rosa fought courageously against the loss of her previous family. But six months later, when a photograph of her foster mother was explained to her, she threw it to the ground in a rage, grabbing us both and yelling "No, no—Sarah, Alice, Sarah, Alice!" We felt triumphant, but our triumph, we realized, came through Rosa's sense of abandonment, and we were saddened by the intensity of this young child's early losses.

Adoption is a complex process and takes a long time. Rosa's entry into our family in 1987 went quite quickly and smoothly, though that only became apparent to us in retrospect and relative to the far more harrowing process that eventually brought Gabriela to join our family four years later. At the time, the waiting seemed endless. Part of the frustration came from the intense paranoid anxiety that accompanied us everywhere as it must accompany those who live in other kinds of undergrounds. I attended a series of group sessions for prospective adoptive parents, and grieved over my aloneness while the married couples surrounding me held hands as they asked questions and made decisions together. We moved furniture in order to create plausible bedroom arrangements for the social worker's home visit. Alice virtually stopped answering the phone, in case it was the agency or the lawyer. Waiting for the call that would tell us we were parents, and then that would tell us we could get on a plane to Guatemala, became a palpable activity. Twice we were told we could leave in a matter of days and made airline reservations, only to learn that one more document was needed or that there had been a snafu in the court system in Guatemala.

We arrived in seedy, desperately poor Guatemala City late on a Tuesday evening, travel-weary and childless but bizarrely laden with a mammoth box of environmentally unsound diapers, an umbrella stroller, and a suitcase full of toddler clothes in an array of sizes. Carlos, our local lawyer, met us and took us to a hotel, calming us and assuring us that our little girl was beautiful—"You will see," he kept smilingly repeating. He promised to arrive with Rosa and her foster mother at 9:00 the next morning. Needless to say, we didn't sleep much, despite our exhaustion. At 9:15, when Carlos called from the lobby, we were pacing the room, stomachs clutched and eyes glazed. Alice busied herself with the camera. Posed as the friend who had come to help care for Rosa while I arranged for Rosa's passport and visa and signed legal papers, she was trying to devise an interested but detached role for herself as this momentous meeting neared.

We blew it, of course. My "detached" friend began to weep as soon as I opened the door, a sentimental turn of events that paralyzed me into a mask of calm. Though tears come to my eyes now as I write about this moment, at the time the knock on the door that so unhinged Alice might have been room service for the amount of emotion I was able to show. Partly, this is how our relationship operates and one of the reasons it works: when one of us is frantic or anxious or sad, the other steadies the family ship. I couldn't go to pieces when I first saw Rosie, because Alice, as was her right, had willy-nilly appropriated the soft mommy script.

The rest of that eight-day stay in Guatemala was magical, weird, terrifying, and fascinating. Our reading had prepared us intellectually but our guts were still left unprotected when we witnessed the military omnipresence, the horrifying poverty, the mistreatment of indigenous peoples and their sturdy resilience in the face of it, and the stunning, lush beauty of the mountains and marketplaces. My Spanish, which I had thought barely adequate for basic politenesses, had to get Rosa and me past three soldiers with machine guns in front of the U.S. Consulate in Guatemala City. Rosie stayed in the room with us, and it seemed to me that listening to her unfamiliar nighttime noises required my full-time attention. I must have slept at some point during those eight days, but it felt as though I had to stay conscious just to will this strange little creature to keep breathing.

Rosie remained cheerfully adaptable to all this change—new care-takers, new clothes, new foods, a different language, hours waiting in lawyers' and consulate vestibules—until it was bedtime. Then her cries were ferocious, filled with the pain of abandonment. Alice and I decided to let Rosie stay again with her foster family while we took a few days to visit some of this ancient country, thinking that we could make an album of photographs for our daughter that would help her to learn about her origins and to understand how our family was created. (She has since taken this album, and various local crafts we brought back, to show off at her school with great pride.) We knew this plan had its drawbacks, and when Rosa returned to us on the evening we got back to the city, she was especially inconsolable, screaming in fury for nearly an hour when her foster mother left for the last time.

That was Rosie's last stand of resistance. She fell asleep toward the end of our ten-hour series of flights home, and slept through the airport chaos at the baggage claim. A friend who had looked after our house during our absence met the plane, and loaded the piles of stuff we returned with into our car, where before our departure we had installed a child's car seat. When we got home, other neighbors came out to greet the sleeping new addition we had all so long awaited, and unveiled the huge "WELCOME HOME ROSA" banner their children had hung across our staircase. That welcome created the first crack in the deep fears we had nursed that this child would never be ours. Over the next weeks, many other friends, neighbors and relatives came to see Rosie or sent gifts, and we began to relax our vigil just a little.

Rosie herself liked the attention; she is a ham without inhibitions, a born performer. Her preschool included a weekly dance and gymnas-tics class, and she was always the first to volunteer to do a solo when there was an audience. Briefly shy when meeting new people, she warmed up to them immediately and was soon on their laps or dragging them by the hand to see a toy or read a story. She was in control of every relationship, and the intense interpersonal dynamics of her commitment to our family dog illustrate this well.

The dog stayed with friends while we travelled to pick up Rosa, and remained with them until things settled down a bit at home. From the minute she returned to us it was clear to Harriet, a large and goofy Airedale terrier, that the terms of her dog's life had altered permanently. She was displaced in our affections, and sulked disconsolately for a few days. As Harriet was twice Rosie's size, we were cautious about their interactions. But within days, our daughter had renegotiated the family/pet system in such a way that Harriet became her devoted slave. She permitted Rosie to drape her with dish towels, put shoes on her paws, feed her by hand. With no protective instincts save a fierce desire to eat the mail when it comes through the slot, Harriet now puts herself between our children and anyone she doesn't know.

Our anxieties about the safety of our parenting lasted until Rosie became a naturalized citizen eleven months after her arrival in the United States and was readopted by the local courts here two months after her naturalization became final. During this process, we were often hostile to the inquiries of strangers. On a beach vacation, we were approached at an outdoor café by two women who had figured out our family structure and beamed up to us wanting to know how lesbians could adopt a gorgeous little girl like ours. We were monosyllabic and awkward initially, then downright rude. Alice especially bristled at remarks that presumed Rosie to be an exotic object one could shop for.

We noticed when Rosa was about three-and-a-half that these unsolicited commentaries had stopped. Rosa can now speak for herself, and she volunteers with pride that she comes from Guatemala, a country whose political struggles we have become involved in and whose fate we feel, quite literally, related to. When our children are older, we look forward to returning there, and to showing Rosie her country of origin in all its beauty, danger, and poverty. She understands now about the cardboard one-room dwellings with dirt floors and tin roofs in one of which she spent the first year of her life. If someone asks about Rosa's origins now, it is usually because they are Latino themselves, and see in her brown Mayan face a bond to their own heritage.

We reside in a community where for the most part difference is accepted and embraced as a positive value. This has taken planning on our part. The city we live in is large enough so that we can keep our private and professional identities separate, an unfortunate vigilance unnecessary for me but required for Alice because of the nature of her work. We live in an interracial neighborhood where people of many different colors and ethnicities mingle in relative comfort. Among our friends are others like us in one respect or another: interracial and gay and lesbian couples with young children; adoptive families; single parent families.

We could be accused of insulating ourselves in an unrealistically liberal world, and it is true that we want to spare our children the discomfort of being the *only* people of color, the *only* children of lesbians, the *only* adopted kids in their vicinity. Oddly, the friends who have had the hardest time accepting our family are childless gays and lesbians who do not comprehend our loss of freedom and the new way we have gone public with our commitment to each other. Married friends with children have had fewer problems understanding, and we have needed to remind them occasionally that despite our new shared interests in the gripping details of toilet-training and kindergarten-readiness, our interactions with schools, camps, doctors, and shop clerks will never quite resemble theirs.

Three hot political issues—international adoption, adoption of nonwhite children by white parents, and adoption (or parenting of any kind) by lesbians and gay men—have polarized many people and affect the marginalized social place of our family.

There are those who misguidedly praise us as saints for taking in malnourished, dark-skinned Third World children. Women in poor, war-torn countries are put in the horrifying position of relinquishing their babies in part because they are exploited as cheap labor by the industrialized West. As privileged white Westerners whose most precious gift has depended upon the wrenching apart of women and their children in Guatemala and Peru, we are only too aware of our inevitable complicity in this imperialist exploitation. We cannot fathom what kind of loss our daughters' birthmothers must live with every day. In the face of that loss, we have gained two beautiful children. But our daughters will have to mourn their families of origin, their histories, their cultures, and their ethnic identities as much as they may cherish their new family, access to education and health care, and economic security.

Can white women be *real* mothers to brown-skinned children? Can we help them to grow up with a healthy identity that includes racial and ethnic pride? *Real* mothers, Alice and I persist in believing, take and instill pride in their children's uniqueness, in the individual forms their beauty, their talents, and their sense of self entails. We are providing a multiracial, multicultural, and international community in which they will grow up. Rosa and Gabriela must define who they are for themselves. Our job is to advocate for them when they are young, and to support their decisions as they grow older.

Our family, of necessity as well as on principle, respects and celebrates difference. We want to make available a range of choices and identities to our daughters—racial, religious, sexual, political, ethnic—without imposing any of them. Our daughters will struggle—to be people of color with white parents, to be Latinos among Jews, to be Indians among Europeans, to be (probably) heterosexuals among lesbians. We can try to clear some of the debris from their paths. But even to do that requires having faith in our love for them and in our own mature sense of who we are. The rest, struggles and all, belongs only to Rosa and Gabriela.

Educating schools about adoption and lesbian parenting and transracial families has been more deliberate than dealing with the occasional thoughtless comments of strangers or the bafflement of some of our friends. After sharing ideas with Rosa's teachers, donating Meredith Tax's children's book *Families* and Lesléa Newman's story *Heather Has Two Mommies* to Rosa's school, and believing our concerns were understood, we still sometimes encountered befuddlement. When one of Rosa's playmates, a boy who lives with his mother and sees his father, to whom his mother was never married, only rarely, teased her with "Rosie doesn't have a daddy!" their teacher reprimanded him by saying "You don't have a daddy either, Jamal." Inaccurate, hardly reassuring to either child, and a sign that the diversity of family structures and the acceptability of all kinds of permutations had not sunk in.

The children themselves, colorblind and unselfconscious in their early years, are better at negotiating difference than adults, patiently explaining to parents and each other that "Rosa and Gabriela have two moms, a Sarah-mom and an Alice-mom." So what's the big deal? But each year new dilemmas arise: we have solved Mother's and Father's Days, how to fill out forms or, better, get schools to revise them to reflect family diversity, what to say to school administrators and intake nurses at hospitals. We still struggle with institutionalized resistances to making the concept of "family" as elastic as we think it must be.

Rosa's and Gabriela's two mothers and racial difference mark them most obviously, but adopted children are also often accompanied by a sense of loss, the fear that they will be abandoned again, and the mysteries of their pasts. We made every effort to gather as much information as we could about our daughters' birth families and medical histories, but pieces of those histories will always be missing. In Gabriela's case, we are sure of almost nothing in her past, including her date of birth. We think Rosa had measles and chicken pox in infancy, but we'll never know for certain.

Rosa and Gabriela were both suffering from malnutrition when they came to us, and Rosa also had an intolerance for lactose and could not digest dairy products. When Rosa came home, she was tiny for her age but could eat as much as any gluttonous adult. You're sending too much food in her lunchbox, her teachers told us when she started preschool. She wouldn't get up from the table until there was nothing in sight left to eat. The school had never seen a child this attached to food before, and they didn't hesitate to tell us they thought we were reinforcing wrong and unhealthy behavior. But Rosa's pediatrician advised us to let her eat as much as she wanted as long as she ate nutritiously, so we worked with her teachers on understanding malnutrition and the catching up Rosa needed to do. With Gabriela, we were more experienced and thus able to be calmer about her even greater need to turn food into a religion.

When Rosa had been home with us for eight months, she started to break her bones. She had fallen while on the climber, but she didn't really hurt herself, her teacher mentioned in passing when she called to say that Rosa was unnaturally cranky. She had fallen less than two feet and onto soft grass, but her left tibia was fractured nevertheless. The pediatric orthopedist assured us that this was a torsion fracture, happens frequently to children under two, nothing to worry about. The school was stunned. Kids fall like that all the time, nothing like this had ever happened before, would we use our health plan instead of theirs so their insurance costs wouldn't skyrocket? And then, with a two-year old wearing a cast from toe to hip, strangers and even some well-meaning acquaintances began to make child abuse jokes. We weren't laughing.

The cast came off after four weeks. Less than six weeks later, I went to pick up Rosie from her friend Jamal's house where she had been playing. Jamal's mother told me Rosa had tripped while running, but didn't seem to be hurt. She cried a lot, though, the mother reported, casually remarking that Rosie didn't seem as resilient about such things as some other kids. Rosa was never a teary child, however, and was almost scarily stoic about pain in her first years with us. Within an hour, her arm had swollen to twice its size, and we were back in the emergency room.

The next day, Rosa's pediatrician called, having received the hospital report. She asked how Rosie was doing, what had happened, etc., and as I chatted with her pleasantly I naively thought how nice it was of her to be concerned enough to call. Then she said, "Of course, I don't think there's any reason to suspect abuse," and I realized abruptly that when a child breaks two bones in three months, her doctor has to investigate. Our state requires adoptive parents to file for a child abuse clearance. We had recently refiled because the clearance has to be renewed annually, and Rosie had not yet been naturalized or readopted in the United States. Our tolerance for child abuse jokes, meager to begin with, became nil.

There have been other health problems, including a skin ailment rarely seen in North American children and the need for serious dental work. A pediatric malnutrition specialist helped us pinpoint one underlying problem, a calcium deficiency, and with changes in diet (Rosa became the yogurt queen in our family), our little girl is now a healthy and growing eight-year-old. It is more terrifying to look back on this early period of injury and illness than it was to live through, since the big picture never came fully into focus while we were absorbed in getting through one day at a time.

The specter of serious health problems made us even more aware of the precariousness of our family structure in the world of institutional officialdom. Alice carries one of my health insurance cards and a document drawn up by our lawyer giving her power of attorney to make medical decisions about Rosa and Gabriela (and me, but that is another battle). Nevertheless, only I am Rosa's legal parent when a signature is required. Alice also carries a beeper at work. We have established a numerological system, ranging in urgency from "call if you have a chance" to "code blue." That means I don't have to explain who I am to her secretary. It also means that Alice has not been able to be present at either child's adoption finalization.

Like all parents, we have been more even-keeled with our second daughter. Gabriela's adoption required two trips to Peru, and this time I went alone. We needed to save Alice's vacation and sick days for my return to work, and we worried about Rosa's safety in Peru, her emotions about having a new sister, and her adjustment to the altitude problems many people encounter in the Andes. Nineteen months old during my first visit to Peru, with scars on her ankles from restraints of some kind, Gaby came to us ill and withdrawn, her now luxurious black hair sparse and reddish-brown from malnutrition. Having received no immunizations, she was assaulted by unfamiliar organisms in the United States and came down with a severe case of mumps a few weeks after getting home. Her mouth became so swollen and sore that she could not eat, which made her frantic with pain, fear, and rage. We thought her a beautiful but solemn child, a diagnosis that amuses us now as we watch our ebullient, feisty, motor-mouth five-year-old adapt happily to anything that comes her way.

Our encounters with schools have changed as the girls have grown. We've been relentless and relatively successful about getting our family arrangements accepted. We are now beginning to confront our daughters' learning differences. They did not hear English spoken until they met us, and before her encounter with Spanish in her foster home in Cuzco, Gabriela's language of origin was Aymara, an Indian dialect spoken in southeastern Peru and Bolivia. We do not yet know what the final legacy of malnutrition, emotional trauma, and language change will be for our girls. We are lucky that the school our daughters attend is willing to work with us as we try to meet our children's needs.

Our privacy has been irrevocably invaded, our leisure time encumbered, our sleep cycles disturbed, our concerns about the ozone layer, nuclear threats, ethnic strife, and world hunger intensified on behalf of the next generation. We visit zoos and go on hikes, string up piñatas for birthday parties, stock extra jars of peanut butter, pack school lunches, go to parent meetings. We have become aficionadas of the local playgrounds, and teenagers on our block have suddenly taken on a new importance as potential babysitters. We have remembered the words to "On Top of Spaghetti," "I've Been Working on the Railroad," and "Rudolph the Red-Nosed Reindeer." We have resurrected our distant childhood knowledge of how to build a snowperson, how to balance on a see-saw, how to steer a sled, and how to play "Red Rover." We drive to piano lessons, put on plays, design Halloween costumes. Rosa and Gabriela have taught us more about survival, humor, flexibility, fragility, fear, affection, awe, and innocence in the last seven years than we ever knew we could learn.

We were careful to play by the rules that require a closed closet door when, in part at Rosie's instigation, we embarked on a second adoption. We knew what we were getting into this time, though nothing could have prepared us for the complications of Gabriela's adoption. We were warier the second time, but also more certain that parenting is a choice that is right for us. Although we felt forced to hide the nature of our household arrangements from the legal system, we take pleasure now in proclaiming ourselves as a public and proud family. We hope eventually that Alice will be able to become Rosa and Gabriela's legal parent.

There are plenty of things for other children to tease our kids about: their adoptions, their racial difference, their small stature, the number of their mothers. But if not those things, then others, and a child can only be hurt by something she feels uneasy or unsure about. Our children are comfortable with themselves and with their family, because we are. We make no apologies for the love the four of us share. And when we worry, we remember the response given by the ten-year-old son of friends of ours when asked by his fifth-grade schoolmates why he had two moms. Amused by the question, he answered with a grin, "Just lucky, I guess!"

The Moment the Two Worlds Meet

Sharon Olds

———————————

That's the moment I always think of—when the
slick, whole body comes out of me,
when they pull it out, not pull it but steady it
as it pushes forth, not catch it but keep their
hands under it as it pulses out,
they are the first to touch it,
and it shines, it glistens with the thick liquid on it.
That's the moment, while it's sliding, the limbs
compressed close to the body, the arms
bent like a crab's rosy legs, the
thighs closely packed plums in syrup, the
legs folded like the wings of a chicken—
that is the center of life, that moment when the
juiced bluish sphere of the baby is
sliding between the two worlds,
wet, like sex, it *is* sex,
it is my life opening back and back
as you'd strip the reed from the bud, not strip it but
watch it thrust so it peels itself and the
flower is there, severely folded, and
then it begins to open and dry
but by then the moment is over,
they wipe off the grease and wrap the child in a blanket and
hand it to you entirely in this world.

Beneath the Skin

Martha Roth

I

I never liked children, and when I was a young woman I didn't like feminists or feminism. I was an intellectual, self-defined, and I thought excellence was gender-blind. If a thing depended on my being a woman, it smacked of mediocrity. Although I couldn't think of a drearier term than "housewife and mother," "Distinguished Woman Anything" came close (this was in the 1940s and '50s, a time when people still said *poetess* and *aviatrix*).

My parents were college graduates, and my mother worked outside the home. They always encouraged me to think of myself as a potential professional and to prepare myself for work that I would enjoy. I didn't want to be a "successful girl"—that phrase included narcissism and lowered expectations. I assumed that fulfillment as a woman, whatever that meant, would come easily, automatically, and therefore I could afford to despise it. I wanted Success as a Person, i.e., a man.

There were plenty of tollgates and detours on the road to success. When we married, my husband and I were both receiving full-tuition scholarships. The university took a look at our status and had the Dean of Women inform me that my aid was being reduced to half. My husband, she said, was regarded by the university as likelier to repay their investment.

It's hard to write this. Intellect, sexuality, and denial wind around each other inseparably in my memory of the fifties, and so does a certain disdain for my body that changed in the sixties. I didn't see anything wrong with living in my head, and it took ten or fifteen years of adult life before I understood the legitimacy of my body's claims. I'm not talking here about sexual satisfaction, for we hard-case intellectuals prided ourselves on understanding "the woman question," including women's orgasms. What I am talking about is softer and more elusive, closer to "the vulnerable feeling self" Susan Griffin invokes in her *Pornography and Silence*—the self that has babies.

In the fifties, "hard" was good: hard liquor, hard reasoning, hard penises. My disdain for "girls" went along with dislike for softness, for the pale, pretty Marie Laurencin prints in my parents' bedroom or the poems of Elizabeth Barrett Browning. I admired Dorothy Parker, Lillian Hellman, Mary McCarthy. Their characters went out and got laid. You never caught them whining about babies. I also admired lesbian friends, who seemed to carry hard femininity to its logical conclusion. I didn't know any lesbian mothers, then.

The first time I got pregnant, in the summer I was seventeen, I borrowed the money for an abortion as fast as I could. I got married at nineteen, in 1957, and a month before the wedding I had a second abortion. I hadn't finished my degree; a baby was out of the question. My husband and I were going to do and be hard, brilliant things. We might have a baby some time, but other things came first.

As my husband slogged his way toward a Ph.D. in American litera-ture, I worked in a downtown office editing copy for a medical maga-zine, returning every evening to the university neighborhood. We enjoyed having more money than most graduate-student couples. When I got pregnant a third time, we could pay for the abortion ourselves.

All my abortions were illegal, and I never felt grief or regret over them. Luckily, all were done by competent people who left me healthy. A couple years later, we conceived again and decided we could fit one hard, brilliant child into our lives.

What we had, of course, was a soft wild baby, and I loved her with single-minded passion. I loved the state of being pregnant and the condition of nursing, and I got pregnant again before our first daughter was a year old. My discovering value and pleasure in my woman's body coincided with larger changes in American culture: the 1960s were happening, and I was happening right along with them, taking organic vitamins, turning on, learning to dance.

For the next ten years, while my husband worked as a university professor, I stayed at home: growing, nursing, and rearing three children. I took in free-lance editorial work that could be slotted between feedings and trips to the playground or the pediatrician. Some of my old friends went South for Mississippi Freedom Summer; I couldn't, because I had little babies. But with the rising activism of Black people North and South, with rock and roll, with Black Pride, I was full of hope for the future. If racial attitudes could change, why not sexual? Some of our friends were starting communes, dropping out of bourgeois life. We drank California wine and marched against the war; I began to write for the underground press.

The sixties really lasted through Nixon's first term. With the end of the Vietnam War and the successful repression of Black militancy at home, the counterculture lost its focus. In 1973, when our youngest child started kindergarten, I went back to work outside the home as a medical editor and writer. One day I discovered the "reproductive history," a technique used by obstetrician/gynecologists for describing and classifying their patients: age at menarche, age at pregnancies, outcome of pregnancies, age at disease or injury to the reproductive organs, age at menopause. I knew the difference between "gravida" and "para"—between pregnancy and childbearing. When I had my first child, for example, I was gravida 1V, para 1. But I'd never taken my own complete history.

I made notes, and later found enough long sheets of ruled paper to do a proper chart. I drew a ten-year calendar and graphed onto it the dates of my abortions. Then I graphed the births of my children. The two sets of lines had the same length: they were exactly the same number of months apart. As though following a schedule, my body had observed the same intervals between the conceptions that were aborted and those that were carried to term.

II

> I remember . . . feeling pleased to be different from
> other women—better—because I was ambitious and
> contemptuous of domesticity and "thought like a
> man," while at the same time, in my personal and
> sexual relationships with men, I was constantly being
> reminded that I was after all "only a woman"; I
> remember the peculiar alienation that comes of
> having one's self-respect be contingent on self-hatred.
>
> — Ellen Willis, "Foreword" to
> *Daring to Be Bad: Radical Femi-*
> *nism in America 1967–1975,* by
> Alice Echols

In the peace movement between 1966 and 1972, I came along with many other women to a feminist awakening. We saw the men we worked with use two different kinds of rhetoric, one for men and one for women; we saw our work valued differently from theirs and our intelligence questioned because of our gender. Whereas none of us ever doubted the ability of a man to counsel a woman about her most intimate problems, women weren't encouraged to become draft counselors because they didn't "share the experience" of being vulnerable to conscription. After years of denying the evidence, I began to open my eyes.

Some women I knew organized separately; they started a women's peace group. Still denying my own experience, I wrote an article deploring their action, but in having to analyze their reasons for organizing separately, I came to understand them and finally to understand that they applied to me as well. My intelligence, my education, and my faith in hard reason had never spared me any of the consequences of my gender.

I began to read about the matriarchal religions of the fertile crescent and their survival in odd places, and I learned to glimpse those seams in the ancient texts where patriarchal culture slides over the worship of the old fierce goddesses: the story of Lilith in the Apocrypha; Apollo's plea to Athene at the end of *Oresteia*. I met with other women who had also begun to read with new women's eyes. The more I read and thought, the more evidence I found for misogyny as a dynamic principle in culture.

Talking about being a woman with other women, for the first time in my life, changed the way I lived in my body. I realized at last that there was no *me* without it; the body that made love and got pregnant and bore children was the same body that smoked and swore and drank and marched and reasoned and wrote.

Women all over the world were making similar stupendous discoveries. Salary inequity— unequal pensions, insurance rates, banking policies— housework— battering— rape— incest— the cultural assumptions of popular art and advertising— the very bases of gender definition were being called into question. Gender roles are constructed in each of us, we realized, to fit the political and economic arrangements of our particular society, and as these change, the patterns of gender would hang too loosely—or pinch. Things could be different! I became a committed feminist.

This major change in self-concept involved letting go of some illusions. Like Ellen Willis, I had thought I was different, exempt (in spite of contrary evidence), and when I discovered otherwise I had to fit my convictions to the new reality. I had a soft body and a soft character; I earned about sixty percent of what men of my age and skills earned; and for all my convictions, my children were going to inherit a world where gender arrangements were separate and unequal.

III

"How can you let him smoke like that?" my mother-in-law would ask, when my husband smoked between courses of a meal, or in the car, or lit one cigarette from the end of another. I just smiled, uncomfortably. She was speaking to me out of a world in which husbands and wives "let" or "made" each other do things—both as in "He lets me do whatever I want," and as in "Look what you made me do." My marriage came from a different place, I thought—from that realm invoked by Rilke when he describes two solitudes protecting one another—and it had survived into the late 1970s.

"How can you let her wear those shoes?" friends asked when our firstborn daughter decided in high school to wear four-inch spike-heeled ankle-strap sandals, the kind they call "fuck-me" shoes.

"How can you stand it?" my mother asked when our second daughter became a rocker, painted her fingernails black and split our ears with the Clash, the Police, Stiff Little Fingers. She dyed her dark brown hair, but she dyed it dark brown just for the dead, lightless quality. "How can you bear it?"

"Isn't it awful for you?" friends wondered when our son's fascination with dinosaurs and monsters modulated into an interest in "gore art." He drew and painted vividly and well, and the subjects of his art were increasingly violent. He began to produce a comic book about the fantasy adventures of his pet ferret; obscene and violent, it also blazed with wit. "How can you let them act like that?"

I lied, of course. I pretended to my mother-in-law that I didn't mind my husband's chain-smoking. "They're his lungs," I cracked, like a tough cookie; I didn't want her to know I was angry and scared.

"They're her feet," I said to my friends, not wanting them to know about the screaming fights I had with my daughter, about my frustration at her struggles to define herself as a woman, a person, a sexual human being—because they took such a different form from my own.

"They're her ears, her fingernails, her hair," I told my mother. "Nothing lasts forever." Although confused and unhappy about how much of my children's behavior was my responsibility, still, I was becoming seasoned in acceptance.

"He's really very gentle," I defended my son. "I think it's his way of exploring violence. I mean, my god, the world deals him plenty."

Our family struggled to balance the needs of two working parents and three working children. We all shared household chores, cooking and cleaning and laundry, on a schedule drawn up freshly every week to take account of football, broomball, softball, dance classes, music lessons, meetings. We tried to talk through our resentments, but when we felt tired and pressed, we screamed at each other. As my children became adolescents, I struggled to subdue my panic at the recognition that I had no control over them.

"Really, we never did have," said my husband in his newfound wisdom.

"But we didn't know it," I lamented. "We acted as though we did— and so did they!"

It hurt me to watch my beloved firstborn tilt and crimp and squeeze her body into parodies of femininity that I had always despised. When my beloved next-born daughter mouthed the woman-hating lyrics of rock songs and told us it was her ambition to be a groupie, I felt I had failed—not only as a mother but as a human. And I felt stricken by my son's desire to draw flayed, decapitated bodies. What did this say about my failure to handle violence? I never bought them toy guns. I tried to talk sanely about violence in their play. In return, he read and admired horror comics that sickened me, drew images that shocked me. I told him how I felt, trying not to inculpate him; I hoped he would use his graphic talent on other subjects.

"You really paint well, but the subjects are too violent for me."

"Well, do you want me not to show them to you?" he asked, at twelve, at thirteen. I felt torn. His talent gave me the thrill Jewish parents call *nachas fun kinder,* pleasure and pride in your children's achievements. But the subject matter . . .

"Of course not," I said. "I want to see how you develop as an artist." For my next birthday he painted an oil pastiche of Whistler's "Study in Grey and Black," featuring as mother a skull-headed figure with suppurating eye sockets.

When our family went out together—rarely—we showed the world two quietly dressed adults, one young woman dolled up like a baby hooker, and two punk rockers in black leather and chains, bondage trousers, multiple earrings, studded bracelets.

"How can you let them go around looking like that?" friends asked.

I just smiled. "Oh well, you know, nothing lasts forever . . . especially at that age . . ."

I still believe acceptance was better than rigidity. Our children knew perfectly well my husband and I didn't like their clothes and music, but we wanted them to know we loved them unconditionally. No matter what they wore or smoked or painted or played, no matter how often they tested our limits, they were our children, and we were proud of them.

I believe that if I had drawn a line, said "Not in this house," I would have betrayed my feminist principles. Isn't *choice* the essence of feminism? Isn't that what our hard-won knowledge is *for?* For my children, whom I love with unreasoning ferocity, I want the widest range of choices consistent with their powers. For my daughters, absolute choice of whether they will bear children; choice of partners, of work, of leisure. For my son, also, choice of parenting, partnering, play and work, and—more difficult for me to think about, because it isn't in my experience—the choice of how to use his penis-privilege, the cultural advantage he enjoys merely because he is male. No one knows how to choose a path who hasn't stumbled part way down several. Who says raising children is easy?

So if I'd said, "You can't wear those clothes," or "No heavy metal music," or "I forbid you to bring those comics or those drawings in this house," I would have been violating this principle. My children were in their teens when they did these things. If I had said, "In the name of feminism, of my espousal of choice, I forbid you the exercise of your choices, through which your judgment will mature," wouldn't I be teaching them hypocrisy?

Their adolescence of course awakened echoes of my own—the agonies of insecurity, the struggles against what I saw as my parents' stuffiness and lack of sympathy. I had rebelled by refusing to adopt a conventional female image; I wore jeans, seldom washed, hung out with radicals, fucked avidly and carelessly. In later years, I kept the politics and the sexual eagerness but let go of the dirt. Our children rebelled (at least partly) against our "political correctness," our Sixties liberality.

Our eldest daughter went through her last year of high school on the edge of expulsion. She could never get up in time for class, and she cut to smoke dope in the parking lot, but she was tops in all her classes. One unforgettable day she was still asleep at two in the afternoon when the mail was delivered, bringing her both a suspension notice (for truancy) and an invitation to join the National Honor Society.

Trying to rouse her from sleep to talk about her contradictory behavior, I found myself shrieking with rage. Heaps of clothes lay on the dirty floor of her room. She had come in very late the night before; she worked as a server at a downtown restaurant and although our condition for her taking that job had been that she be "in bed by midnight," she often went out after work.

"Look at this room! It stinks of dirty laundry. You were drinking last night, weren't you? They're going to expel you!"

I screamed these and similar words until she was awake and screaming back. This scene played two or three times during her senior year, with minor variations, and it was effective only in straining my throat. With the second daughter, I could be cooler: she was suspended one day when she arrived in class (on time) wearing blue pancake makeup, blue lipstick, and blue nail polish to match her blue dress, blue stockings, and blue shoes. She and her friends belong to the scavenger generation, haunting rummage sales and resale stores to assemble their amazing outfits.

"How could you let her come to school looking like this?" the assistant principal asked, when I went with her to his office.

"I don't monitor what she wears. She's clean and decently covered," I said. "Beyond that, it seems to me that what she wears is her own business."

"It's not appropriate dress for high school."

"I don't feel able to say that so confidently."

"Well, she can't wear it here."

My daughter and I looked at each other. "It's his sandbox," she said. I nodded. She washed her face, changed her clothes and went back to class.

Of course, real dangers threatened them. Our son, small for his age and defiantly shaven-headed, got his nose bloodied on the way home from school. I applied ice, tears, kisses. For weeks afterward I quaked whenever he left the house. I quaked for them all, off and on, because they were always also the babies I had borne, the gurgling infants, the toddlers who mastered symbol systems and applied physics with lightning speed. My gore-artist son was the little boy who used to climb my body like a tree frog and the kindergartner who announced one rainy day, "My self is wet!"

Our punk rocker was the curly-headed tomboy who slept with twenty-four stuffed animals and two live cats ranged along her bunk. The young woman in torture-shoes and too much lipstick was the diapered angel who had said goodnight to John, Paul, George, and Ringo before she could say Mama and Daddy. They were my kids. Did I err in setting limits that were too vague, too elastic? Were they confused about our expectations, and did they have to parent themselves? Their father and I expected them to play around with sex and drugs and rock 'n' roll, because we expected that teenagers would be curious and rebellious, as we had been. Would I want my children to be timid or indifferent to experience?

I don't really believe that our expectations pushed them into danger. We did the best we could, modeling adult tenderness for them, talking to them, listening to them. We didn't provide a drug-free household while they were growing up, but the world isn't drug-free. After the fact, I'm glad they know people use drugs, and drugs can be dangerous, and for some people they are too dangerous to use.

Peter DeVries somewhere says that the amazing thing about parenthood isn't that adults make children, but that children make adults. My children had to go through my maturing process with me, and no doubt there was wasted pain in it along with light and warmth and solid growth. But I can't have it any other way. And—though they're healthy, intelligent, aware adults—perhaps I shouldn't be surprised that they didn't catch the feminism I got so late.

IV

When I saw my son's first gore comics with their images of gouged eyes, spilled brains, disembowelment, I dealt with my revulsion by thinking, Hey, maybe he's going to be a doctor! This is close to the scientist's curiosity about what lies under the skin. Kids' cruelty begins in investigation, and investigation, I'm sure, begins in anxiety about our little bodies.

Gore art even mocks this anxious curiosity and reduces the scientific impulse to absurdity. If I listened, I might find a similar self-reflexive, self-critical meaning in rock lyrics. Postmodern style incorporates send-up, camp, satire in the presentation of the thing itself; everything spoken is "quoted." Of course satire, like camp, is a safety valve that ultimately sustains a status quo. That's why revolutionaries are regarded as humorless: "None of you feminists can take a joke!"

In exploring misogyny as a dynamic cultural principle, I've come to see that male or female, all we mother-raised creatures acquire a need to oppose women that is maintained in society and sharpened by every item of role definition that differentiates women from men—our styles of speech and persuasion as much as our clothes. My own disdain for women and children must have come from this need; the fifties woman who thought, drank, and wrote like a man was my generation's way of denying the value of femininity. My children have found other postmodern ways. I got over mine; there's hope for them.

My children are professionals now, in academia, in film, in video, and I still worry over the connection between sensuality and violence. I know this connection is made in us long before we have the language to describe it or defend against it, and I remember how long it took me to accept the soft, unappeasable hunger of the flesh.

I used to enjoy fantasies of cruelty, as my brilliant children appear to do still. The body that bore them is the same body that refused to bear three earlier ones. Maybe the curettes and the steel bowls of blood in the abortionists' offices were necessary before I could fully choose my babies' translucent fingernails, their perfect little genitalia. Perhaps refusal must always be a prelude to acceptance.

A Feminist Moment

Kimiko Hahn

One of the most important "moments" of my feminist education came in the contradictions of childbirth: a body swollen beyond recognition (the past body once so sexual, now spent and turned into a vessel, yes) now on the brink of a transformation from woman to mother/woman. The contradiction of the pain and the elation of seeing the child. The need to relax and be in perfect control. But these contradictions were small compared to the social one: the need to be self-absorbed and in complete partnership with my husband. When fear told me to stay put, to trust his urgings to squat or walk or lie down in a different position. To put a piece of ice in my mouth. Lean against his chest and cry. To shout during contractions—shout like this usually reserved but sassy body never shouts. My trust in him enabled me to relax. To focus the pain. To abandon pain. That depth of trust in the opposite sex is rare, profound, and ultimately necessary for political change.

For E

Kimiko Hahn

Jonathan and I have both been working all day: he, at his program for "juvenile offenders," me at home, art administrator one minute and mommy the next. Deadlines are in the air. Art work awaits the children's bedtime. Until then it is dinner, park, bath, stories, songs, tuck-in. We decide it's too hot to cook so pack restaurant distractions: a book for the older one and a bottle for the baby. As soon as we hit the street Aki demands to ride on Jonathan's shoulders. Kei screams until we give her the bottle.

We choose the Chinese-Latin restaurant and sit close by the big fish tank. The two race over to watch the carp, big as their own heads, blow bubbles and bump into the glass. When they're finally seated we notice little hand prints across the tank. Dinner comes: the baby attacks the *ropa vieja* so half goes in her mouth and half scatters confetti-like on the floor.

Before I take a bite, a friend comes over to tell me a young woman who used to cut hair in my apartment died last April. She was either pushed or jumped off a roof near her parents' Bronx home. I think: *She couldn't have jumped. I know it. This fucking society. Maybe she chose jumping over rape and strangulation.* I am distracted by the children's feeding frenzy and dinner is over in fifteen minutes.

On the way to the park, Aki begs to ride Jonathan's tired shoulders again. I distract her by pointing to a row of flowers along a building. *Aren't the flowers pretty!* Then I notice a rolled-up condom on a shrub. *Yes, and one has a hat,* she replies. When I laugh she says, *Don't laugh.* I shake my head and buy the two their promised Italian ices.

We make it to the park. The girls are sticky, sweet and happy. Jonathan and I open the lids off a couple decafs. The sun seems high for 6:30. *Mommy forgot the sand toys.* She couldn't have jumped, her daughter would be going on four also.

Maternal Boundaries; or, Who Gets "the Lap"?

Shirley Nelson Garner

I was the first woman in my family to want children when I had them. For the most part, the women in my family were maternal: they would sooner or later have wanted children. They were supporters of marriage and the family. But the children came too soon or too close together, or there were too many. My grandmother gave birth to my mother when she was fifteen, and four more children came one after the other, only a year or two apart. Her mother, my great-grandmother, was the child of what was then described as an "illegitimate" birth. My aunt and my mother had planned to wait longer than they did before becoming pregnant with my cousin and me. But my aunt became pregnant on the brink of the Depression, and my mother became pregnant during a rift in her marriage. Attending a girls' school in the fifties, my cousin had to leave college when it was discovered that she was married and pregnant. My mother told me of my second cousin, in her late teens and trying to finish college, "She cried when the doctor told her she was going to have twins."

Growing up in the fifties, I struggled to hold on to my virginity out of a fear of pregnancy. The disgrace of becoming pregnant "out of wedlock," as it would have been phrased, haunted me. But I also knew I had to go to college, I had to get an education. My father deserted my mother as soon as she became pregnant, though he would have done so sooner or later in any case. She bore the burden of single parenthood at a time when it would never have been a choice and when she had little company. She struggled as a teacher and a secretary to support herself and me and to find a decent place for us to live. Landlords weren't eager to rent to unmarried women, much less unmarried women with children. According to my mother, it was always assumed that single women would have affairs and bring scandal; if they had children, it was suspected that they had never been married.

Given my history and the stories that were told in my family and elsewhere, I knew that marriage and the family held no security. I knew from experience and quite consciously that I needed to know how to support myself. I remember noticing in my junior year that the skirts of one of the most beautiful girls in my high school were beginning to pull at the waist and then feeling sick when I heard that she and her boyfriend would marry. I thought of it as the end of everything for her. As I began to date and to feel the promptings of desire and know the pleasures of satisfying it, I was terrified that I would give over to it utterly and become pregnant.

I don't know whether it was the need to feel sure I could maintain myself independently through meaningful work or growing ambivalence about my husband that prevented me from having children during my first marriage. But when it ended in a divorce that we both wanted, I was grateful that there were no children. I could walk away without looking back. And I did. By the time I recovered from the ill effects of a bad marriage, secured an assistant professorship in English at a university, and was nearing completion of my doctoral dissertation, I was thirty-five. By that time, I was worrying about the direction of my life.

I had had serious romances and had fallen in love several times, but, for a variety of reasons, had never remarried. I remember at some point knowing that I wanted to remarry and have a family. I wasn't sure whether I would like having children, but I knew it was something I wanted to try. Having children—all of it: the pregnancy, giving birth, mothering—was an experience open to me, and I didn't want to miss it.

Sometimes when I said to a lover that I wanted to remarry and have a family, I could feel him begin to recede. A psychologist with whom I was in therapy in California after I got a divorce and was finishing graduate school suggested that I was too direct for most men, that my straightforwardness scared them. He said I needed to give them "an out." I think he meant that I ought to seduce them into marriage. He seemed to assume that many men, perhaps most, wanted to marry and have children, but that they couldn't face that desire openly. He thought that if I found a man who wasn't frightened, it would mean that the man had a strong sense of himself, which would make him a good mate. Yet he believed that it would be hard for me to find such a man. I argued at the time and still believe that leading a man from romance to the everydayness of marriage unawares would be a disastrous mistake. Yet the psychologist was right. It took me a long time to find someone who loved me that I could love back and who also knew that he wanted to be married and have a family.

By the time I remarried at thirty-seven, I knew that if I expected to have children, we would have to hurry. As soon as we decided to marry, Frank and I abandoned contraception and began trying to have a child even before our wedding at Thanksgiving. As time went on, and I didn't become pregnant, I discussed the matter with my gynecologist. He recommended that we begin fertility tests since there was not a great deal of time. After eliminating all the simple possibilities for our infertility, my doctor performed a laparoscopic examination to discover inhibitors that were invisible clinically—endometriosis and a benign ovarian cyst that was pressing against a fallopian tube and diverting the path of the egg. Once these obstacles were removed, I was hopeful of becoming pregnant and the doctor was optimistic. But it didn't happen right away. In 1972 radical reproductive technologies to which we have now become accustomed were not in place or were not ordinarily available. My surgery was then the last step toward fertility. At first, I became anxious. Then depressed.

The operation had occurred in the summer of 1973, and by Thanksgiving, when I had not become pregnant, Frank and I were discussing adoption. Earlier, he had said that he would be pleased to have an adopted child, but with the real possibility before him, he began to waver. Over the holiday and our wedding anniversary, we went to Texas to the wedding of Frank's niece. Away from work, cloistered in a hotel room overlooking the Austin hills, I suddenly felt a cloud lifting. I knew that whatever was to come would be all right. It was one of several epiphanies I have experienced, when I have felt diamond-sharp clarity. I knew that whether we decided to adopt children or not to have any, my life was filled with richness and possibility.

Maybe I had simply begun to count my blessings. I remember thinking that my life could take various courses, and its direction, and therefore I, would be different if I did or did not have children. No better or worse. Just different.

Whether it was the letting go or the biological course of things, I probably conceived that weekend, for I became pregnant with my son, Hart, who was born on August 23, 1974. I do not know if I would have had to struggle with a recurrence of depression had I not become pregnant. I am not certain that I would have maintained the peace of mind and contentment I felt that Thanksgiving weekend in Austin. Yet I believe that ultimately I would have accepted the circumstances of my life whatever they were. I don't believe I would have settled into depression, despair, anger, or grim resignation had I been unable to have children.

As time has passed, I have felt grateful for the difficulty I had becoming pregnant. Thinking I could not have children and imagining I could live well without them gave me a sense of strength; it let me know that I mattered in myself. Thinking I might not have them also let me know how much I wanted them. Having to go after them freed me from ambivalence or the illusion of ambivalence. When Hart was born, he came as welcome into the world as any child and more welcome than any of the children in my family. My daughter, Celia, born two years and eight months later, was particularly desired because we wanted a girl, and amniocentesis assured us that she would be one. I recount this history at some length because what I am about to describe about the experience of motherhood depends on some understanding of the pleasure with which I undertook it.

I also became a mother in privileged circumstances. Frank and I both worked, so we were economically secure. We could afford baby-sitters, daycare, and cleaning help. Our jobs, particularly mine, allowed some flexibility of working hours so that having a child didn't put us under unbearable pressure at our offices. We were, of course, busier. We were old enough to feel committed to both our personal and professional lives. We didn't have the anxieties and doubts that plagued us when we were younger.

Most importantly, my mother came to visit for two weeks after Hart was born and agreed to stay the year to help out until Frank and I could adjust to the changes in our lives. When that arrangement worked well for us all, she agreed to live with us during the academic year, going home to Texas in the summer and occasionally for holidays or visits. This meant that we avoided many of the strains that working parents generally have: anxiety about childcare, the complications of numerous arrangements, overtiredness and tension when anyone is ill or under pressure at work. I remember telling a friend that it seemed to me that each child needed three people to take care of it. Having three children, she laughed knowingly and responded, "Now I know what our problem is: we're missing seven people in our household!" For the first time, I was grateful that I was an only child, that my mother and father were divorced, and that my mother had not remarried. All of those circumstances freed her to be our live-in grandmother.

I had never imagined that becoming a mother would be wholly wonderful. I expected tiredness, hassles, lack of freedom along with the pleasures. But what I had not expected was some loss of my self, a feeling of being overwhelmed. Recalling Renaissance poets' configuring of a woman's body as fort, castle, city, or country, I don't think of enemies intruding or attacking. Rather I think of a castle without a moat, a town without a wall or with its gates open, or a country without borders. As a mother, I was something to those around me I had not been before. I didn't lose my freedom simply because I couldn't come and go as I wished and because I had added responsibilities. I felt newly permeable, taken over in a way I had never experienced.

Becoming a mother meant experiencing my body and understanding myself in a different way. It meant becoming conscious of boundaries between myself and others both literally and figuratively. On an almost daily basis, I find myself needing to define my boundaries and negotiate space for myself, actually and metaphysically. While this need may arise in other situations, my role as mother creates it most profoundly. While I began to know this feeling when my children were young, it continues though they are now teenagers.

I became aware of how literally my children understood my body as their property only as they began to lose their infants' dependency on me and assert their own independence. I remember preparing my children's breakfast one morning while they sat at the table. My son must have been approaching five, and my daughter two. As I stood at the counter buttering toast and sprinkling it with sugar and cinnamon, they both left their chairs and came to watch. Celia grabbed my right leg and clung to it; Hart pushed her away. Beginning a tug-of-war over my leg, they threatened to tear my nightgown and make me lose my balance. They were surely going to hurt each other. Celia screamed, "I stand by her!" Hart yelled back, "No, I do!" As they pushed and shoved

trying to take possession of my leg and I tried to calm them and separate them and myself from them, Hart drew himself up authoritatively
and asserted, "Celia! Mother told us not to fight over her body!"

I thought I must have said that, and I remembered the moment. I
had taken my children to a movie at the University Film Society. I don't
remember now whether it was a movie I thought they would enjoy or
one that was for my pleasure, which I hoped they would tolerate. Seated
on either side of me, one of them climbed into my lap; then the other
one tried to climb up as well. They began to push and shove and hit at
each other. One of them cried, "*I get the lap!*" Then the other shrieked,
"*No!* I get it!" Then they both begin to insist, "It's *mine!*" "*No!* It's *mine!*"
Growing up as an only child, I was unprepared for such tempests of
sibling rivalry. Surprised and amused, I had to work to take my children seriously and concentrate to stop the scene they were making, as
the people on either side of them began to lean away uncomfortably
and those behind us begin to change positions in their seats and
whisper to each other. Another moment flashed before me: when my
children had once fought over a two-inch scrap of waste paper so
desperately that I thought they might injure each other. That is how
they were quarreling over me. I was a contested piece of property.

I have often reflected on that moment and what I mainly was to
them: the lap. A comforting presence, warmth, a supplier of needs—
whatever those happened to be. Their thinking of me as "the lap"
depended upon some continuity they felt between their bodies and
mine. My body was theirs. *I* was theirs. To some extent, I am *still* theirs.
As theirs, I do the grocery shopping, cook the meals, do the laundry,
oversee the housekeeping, arrange all the doctors' appointments,
transport them almost everywhere beyond walking distance, and more
or less direct everything, even when my husband, their grandmother,
their friends' parents, or others actually do what is to be done.

Though I work full time as a professor of English and bring my job
into our home in the form of papers to grade, essays to write, phone
calls to make, colleagues to visit me; talk about events and problems at
the University; express the usual pleasures, anxieties, and angers of a
person who works outside the home in an atmosphere that can sometimes be benign and other times ruthless and politically charged—that
is not the me that is theirs or even that they pay much attention to. As
their mother, they see me in the ways I fulfill the stereotypical mother's
role of giver and nurturer.

A story will illustrate. For sixteen years, my mother has been our "angel in the house," sharing with me many of the usual mother's responsibilities. This fall after she, at eighty-five, had a heart attack, I took over most of the jobs that she had assumed wholly or shared with me. When I was describing the situation to my cousin and talking about how I was having to relearn how to schedule so many household duties into my life, like doing the laundry, watering the houseplants, cooking breakfast, my son entered the conversation and referred to the time after his grandmother's heart attack as the period when I became a "real mom."

No matter how much our lives cut against it, this *real* mom lives in all of our heads. When my children were much younger, Hart, Celia, and I were sitting around the breakfast table talking. In the course of our conversation, Celia said that when she grew up, she wanted to be a fireman or an artist. Hart said to her with great disdain, "*You* can't be those! You have to stay at home and take care of the babies!" Not believing what I was hearing, I intervened, "What! Such a thought! In *our* house? *I* don't stay at home all day—I work. So will you and Celia!"

But the *real* mom, who cooks and cleans and comforts everybody, still belongs to them as surely as I did when they thought of me as "the lap." What is mine is theirs, and they still assume a certain familiarity with me physically that both pleases and irritates me. They play a game in which they try to *get* each other; whoever *gets* the other receives a point, and they keep a running count of their ever-increasing scores. Taught them by a friend, the game involves one person's taking the other by surprise, brushing him or her underneath the chin with the top of a forefinger. If you want to tease and irritate someone, this is surely the way. Nothing is more annoying than having someone come up from behind and stroke your underchin or to be talking to someone and suddenly have him or her reach out and brush you under the chin. Not only is the surprise and distraction bothersome, but the feel of this gesture is also unpleasant. My children often exclude me from their world, filled with adventure and a myriad of secrets. When Celia was younger she once said to me quite cheerfully and disinterestedly, "I tell my friends my secrets. I don't tell you my secrets because you're my mom." But they take me into their chin game. They do so because we like each other, and they want to have fun with me. I know that, and yet sometimes I think I can't bear one of them startling me with this gesture when I'm busy or deep in concentration.

I notice the way my children still merge with me in little ways. This summer when we took a four thousand-mile driving trip we got along splendidly. I loved having encapsulated space with them during the drive—no telephone calls, no interruptions, only limited plans to make. We managed our differences with amazing ease. We took turns playing tapes during the drive. We shared or divided various responsibilities; we discussed possibilities for sights we might see and places we could eat and either reconciled our differences or followed one of our preferences now, another's the next time.

We had agreed to share things when we packed—shampoo and toothpaste, for example—so that we could travel as lightly as possible. But for no clear reason, my son continually used my comb. He said that he had brought one, but couldn't find it. When I offered to buy him another, he said it wasn't necessary. I wouldn't have minded, but his hair was usually wet and mine wasn't. I would often absentmindedly run the comb through my hair to find its wetness had spoiled my curls. Sometimes, he would carelessly put the comb in a different place, and it would be lost for a day or so. Then I would have to use the small comb I carried in my purse or just brush my hair. I could never get him to respect my wish to have my own comb; it was as though it was his *right* to use it.

When we went to buy travelers' checks before the trip, I bought checks for both Hart and Celia as well as several denominations for myself since we might be gone as long as a month. Both children were understandably curious to see them, how checks for various amounts differed. As I was trying to see that everyone had the right checks to sign, they leaned over me, picking up one book and then another and exchanging them, confusing one with the other. I was trying to complete the transaction, sign the right checks, and honor their curiosity by enduring it. But to keep from yelling at them in exasperation, I had to repeat to myself the title of one of Adrienne Rich's books of poetry: *A Wild Patience Has Taken Me This Far.*

But it has not only been my children who take me over. Both my husband and, to my amazement, my mother saw me differently and began to have expectations of me that fall peculiarly on mothers. Having grown up in an extremely patriarchal family, my husband was accustomed to the usual division of labor between women and men. Yet he supported me as a professional person and took on many of the responsibilities of childcare—more than I might have hoped. I began to realize, however, that he always expected me to be in my place: to be able to find me when he wanted me. This had not been the case before we had children. He always knew my schedule; I did not necessarily know his. No one thought anything of it if he worked late, ran errands after work, or arrived home half an hour later in the evening. If I stayed late for a meeting or to finish something and came home later than expected, the atmosphere was different when I arrived. It wasn't that he was angry or annoyed, but household order and direction suddenly had become tenuous without reason and I could generally feel some vague, collective anxiety beginning to gather.

Much to my amazement, my mother began to see me as her "rememberer." She might ask me to remind her to call Auntie Bill on the weekend, help her remember her appointment with the eye doctor the next week, not to let her forget to pay her bill when we went to the drugstore, and on and on. When my husband began to pick up this habit, I recall saying to them crossly: "I'm *not* the family rememberer!" I bought my mother an appointment book, but she never used it. I lectured my mother and husband about keeping up with their own responsibilities and appointments. I began to ignore their requests willfully and let them miss dates and forget things they wanted or needed to do. I treated them as the experts told me to treat children: let them learn through experiencing the consequences of their behavior. They never started making lists and don't keep appointment books, and they miss and forget a lot of things. But they no longer expect me to remember for them.

My husband also began to want me to be the "finder," especially in the kitchen. "Where is the Teflon skillet?" he might ask. Or, "Where do you keep the soup ladle?" "What drawer is the Saran Wrap in?" Tired by all this, I finally realized that as the mother I was supposed to run the house, know all about it. I was supposed to have a different relationship to it than the rest of the family. The appropriate response finally came to me: "You live here just as I do. Why do you expect me to know where it is if you don't?" Or, "The soup ladle is in the drawer where it always is." I simply stopped helping everyone find things.

But the feeling of being taken over has another side, which is attractive and seductive. It is the exhilaration of feeling larger than life, of dwarfing everyone around you, of thinking that you are at the center of everything, of believing you are all-powerful and that you can control everything. Once I said to my daughter, "You are an intelligent girl, a pretty girl, a nice girl, and I love you a whole lot!" When she looked mildly disappointed, I asked her if there was something else she wanted to be. Her face brightened visibly as she said with enthusiasm, "A *magical* girl!" Once she told me that she was not clever, but that she "could do many magical things." It is precisely this fantasy—that you are magic—that you sometimes get to live within as a mother. Everyone's crossing your borders, clinging to you, expecting the impossible of you, assumes it.

Once when my son fell and cut his lip only slightly, it bled profusely and frightened him out of all proportion to his injury. He kept pointing to his bloody lip and pleading, "Kiss, kiss!" believing I could stop the bleeding. We once had a conversation that reveals the fantasy:

Hart: What if we're dreaming our lives and we're really somewhere else?

Me: Shakespeare occasionally imagines something like that. Where do you think we might be, if we're only dreaming we're here?

Hart: What if we wake up in the king's palace?—Or, what if we wake up and we *are* the king and queen?

Magical. Queen. Once when Celia wanted to know whether the tooth fairy would bring her the dollar she was hoping for, I assured her that there was no reason to doubt it. When she wanted to know how I knew, I decided it was time to disabuse her of the myth of the tooth fairy—she was getting too old for it and probably didn't believe it anyway, I reasoned. I replied, "Because *I* am the tooth fairy." Her eyes danced with excitement as she exclaimed, "You *are!*" She thought that I was telling her that I was the tooth fairy for the whole world, rather than that there weren't tooth fairies. Where else except in this kingdom of my family would I ever be mistaken as a queen or a fairy of any kind? Where else believed to possess magic?

As a mother I frequently feel oppressed. I sympathize with and partake of the yearnings of my friends who had children early, before they were really ready for them, or those who had more than their temperament could easily sustain. One of my colleagues and friends, recently divorced, bought a house and furnished the downstairs with white carpets. Given the wet and slush of Minnesota's winters, I thought she was crazy to furnish a living room with white carpet, but she laughed with pleasure at the thought. Now that her children were in college, she told me, she could risk such pristine elegance. I think of the friends who had moved to Minneapolis and bought a condominium after their four children had left home. White carpets, white walls, uncluttered glass and polished wood tables, sofas and chairs in silky pastel fabrics that even a sweaty palm might smudge. My first thought when I saw it came immediately out of my mouth, "You can tell children don't live here!" Teasing, I asked them if I could come there and meditate sometime when they were out of town.

These friends could realize some version of a fantasy I had heard expressed long ago. The wife of one of my professors in graduate school and the mother of four children told me that when she and her husband retired they didn't expect to "settle down to become grand-parents." They planned instead, she said, to buy a white convertible and travel everywhere in white linen suits. She was the first parent as well as the first mother I ever heard speak honestly as a parent, to acknowl-edge that caring for children might be difficult, tiring, or boring, that an "empty nest" might offer promise. When I remarked on the fact that all four of her very bright children were going to summer school, she replied, "Oh, they don't all *want* to go to summer school, but we'd all go mad here in the house together for three months!"

After my colleague, a feminist theorist, told me about her white carpets and the children who had gone away, she remarked that we needed to consider how to make motherhood "less intrusive." Her words struck me at the time and continue to engage me. "Intrusive" wasn't the word I would have used. But I knew what she meant. Maintaining your sense of yourself, not being overwhelmed by motherhood, means realizing that you have limits and needs and that you are not omnipotent. It means helping your family to see you as you are. You must give up some of your magic, making *the* lap *your* lap— "Mother told us not to fight over her body"—and only one of several places to find comfort.

In bleak moments, I try to hold on to other times. When I recog-nized that I wouldn't be better or worse with or without children, just different, I didn't know what the difference might be. But my children have taught me things. Things I thought I knew. The most profound wisdom they have given me is a respect for human vulnerability. I have known that people are resilient, but I didn't appreciate how fragile they are. Until children learn to hide their feelings, you read them in their faces, gestures, and postures. The sheer visibility of shyness, pain, and rejection let me recognize and remember them. Hart and Celia also had an incredible capacity for telling me who I was. Once at a restaurant, when I was explaining to Hart that he was supposed to break his bread and not pick up the whole large piece, Celia said to me, "Mom, you seem to care a lot about little things." Once in a sentimental moment, I told Hart that no matter what happened and what friends deserted him, I always wanted him to remember that I loved him. He replied, "Mom, that isn't the way you love someone."

What I imagine as possible assumes certain minimum circumstances. It assumes reasonable economic comfort and freedom from basic fears. If you are worried about where the next meal is coming from or how you're going to afford shoes and coats in the winter, then your relationship to motherhood will be different and more taxing. If you're going to go to work each day and leaving a young child behind without care you feel is adequate, your sense of boundaries will undoubtedly diminish. If you are a battered wife or live in otherwise threatened space, then worrying a great deal over many of the matters I write about here will seem a luxury.

When I'm feeling overwhelmed, I call up as amulets to give me courage two conversations with my children. Coming to the end of a long Minnesota winter, Hart looked out an upstairs window to observe the melting snow and clapped his hands with delight: "Look! Look! The sidewalk is coming, springtime is here!" One Ash Wednesday, Celia noticed that all the people around her school, the roots of which are Episcopalian, were walking around with black smudges on their foreheads. In response to her bewilderment, I explained this pre-Easter ritual. She looked at me doubtfully and said with great assurance, "I wouldn't let *anyone* put ashes on *me!*"

Counting Cost

Akasha (Gloria T.) Hull

---

i.

Walk out the door

Too much pain
too much limitation—
Leave that woman-thing
                that mother-bind
behind

ii.

Images:

I.
Fifteen months old—
Us returning from the interview trip
                to Midlands, Michigan
                to Elizabeth, New Jersey
                to Chicago, Illinois
One:
the red bib coveralls
the red piano
unplayed

no smile of greeting
no outstretched arms—
taking what was given
as early as that point
reaching out for nothing
which was not there

Times two:
The swollen face
blueblack from eye to chin—
The babysitter said he fell,
her spare white face
nipped and frosty language
offering no details and less apology

His face
the same passivity
uncried questions
                in the old man eyes

The rational approach to childrearing requires:
no angry accusations, no alarm
no swooping arms of pity
no tears, never
no tears

Without really looking at one another
we collect the child and go on home

II.

Fifteen years old—
In the house of empty rooms
full of nothing but furniture
and fancy shades pulled down
against the evening sun,
dustbeams caught in yellow light
the only signs of life

My timid rescues are slight
                and temporary
Aloneness is the dependable order of the day
Cheery goodbyes
which did not fool the silence—
By then the old unasked, unanswered question
not even a feeble echo in the void:

"Mommy, can I come
            and live with you?"

iii

Walk out the door—

Away from meals
of fried pork chops and frozen string beans,
of the feminine mystique turned black—and blue
Needing a larger self
a whole, new way of being
in that tragic drama
where all the characters
play the parts of ghosts
and end up dying
as the world turns,
as the curtains fall

Cry all the unshed tears many long years later
Look the damned and bloody monsters
                in their midnight face
Count the cost
feel the pain

Cry it all out—
Unblock the aching head
            the clouded eyes
            the choked-up throat
            the banded heart
            the knotted entrails
            the swollen womb
            the two tied tubes

            the way to health
            to self—
            forgiveness
            love
            and joy

Discoveries Through Our Children

Nancy Spero

Section II

Discoveries through Our Children

Mothers thought their children would learn about the world from their parents' experience, but found that learning also happens the other way. Several writers in this section thought they had learned the lessons of gender, color, and class, but learned even more from their children's encounters with these hard facts of life. Maureen Reddy's children ask questions that conflate gender and race, because their parents are an interracial couple; "Race-ing Love" tells how she answers these questions and what she has learned from them.

Children give mothers echoes of their own childhoods, and they confirm mothers as adults, as Vera Williams shows in a delightful drawing.

When children are not born healthy and perfect, they introduce their mothers to a special kind of sorrow and anxiety. When children die, maternal grief is of a depth never before imagined. Linda Aaker, in "Birthing Death," writes with rage and grace of the feelings of a woman poised to welcome motherhood who then encounters the awful blankness of death instead of new life.

Mothers' emotional connection to their children characterizes this section, the surprising freshets of spontaneous, unconditional love at their births and the anguish with which mothers have had to let them go. In "Jessica's Poems," Madelon Sprengnether reports on some of her young daughter's responses to the transformations she perceives around her. Amy Sheldon, in "Kings Are Royaler Than Queens," discusses how young children, especially her own daughters, learn through language the inequities of gender in our society. Wanting a perfect world for their children, mothers are surprised by a feral urge to protect children from ordinary misfortunes, as in Linda Hogan's poignant poem "Shelter." Feminists are committed to freedom of development for all individuals; children's needs for guidance require constant reinventions of this commitment. Nicole Hollander's Sylvia speaks to this reinvention. In Jane Lazarre's "Black and Blue," a biracial adolescent encounters invisible barriers for which his parents could not prepare him, and which they must confront with him.

Children often lead mothers into deeper self-understanding, as Sheila Fay Braithwaite illustrates in her recovery narrative. They also widen mothers' emotional range and test maternal convictions, as Marilyn Hacker describes in her poems to her daughter, "Three Sonnets for Iva." Kathryn S. March's essay about her struggle with the grief of infertility and child death, "Childbirth With Fear," concludes this section.

Race-ing Love

Maureen T. Reddy

"**M**ommy, I am Roo and you are Kanga, okay? Just pretend. And Daddy is Piglet, and Brendan is Tigger." Caught in the spell of the Winnie-the-Pooh stories, two-year-old Siobhan casts her family in an imaginary, long-running play. Siobhan calls me "Kanga" for nearly a week, refusing to answer to anything but "Roo" for that whole time. Even when she wakes up in the morning and wants to be rescued from her crib, she calls out, "Kanga? Kanga?" or, if she wants Doug, "Piglet? You there?"

Just as I begin to despair of ever again finding my way out of the hundred-acre wood—will I start to think of myself as Kanga soon?—Roo/Siobhan announces new roles over dinner one night: "Mommy, you are not Kanga now. Now you be the dumb policeman, okay?" Surely A. A. Milne did not inspire the "dumb policeman" idea? I burst out laughing, angering the intensely earnest Siobhan. Banging her fork on the table to emphasize her seriousness, she says, "No laughing. And Daddy, you are the butter man." Brendan/Tigger, who is ten, wants to know his new role, too: "Who am I, Siobhan?" She leans across the table toward him and whispers conspiratorially, "You are *my brother!*"

This is one of the best parts of mothering: glimpses into my children's imaginations that often hint at a sense of the world entirely different from my own, a place where fewer possibilities have been closed off. When Brendan was about the age Siobhan is now, he told me that he wanted to be a cow or a pig when he grew up, because then he could play in the dirt all the time. This came right on the heels of a few months in which "eight tiny little reindeer" (invisible, of course) accompanied us everywhere. When Doug picked Brendan up at the child care center, he would have to open the car trunk, wait a few seconds, and then check with Brendan to make sure all eight had made it in safely for the trip home.

Two is also the beginning of years of questions, asked confidently—at least for the first few years—by someone who thinks parents really have the answers: what is the sky made of? where does the night come from? why do we wash our hands? why is it bed time? why do you say "oh, shit"? why? why? why?

Siobhan is now nearing the age when Brendan began to ask the questions that changed my life: why do white people have vaginas? what is older—dark skin or light skin? why do boys have curly hair and girls have straight hair? And later: what does "nigger" mean? why do some boys think they're better than girls? why were there slaves? why are so many white people racist? And just last year: why do pictures of Jesus show him as white? Last month: why are all the people in *Mrs. Doubtfire* white? Last week: is saying "Mammy" always racist, or is it only racist if you're not talking about your own mother? Siobhan's questions will probably differ from Brendan's. She is unlikely to ask why white people have vaginas, for example, since she has a vagina but is not a white person. Although I cannot predict her precise questions, I hope that she does soon ask why all but one of Milne's characters are male. And I am almost certain that her questions will teach me a new balancing act on the race and gender axes.

I am white, my husband is black, our children are biracial. Although I had understood intellectually before Brendan's birth that my children would lead lives some of whose most salient factors I had never experienced, I did not *feel* what that meant until much later. When Brendan began to ask questions about race at about age two-and-a-half, I had to confront the disjunction between what blackness and whiteness mean to me and their broader social constructions.

Most painfully, I had to grapple with the social meaning of my own whiteness.

Until Brendan began to ask those hard questions about race and gender, Doug and I had treated race as an issue for both of us in the outside world that shed its public significance at our apartment door. In some strange way that is difficult now to reconstruct, I think we considered ourselves "de-raced" in private, "raced" in public. I did not think of Doug as "my black husband," but simply as Doug, just as he did not think of me as "my white wife," but as Maureen. Yet we often discussed race, particularly because we were both active politically in organizations working on racial issues; however, we did not discuss race as an issue *between* us. Our home was an oasis of sorts, a refuge from the racial hostility festering around us. We knew that we would have to help our child to negotiate a racist society and thought we understood what that would involve.

And then Brendan's questions "re-raced" us by reminding us that we are *always* raced and by demonstrating that we had taken too much for granted, including the notion of race itself. When Brendan asked what made me light and his father dark, for instance, we knew "melanin" would not be a useful answer for a small child. Similarly, when he asked why we called some people black and others white when most people looked brown or pink to him, we had to consider how to explain race as a social, as opposed to a biological, category.

Like most white people from progressive families, I seldom thought of my race while growing up; race had no conscious role in my self-identification. As the daughter of immigrants who spoke always of Dublin as "home," and whose American-born children all did the same, I thought of myself as Irish, certainly, but never as white. Even as an adult involved in an interracial relationship, I did not fully confront what my whiteness might mean—socially, personally, politically, symbolically—until my son's questions pushed me to interrogate myself.

This absence of analysis itself reveals one of the meanings of whiteness: being white means never having to think about race in relation to oneself unless one *chooses* to do so. One of the great privileges of white skin is precisely this lack of racial consciousness. That is one privilege—and a dubious one, to be sure—that I lost through becoming the mother of black children.

Explaining the difference between girls and boys initially was much simpler than answering Brendan's race questions, because sex has biological criteria that can be simplified without total distortion. "Girls have vaginas, and boys have penises," we told him, and that seemed satisfactory for a while. Some of his early questions—why do white people have vaginas? why do boys have curly hair?—showed that he confused race and sex. That confusion demonstrated to me in practical terms the interrelationship of race and gender. It also sharply reminded me that both are indeed social constructions whose meanings are dependent on circumstances and therefore constantly in flux, but in flux *together.* One learns one's race and gender simultaneously, in the sense that one learns to be a black female or a white female, a black male or a white male, not first how to be black and then how to be female, for instance.

Once Brendan began to ask questions about gender, as distinct from sex, Doug and I had to confront our own hard questions about social constructions of black maleness in order to figure out how to help our son to resist the soul-destroying stereotypes of black masculinity current in the United States. Because systems of oppression seem to favor Brendan on one of their axes—he has the (largely illusory for black men) privilege of maleness—we decided the safest course would be to insist on entirely biological criteria, to emphasize sex over gender.

When Brendan was four and began to run into explicit articulations by peers of girls don't/boys don't rules, we reminded him that if he did it, it was something boys do. So, for example, when a kindergarten classmate jeered, "Only *girls* play with 'My Little Pony.' Are you a *girl?*" Brendan responded calmly, "No, I'm a boy. I have a penis," and continued to play what he wanted.

As Brendan gets older, resisting gender role limitations gets harder, and he often finds himself out of step with the views of his peers. Ironically enough, Brendan's resistance of gender stereotypes has been made easier for him than it might otherwise have been because he meets several gender ideals: he is tall and strong, athletically talented, extroverted, and quick-witted. Deliberately standing outside conventional gender requirements has not meant that Brendan stands alone; he has many friends, some of whom share his views and others who tolerate them as part of Brendan (I think Brendan sees these last as potential converts). I sometimes wonder if Doug and I would have persisted in teaching Brendan to reject gender-role limitations had he been small, shy, physically inept. Would our principles have withstood the pain? We have been lucky that our son has not suffered much as a consequence of his perceptions of gender, but he has suffered some.

Many of our family's dinnertime conversations center on what happened that day at work and at school—our own nightly news. For the past three years, talk of what went on at school has often led to talk of gender. We heard that the boys didn't want to play with the girls and vice-versa, leaving the few children who had friends of both sexes (such as Brendan and his best friend, Luz) in a difficult position. Certain conflicts are more disheartening than others; the worst for me are when adult women reinforce gender stereotypes.

When Brendan was in second grade, for instance, the bus monitor was a female patriarchal enforcer, who created her own silly rules about the girls entering and leaving the bus before the boys. Brendan was perpetually annoyed by this unfairness, believing that a "first-come" rule was fairer, and also by the monitor's insistence on sex-segregation (girls on the left side of the bus, boys on the right). We suggested that he discuss the rules with her, but that didn't work; she announced they were just "good manners" and reminded him that she was "in charge of the bus," so he would have to do what she said. This turned out to be a good practical lesson in dealing with petty rules and deciding when to resist. According to Brendan, the girls liked the rules, so none of them complained. I hope some of their parents helped them to understand that this unfair privilege had a heavy price, that "special" treatment is based on a false and limiting view of difference.

I think the bus struggle had special significance for Brendan because of his interest in the Civil Rights Movement and the hold the story of Rosa Parks had over his imagination. When he first heard about Rosa Parks at about age four, he related very personally to Jim Crow laws, telling me one night, "I would be sad on those buses, because you would have to sit in the front and couldn't sit with Daddy and me. People must have been sad."

Doug and I explained that people weren't sad, they were *mad,* and getting angry helped them to change things. One evening not long after this discussion, Brendan brought me a sort of stick that he had made by putting tiny Legos together and asked me to guess what it was. A stick? a snake? a ruler? a road? No. "It's my idea of what the buses looked like before Martin Luther King had a bus boycott."

Only then did I notice that half the stick was made entirely of black Legos, the other half with white, yellow, and gray ones. A few nights later, I heard Brendan singing in the bathtub, "The South Africans are free because I took away all the missiles! We have our freedom!" This fantasy demonstrated some confusion between racial oppression and nuclear war, but I was impressed that he made the connection between social justice and peace, and that he thought of black people the world over as "we."

But the "we" is also problematic because Brendan is also white: black and white are not binary opposites in our family, but fused and fluid categories. I know that other people reduce this complexity and see Brendan and Siobhan simply as black, but I want my children also to have a sense of their own Irishness and not simply to read the world as divided into color-coded sides. At the same time, though, I want to encourage Brendan's and Siobhan's identification as African-American and to have an understanding of what that identity means. Sometimes these doubled desires lead to absurd confusion. Explaining to Brendan, then eight, what an "Uncle Tom" is, I heard myself concluding, "So don't go kissing up to white folks." Well, I *am* "white folks," of course, and I *do* want him kissing up to me!

Mothering Brendan and now Siobhan means that I am constantly aware of race; I have become alive to the byzantine workings of race in everyday life through loving and feeling responsible for children who lack the privileges that protected my own childhood. In relation to my children, I frequently have to ask myself the question that I think may be a near-constant buzzing in many black people's minds: is this racial? When Brendan's third grade teacher complained that a comment he made about a classroom rule was "outrageous," I wondered: is this racial? When the bus monitor told me that Brendan talked too much: is this racial? When a fellow student said to Brendan that "everyone knows" Brendan (who was one of the smartest children in the class) would never go to college: is this racial? When a white boy called Brendan a "monkey" during a dispute: is this racial? When Brendan and I were ignored as we waited for service in a deli, while white customers who entered after us placed their orders: is this racial? And if it is racial, what should we do about it? Is it worth a battle, or do we need to let it slide? ,

And I wonder how Siobhan's struggle with the vexed nexus of race and gender will reshape us all, what battles we will choose to fight and which will be forced upon us. I think a lot these days about the tension between black and white women, especially in the context of the feminist movement. And I worry about the (inevitable?) personal fallout from many black women's anger at white women who marry black men. My relationships with my children—like *all* parent/child relationships—exist within a swirling vortex of political and historical forces. Being a white mother of black children does not create those forces or bring them into play; it simply makes one aware of them, unable to ignore their shaping power.

The summer of 1990, when Brendan was six, we spent sunny mornings at the local park, where he zoomed around on his scooter or climbed trees while I read with one eye on my book and the other on him. One day, I noticed that Brendan and his friend George were in a turf dispute with two little girls, who apparently had laid exclusive claim to the jungle gym. George shouted to the girls, "We can play on it too! It doesn't belong to you! It's a free world, you know!" At this, Brendan turned away from the girls and said to George, "Well, actually, George, it's *not* a free world. They *say* it's a free country, but it's not a free world—just think about South Africa." George stood silent for a few seconds, looking baffled, and then he and Brendan abandoned the jungle gym battle and wandered off to do something else.

At first, Brendan's comment simply filled me with pride. It showed that he paid attention when his father and I talked about world events, and that he understood enough to explain it to another child. We had seen Nelson Mandela in Boston a few weeks before, so South Africa was much on his mind. But Brendan's comment also saddened me, as it demonstrated anew the truth that black children lose their innocence early, and seldom have the sense of entitlement or belief in the world's basic goodness that seems to come so naturally to many white children. Not that a false sense of entitlement or a mistaken confidence in universal fairness are good things—indeed, I understand well how dangerous they can be; nevertheless, some part of me mourns that my children will never feel the sense of personal power both of these beliefs bring. On the other hand, perhaps they will feel a more useful and realistic sense of power in collectivity, will recognize early the necessity of working with others to effect change.

Mothering Brendan and now Siobhan has allowed me to experience the link between feminist politics and anti-racist politics, to feel what used to be for me an intellectual grasp of race, class, and gender as interactive categories, to live with a heightened awareness of varieties of oppression. Being the white feminist mother of black children has sensitized me to the interdependence of social changes and to the absolute fallacy of separating racial, sexual, and economic justice. In *Maternal Thinking* Sara Ruddick describes the potential for a politicized maternal thought as a resource for peace, if that way of thinking is informed by a feminist consciousness that could help mothers extend their commitments to their own children into a commitment to *all* children. Too often, loyalties to one's own children can result in a *lack* of care for others, in a limited perception of the best possible future for one's own children. This limited—indeed false—perception remains widespread among white people, even among those who have suffered other-than-racial forms of oppression themselves. Would I understand this if my children were white? I don't know, but it's possible that I could learn it. That possibility, that hope, is what animates all my work now, and for it I am grateful to Siobhan and Brendan.

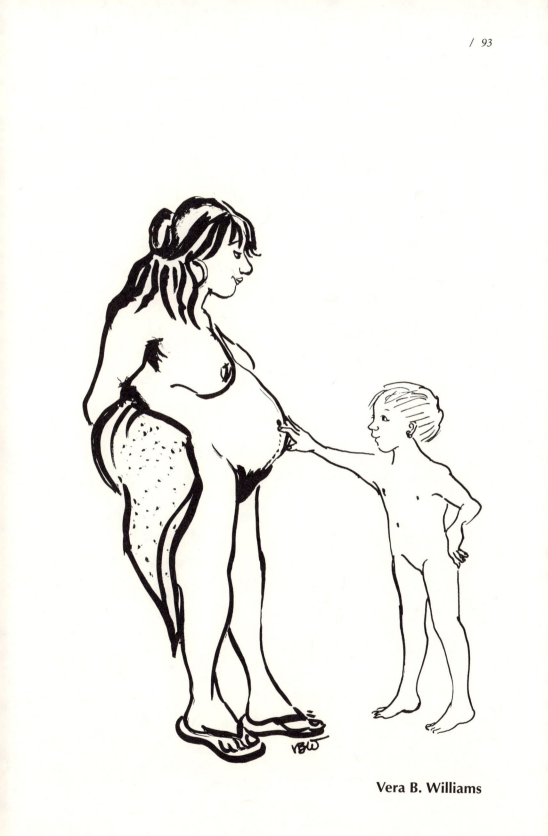

Vera B. Williams

Birthing Death

Linda P. Aaker

June 22—The Autopsy Conference

We sit solemnly in the waiting room at Children's Hospital. Although we have arrived separately, my husband Monte and I have not greeted each other. We have come to discuss the extent of Sarah's deformities. From here I can see the door to the room where she lived her entire life. Sue, the perinatal social worker, comes and leads us through a labyrinth of rooms and hallways to the conference room.

I follow mechanically, rehearsing the questions I want answered. When was her last moment of consciousness? Was I with her then? Did she pass from consciousness sensing my absence, not hearing the voice she had come to know during the thirty-eight weeks she was part of me? Did she die knowing that I loved her so much she did not have to keep trying to live in order to fulfill the dreams I had for her? Did she know that I loved her so much I could not tell her to die . . . that in the anguish of meshing her needs for peace with my dreams for her, all I could say was, "Sarah, I love you . . . You choose"?

We arrive at the office for Neonatal Medicine. From the small reception area, I can see Dr. Cosel, Sarah's neonatologist, sitting at his desk, wearing his white coat, and talking on the telephone. He smiles cheerfully, waves to us, and promises to join us in a minute. A copy of *Triathlete* magazine lies in the reception area. I numbly pick up the magazine to see who is the subscriber. I compare my pre-pregnancy body with my present waistless state. My dough-like stomach is an unwanted souvenir . . . a portable reminder that although I have no baby, I did, in fact, give birth.

In some ways the soggy stomach has helped me. Hundreds of times I have gone and looked at it in the mirror just to assure myself that she was born, that she really existed. I have woken from my sleep thinking, "Oh my God! I've got to call the hospital. I haven't felt her move for hours." Once awake, I go to the mirror to check. The sagging flesh has always confirmed the dreaded truth with rude honesty. My mind drifts to the suits waiting for me to recall them from storage at the dry cleaners. Can a waist stretched by the excessive amniotic fluid of my polyhydramnios state ever return to size ten?

Sue clears the conference room. The three of us enter. A pregnant woman joins us. "Hi. You may not remember me, but I'm Nancy from the Cardiology Clinic." I'm astonished that she actually thinks I may not remember someone so pregnant.

Since Sarah's death, I have avoided public places to assure that strangers would not ask me when I am due. Initially I welcomed this question as an opportunity to talk about her. "I've had my baby, but she died," I'd explain. Quickly I learned that their interest was only in live babies, not dead babies. Many, appearing embarrassed, replied, "Oh! I thought you were still pregnant." One woman, a hostess in a restaurant who was herself pregnant exclaimed in reply to my explanation, "You mean I'm going to have to look like that?" But the most painful response to the explanation that my baby was dead was the one most people had . . . silence.

Dr. Cosel enters still wearing his white coat and carrying Sarah's chart as if he has needed to review her case in order to recall who she was. Sarah's death is a professional incident that is behind him. I am jealous of his detachment. A tension has entered the conference room with him. Today I am feeling that he knows a great deal more about me than I know about him. This is a tension that exists when two people who hold their cards closely are together, but one has shown her hand without seeing his. He was present at Sarah's birth and heard my pleas to see her before they whisked her away to the Neonatal Intensive Care Unit (NICU). He has seen me weeping uncontrollably over the plastic top of her incubator. He has seen me rush to her side, kiss her paralyzed little fist, and sob to her that I loved her and that she could choose to live or to die. He has stood by as I held her dead body, stroked her hair, and rambled on and on about some of the dreams I had held for her. In the stupor of pain, I have turned to him and asked, "But what about my milk supply? What am I going to do with that now that she is dead?" He has seen all of this, treated me with respect, but never revealed how he felt. He has seen my hand, but I have not seen his.

Until now, I have not experienced this tension, but it seems to be present today as a byproduct of the overwhelming feelings of failure I have been having recently. Before Sarah's birth, Cosel's partner, Barnes, had told us, "If it's not genetic, we can fix it." Well, her defects were not genetic, but they couldn't fix her. I have seen her death certificate. Her heart had only one ventricle. I have friends who are doctors. They have told me how very rare such a defect is. She had a rare and fatal flaw, and I feel responsible. I feel badly that Cosel had to try so hard to save her when that was not even remotely possible.

Dr. Benger enters. He is a man of stature and warmth, and his entrance breaks the tension. His open warmth contrasts with Cosel's cordial yet reserved style, and the fact that he is a pediatric cardiologist suddenly strikes me as a splendid fit for this man with his kindly, open personality. I study his face closely to assure that each feature matches the face of the man who carries Sarah's dead body in the nightmares I have been having. The match is perfect.

"You look great. You're doing fine," he says as he warmly shakes our hands.

His pronouncement surprises me. I cannot eat. I have difficulty sleeping. When I am able to sleep, it is fitful and provides little respite from the reality of her death. When I arise, I feel like retching.

"I really don't feel like I'm doing so great . . ." I try to protest, but he interrupts me.

"Oh, no. We can tell. They're doing great, right, Mike?"

"Yes," Cosel replies perfunctorily.

Benger remains standing and begins, "The reason we're meeting is to tell you what we learned from the autopsy. The primary thing we learned . . ." His voice seems to break, and he turns to Cosel and says, "Well, why don't we do this like we talked about."

Benger sits, and Cosel begins, "Well, the first thing we learned is that when we removed the respirator at the end, that was the correct decision. The necrotizing enterocolitis, or 'the NEC' as we call it . . ."

His decision to add parenthetically the nickname neonatologists use for this condition where the intestines and colon are actually dead seems odd, but he has communicated clearly and succinctly that the condition is viewed as a dreaded deadly enemy for all neonatologists.

Cosel's presentation is short, and the message clear. Nothing more could have been done for her. The necrosis had spread throughout her body.

My mind drifts back to those last hours. Why did I let her suffer so long? Why didn't I insist that they give her some morphine? Cosel gave her some as they were removing the respirator. He had to believe she was in pain even at the end.

Sarah, did you die thinking I let you suffer? Cosel's mission was to save you. Mine was to protect you.

Benger stands. He begins, "You know on the Monday before she died, we thought . . . well, maybe I should use the blackboard here." He moves to the head of the table and draws a simple diagram of the heart. Although he turns to glance at us, he no longer faces us as he talks.

He continues, "On Monday we thought that she had this A-V canal and this patent ductus arteriosus . . . On Monday afternoon we talked about closing the ductus with the drug indomethacin . . . But on Tuesday she developed the necrotizing enterocolitis, and . . ."

As he speaks, I feel that those last few days are so close to him that he is actually reliving them. He is not saying "First we thought . . . then we thought." Instead, now more than a month after her death, he recalls the specific days of the week on which the events surrounding her death occurred, and, unlike Cosel, he has come to the conference without notes.

I recall him standing next to her that Monday before she died. "If I didn't try the most conservative route with this drug first . . . if I tried surgery without trying to close the ductus with this drug first, and if we didn't try to get her weight up before surgery . . . and if she died, I could never look myself in the mirror again," he had told us emphatically.

He continues seeming to question his past judgment. "We don't know, and believe me we really don't know. This is a very rare defect that we're talking about. This is the third conference I have had—the other conferences have been with cardiologists—in which I have discussed what we could have done differently . . . but hindsight is 20/20. But even if we had tried the surgical procedures and been successful in keeping her alive longer, ultimately she would have been a transplant candidate, and we all know how speculative those are."

He returns to his chair but remains standing. Until now, I have felt sorry for the burden Sarah's defects placed on Cosel. I have felt badly remembering Cosel's jaws clenched with tension and his face ashen with fatigue the day Sarah was clearly moribund. Although Benger, unlike Cosel, was not physically present during those final desperate efforts to save her, I sense that her death was difficult for him.

I look at Cosel. Once during the conference he has politely excused himself, then quietly returned. Today he seems bored with the dead and anxious to tend to the living. Her death is behind him.

I look at Benger. Twice I think I have heard his voice break as he has talked about her. Her death is not yet behind him. The fact that he seems to care so deeply makes me feel a connection with him. Yet, I feel badly that I have put him through this. At least three times during his presentation, he has repeated his ". . . but hindsight is 20/20." I wonder whether he has some doubts about our confidence in the care he gave her.

"Well, we feel she had the very best care, and we are very grateful for that," I tell him in an effort to assure him.

"Thank you. Thank you. We appreciate that very much, BUT THIS IS AN INTELLECTUAL CONFERENCE," he proclaims.

He is towering over me. He has stated his edict, and the conference is over for me. I no longer feel a connection with him. I am uncertain of my previous analysis of him. Why did I foolishly believe he is sad that Sarah died? I am not sure of anything except that I have produced this badly deformed child, and now I have said something that is inappropriate . . . the inappropriateness of which appears to be obvious to everyone.

I can feel the lightheadedness of shock giving way to tears. One thing is clear. I've got to get out of here without openly sobbing. I focus on the cover of a nearby magazine. I focus on the lavender border on its cover. I think of the pale lavender baby blanket, now placed out of sight in the cedar chest, that was for her trip home. My chin quivers. I concentrate on the fake wood grain of the plastic top of the conference table. I think about the particle board beneath, silently releasing formaldehyde into the air.

Sarah, Sarah, was it that I unknowingly exposed you to formaldehyde?

I can feel my chin quiver again. I scan fruitlessly for another focal

point. I recall the last line of the e.e. cummings poem on the announcement we had printed for her birth/death: " . . . rarely beloved a single
star is uttered and I think of you."

Benger is now sitting at the table and talking. "You see, if a tree grows
crooked, we can accept that, but when a child is born defective, we cannot accept the fact that such defects are also a part of nature. Oh, sure,
we know of some environmental insults that can cause heart defects, but
for the most part, we must accept that nature is not perfect . . . "

First he proclaimed this to be an intellectual conference, and now
the message I get is that there are to be no questions about possible
causation. A gush of rage engulfs me. He speaks in a vacuum. He
knows nothing of my medical history, but he has said that there is no
explanation except that her defects were a cruel quirk of nature.

I am an attorney. I am trained to ask questions, but now it takes all
my courage to ask a question about possible causation. Feeling that I
am being defiant, I begin in a barely audible voice, "When does . . . "

He interrupts, "Were you going to ask about when an echocardiogram could have been done?" Sue and Nancy laugh nervously. He
waits for my reply. He has interrupted me, and now I am profoundly
disoriented.

"I don't know what I was going to ask," I reply looking at the fake
wood grain of the table top.

I hear only snatches as he continues. " . . . echocardiogram at
sixteen weeks . . . soon enough for a therapeutic abortion . . . "

Until this very moment, I have never thought about whether Sarah
might have been aborted. Perhaps he believes he is talking about future
pregnancies, but I think about Sarah. I love her . . . freak little heart
and all. Doesn't he know having her at all was worth all the pain of her
loss? I recall Monte telling me as Sarah went to surgery the first time, "If
we have her for an extra hour, it's worth it."

I look at Benger as he continues. He is oblivious to the connection I
am making with Sarah, but I hate him for salting the raw wound of
Sarah's death with this discussion of abortion. A few minutes ago, his
warmth and caring comforted me, and I adored him. Now that
adoration is churning in painful dissonance with the rage I feel for first
cutting off my effort to thank him and now interrupting me and
answering a question about abortion, a question that I never had.

Somehow I mumble a jumbled question about causation and the
likelihood such factors run in families.

In a clear determined voice, he states, "In my family there has never been a child born with a heart defect, so if a woman in my family were to become pregnant . . ." He continues, but I only hear vague segments of the statistics he is quoting. His genotype is pristine. Mine is flawed. I have seen them everywhere. Healthy rosy-cheeked children. You see them with tear-streaked little faces and sticky hands being dragged by sixteen-year-old mothers with painted faces, skin-tight jeans, and cigarettes in the sidepockets of their purses. Sixteen-year-old children can do it. Benger's family can do it . . . but I couldn't. I don't care about your statistics.

As a follow-up to my inner analysis, I turn to Cosel and ask him directly how many babies survive NICU.

"About ninety percent," he replies.

So even ninety percent of those babies with the most critical problems survive. Sixteen-year-olds can do it with reckless disregard for even minimal prenatal care. I had tried to follow all the rules. Benger is right. Nature is flawed, and the flaw is inherent in me.

I manage another garbled question about how much awareness she had at the end. Cosel makes sense out of my muttering and answers the question in spite of the unintelligible way I have stated it.

"Oh, I see what you mean. I honestly think she was so sick the last twenty-two hours of her life that she didn't know anything." At once I experience relief that she wasn't in pain but profound distress that she died without knowing I was there. I toy with the idea of asking why he had the nurses give her morphine when they removed the respirator if she wasn't in pain, but I decide against asking.

I want to leave. I can hear myself muttering irrelevant anecdotes about our five-year-old daughter, Elizabeth. If this were a courtroom and I were a witness, the examining attorney would be shouting, "Objection! Irrelevant!" Somehow I can comprehend all this, but I do not stop. Cosel and Benger rise to leave. Benger states that our relationship is not over and that we should feel free to call him with questions.

Cosel says good-bye. Despite his bland tone of voice, I feel he must care more than he shows. He has listened closely to me and answered my questions no matter how garbled.

October 13—Just Checking

Perhaps others would be at a grave in a cemetery at a moment such as this. But on this the day that marks the fifth month since my baby's death, I have stopped my bike here in the dark of a rugged part of town, and am peering through the windows of the Neonatal Intensive Care Unit of Children's Hospital where she spent the entire fifteen and one-half days of her life.

Irrational . . . I am an attorney. I could be arrested for window peeping. I know it's senseless and impulsive, but I need to check. I am looking into the windows on the west wall. Sarah's isolette was in position number three on the east wall. Isolette position number three . . . who is there now?

Sarah. Oh, Sarah. If only your death was a bad dream. I am awake now. Are you there?

A nurse approaches and gazes up toward the window where I stand wearing my bicycle helmet. If she sees me, she will gasp. I slowly step backwards fearful that the fluorescent light from inside will illuminate the reflective tape on my helmet and alert her to my presence. She raises her hand, but her expression does not change. I exhale with relief. She does not see me. Her gaze is fixed immediately below the ledge of the window sill. I get it. The monitors are immediately below the window ledge, and she has just pushed one of the buttons to stop the blinking. While she appeases the monitor by adjusting the lines leading to the isolette below, I envision the monitor with its squiggly green lines moving from left to right across the screen. Am I really hearing the high pitch of the monitor's beep warning that death might be nearby? Or is the sound in my head still resounding from those final moments when her doctor said, "It's time now," and ushered me away from her, leaving behind the wailing monitors that one-by-one fell silent to announce death's arrival?

The nurse turns her back to the window. I move forward again. I look at the baby she is tending. She is only slightly smaller than Sarah. Her little chest rises and falls rhythmically. She is on a respirator. I imagine the familiar hiss as the exact mixture of air and oxygen is pumped into tiny lungs with a mechanically stolid pattern. But unlike Sarah, who during the last hours of her life had been given a drug to paralyze her so she would not "fight" the respirator, this baby is not paralyzed. The arms of this baby stretch and flex.

Sarah, oh, Sarah. My own life I would give to have this baby be you.

Next to position number three is the door to the breast-feeding rooms where we held her when she was dead. I cannot see more than a few feet beyond the door, but I can envision those last moments when I held her on my shoulder with my cheek resting on her soft fuzzy head as rigor mortis crept into her splendid little body.

Another nurse joins the nurse tending the baby that lies beneath the window. I watch as they smile and chat. Are they talking about the latest antics of their own children? Each has the latest hairdo carefully styled to look wet. I check for wedding rings, but find only freshly painted nails. Are they talking about the dates they had last night?

I grip the padded handlebar of my bicycle to stifle my impulse to strike the window and scream, "How can you smile in this room? Don't you remember that she lived her entire life here? You gave her your formula rather than my milk. You entrusted her to your machines. You paralyzed her with a drug to assure her cooperation with your machines. And then she died, unable to cry out in pain. Just a few feet from where you are standing, she died. How could you let her life pass with only the mechanical protest of the monitors? She deserved some human fanfare at the end. What about a tribute of tears?"

I look again at the nurses' faces. They were not the ones with her at the end, but their casual conversation still seems irreverent. I will never be in the room where they are now. I cannot visit this isolated room where my daughter lived her entire life and died. If they were mothers, surely the ghosts of unfulfilled dreams that haunt the room where they now stand would make them solemn.

I look again at the isolette in position number three. The isolette is empty. The warming lights are on indicating that it is ready for its next occupant. Relief. I shut my eyes.

Sarah, it's not too late. Please be there when I open my eyes.

I ride away on my bike. I look over my shoulder to assure that no police or security guards are there. In the dim light I cannot see well around the shadowy hulks of construction equipment that loom near

the hospital waiting to begin another day of building the nearby inter-
state highway. A blackened outline of a huge bulldozer blocks all light
from the nearest street light. A fear of the dark shadows ahead overcomes me. I pedal faster. If I can make my way through the shadow of
this last piece of equipment, I will surely be safe.

As I pass the bulldozer, I anticipate the uniformed man who will
step from the shadows and block my path. I rehearse my answer to his
demands to know why I had been peeping into the nursery window.

"I was just checking to see whether my daughter might be there.
You see she was born almost five and one-half months ago, and I miss
her so very, very much. As soon as she was born, they took her from
me and put her in that room back there. They told me to trust them,
and I did. I did not protest when they told me that she needed formula
rather than my milk. I always waited for their permission to enter the
nursery to be with her. I followed all their instructions. And she died.
You see, now much of what happened doesn't seem real. Sometimes I
feel like I'm still pregnant . . . like her birth never happened. So I came
back here tonight just to check . . ."

No. A policeman would need a different explanation. I rework it
several times as I pedal faster and faster past another bulldozer. As I
emerge from the shadows into the dim light, I realize that I am no
longer rehearsing my explanation to a police officer, but rather to the
neonatologist who was Sarah's doctor. It is his hospital, and he needs to
protect it from intruders.

I begin my ascent up the hill that will take me home. I pass a liquor
store. It has those chain-link grates that at closing are lowered to
protect the door from the habitants of this area of town. I coast my bike
through the door and ask the clerk if I can leave it against the counter.
He nods keeping his eyes glued on the screen of the black and white
television behind the counter. Uncertain of what to do now that I am
here, I ask him where I can find his California wines. A voice within me
is screaming, "Hey! My daughter died just five months ago today. She
died just a few yards from where you are standing. She was beautiful.
She had fuzzy teddy bear hair, and she had a little rosebud mouth. . ." I
look at his face. I say nothing. He is oblivious to the tiny bodies that lie
just a few yards from the counter where he stands watching the World
Series. Does he even know a hospital for children is nearby?

I leave. Once again I begin the ascent home.

Now what?

Jessica's Poems

Madelon Sprengnether

I consider these poems to be co-authored with my daughter, Jessica Gohlke, who was around four years old at the time of their composition. Like most children of this age who are not actively discouraged from speaking their minds, she was in the habit of saying out loud whatever came into her head. I was so astounded by some of her free-form (and also quite rhythmical) meditations that I wrote them down almost verbatim, changing at most the placement of a word or two and arranging the whole into verse form. I wanted us both to have some record of what she thought, to be able to remember together the world she once inhabited.

But then I put the poems aside. For many years I effectively lost them, and in the meantime my daughter became more reticent, more inward and contemplative. I no longer had such sharp glimpses into her states of mind, themselves now changing under the varying pressures of growing up. Her adolescence was difficult for us both, the process of communication halting, sometimes even explosive. We struggled to stay in touch. It is a measure of our success, I believe, that when I rediscovered these poems and considered submitting them for publication in *Hurricane Alice: A Feminist Quarterly,* my first thought was to show them to Jessica, who was by then a senior in high school.

Our talking about the poems and how they came into being initiated a new kind of conversation between us—as I tried to express how much I loved her cheekiness, her forthrightness, her clear sense of self from those first years. She had always known where she stood. When we found ourselves in conflict, we at least shared some ground rules: we each said what we thought.

When the poems were published, Jessica showed them to all her friends, who thought they were fascinating, but weird. She even took them with her to college, where she pinned them to her bulletin board in her room, creating something of a stir. She acquired a minor celebrity on her small college campus, as the originator of these strange productions. A friend even went so far as to create a performance piece based on one of them.

We still talk about these poems from time to time. They have become a special channel of communication between us. Jessica's easy way of speaking her mind as a child and my attentive listening have by now transformed themselves into a different kind of adult conversation. But I believe that our current pleasure in each other's company also has roots in those early moments when something she said would catch my ear, and I would try to transcribe it on the fly—before it vanished from both our conscious memories.

Jessica's drumstick

This animal hurts.
I am eating him.
Eating is another word for dying.
If you cut an animal, there's blood.
If it's too big, it won't stop.
I've seen people die before
at Grandma's house.
After Christmas
the robber killed the boy.
I'm eating an animal.
I'm eating his bones.

Jessica's fantasy

Who eats vaginas?
The vagina monster.
He has vaginas all over:
on his arms, his legs, his belly button
his eyelashes, his forehead, his penis
his fingernails, his hair, his toes
and he eats vaginas everywhere
on the table, on chairs
on cereal, on french fries, and hamburgers.
He eats vagina seeds.
He eats them on toast.
He eats them on the ceiling
and he eats them on the floor.
He thinks they're diamonds.
He thinks they're rubies.
He thinks they're gold.

Jessica's lament

Once there was a farmer.
The farmer had a pig.
The pig ran away
into the field.
The farmer killed the pig
because he wanted what was inside.

Then there was a dragon.
The farmer killed the dragons
(there was more than one)
with a knife.
Then the farmer died.

This story is hard.
You have to sing.
I can't tell it again.

The farmer died.
The farmer died.
The farmer died.
Aaah.
Aaah.
Aaah.

Jessica's stories

First story

Two dinosaurs are looking for mud
but they can't find it.
They don't know where it is.
It's over here and it has toast in it
and they don't like that.
It's in their mouth
and it's blood.

Second story

An old fairy lives in this house.
Two dinosaurs knock on the door
and she lets them in.
They like her because she's nice,
so they kiss each other.

Third story

This part you have to sing.
A little girl is pulling her wagon.
A dinosaur comes and chases her
but she is too fast for him
and runs to the woods.
She is Goldilocks.

This part you just talk.
The three bears come back
and say in a loud voice, like this,
"Who ate our cereal?" or else
they slice her up
and eat her for dinner.

Jessica's lullaby

Here's a piggy, sweet little piggy.
Put him under your blanket.
He's under me and he's under you.
Will baby foxes hurt you?

Don't cry honey.
It's all right.
I killed the bear and the crocodile.
I'm not a robber. I'm your mother.

"Kings Are Royaler Than Queens"

Amy Sheldon

E arly childhood experiences socialize children into their gender roles. One component in this socialization is the English language. Our language reflects sexist, male-centered attitudes that perpetuate the trivialization, marginalization, and invisibility of female experience. It sets the male experience up as the norm, the normal. This is one major way that women are diminished in our culture. The invisibility of the female experience has a direct bearing on early childhood educators, as well as on children. For example, child-care professionals, like other women in the work force, are consistently paid forty percent less than their male counterparts. The reason we are now struggling to raise the consciousness of our nation about the need for quality child-care and appropriately paid child-care professionals is because our society has long devalued what it considers "women's work." The English language reflects our culture's negative attitudes toward women and passes these attitudes on to our children.

A few weeks ago my six-year-old daughter, Nicole, was talking about one of her stuffed animals. She described it as a "he." The animal has no genitals and no clothes. I asked her why she had called it a "he." She said that she likes "he's" better than "she's" and "anyway there are more 'he's' than 'she's'."

I pondered this on and off for a few weeks. Her assertion that she likes males better than females is not supported by her behavior. Her good friends at school are girls, as is her special friend at home, her three-year-old sister, Talia. Yesterday, Nicole told me that she doesn't even like boys. As for her second comment, there aren't more males in the world than females, not even in her particular day-to-day world. Almost every adult at her school is female, and there are exactly equal numbers of males and females in her classroom. The population of children at her small school is pretty equally divided between boys and girls; I even checked this on the school list that we have. In her home neighborhood, there are more girls than boys. Furthermore, Nicole lives in an egalitarian household due to the continual efforts of both of her parents. This household contains three females and one male. So from where does she get the impression that there are more males than females?

It's no secret that the male characters in children's books and television programs outnumber the females. One trip to the children's book section of a library or one session watching children's television programs will teach the novice parent that fact. However, in our house, my children's books are screened to make sure that female characters are in abundance and are doing important, exciting things. And my daughters' television-watching is limited and also "guided." We have tried to minimize the male-dominated world that is fed to her by these forms of media and to provide female-centered alternatives.

But there is still one source of information about our culture that she comes into contact with constantly: our language. I am sure that the language that she has spent the last six years speaking, hearing, and becoming competent in has reinforced her belief in the preponderance of "he's" over "she's." Just about everybody uses *he* more than *she* in English. That's because we use *he* to refer to someone or something that may not even be male:

"What color is that bird in the backyard?"

"He's blue with a white chest."

What I see happening with my daughter is that this convention in her language is causing her to think in a child's very concrete sense that more "he's" than "she's" actually exist out there in the world. Females become invisible if you rarely refer to them. So Nicole is right about English, but she's not right about the world in which she lives. Due to no fault of her own, she has been led to misperceive or misconstrue ordinary daily events because of the powerful influence that language has on us. Put another way, her language has been tricking her. It's been tricking us all.

Today, she did it again, but I was prepared this time. She received a present in the mail. It was a white teddy bear wearing just a red scarf. No genitals. She kept referring to her new bear as "he." I asked her why she was doing that. How did she know it was a "he"?

Nicole: I'm more used to "he."

Me: Why?

Nicole: Because I always *say* "he." Because *you* say the turtle is a "she" and *I* say the turtle is a "he." Why are you so fussy? It's just my imagination.

The reference to the turtle goes back a week or so when our family had been out on a walk and had seen a turtle swimming in a canal. Someone referred to it as a "he." I said that it was a "he" *or* a "she," and we didn't know which because we couldn't see its sex. To balance out our conversation about the turtle, I then started referring to it as a "she."

I have been keeping fairly close tabs on Nicole's language development. It started as an extension of my linguistic research in child language development. As her language has become more adult-like, I have seen how it has been eroding my efforts to provide the female-centered counterbalance to this male-centered world that every girl's and woman's life needs. This struggle against the erosion of the feminine in my children's lives has made me an activist. Language is one of the areas that needs change.

My activism takes the form of drawing the attention of my conversational partners to their use of language in situations where they assume that someone or something is male. For example, when we can't tell the gender of some animal or toy (or whatever we are referring to) because it is unspecified or hidden from our view, why don't we acknowledge this? Although it is conventional to say *he*, our language doesn't force us to; we have other choices. For instance, we can refer to what we are talking about as *it*. Or, we can alternate and sometimes call it a "she" and sometimes a "he," rather than *always* assuming it is a male. We can always call beings *she* just to get people's attention and to force them to rethink their habitual choice of *he* and the expectations and assumptions about gender that underlie that choice. Using *she* can be a way of equalizing the current imbalance that the overuse of *he* creates.

All of these ideas work nicely in theory, but in my house, even though my children are used to hearing me say *she* when others say *he*, this has had—at best—an uncertain effect on them. Sometimes, they acknowledge that I am right. Other times, they resist me. As generations have discovered before, a parent's influence on how their children use language is limited. What is most distressing about the sexist way that my children are being shaped by English is that I catch them denying the reality of what they are actually seeing. This happened when Nicole insisted that there were more "he's" than "she's" in her world. It also happens when they, like the adults around them, address an all-female or mixed-sex group of friends as "guys." At a demonstration we attended at the South Florida Science Museum, the group leader referred to each of the marine animals we handled as "he" or "this guy." In fact, they were mostly hermaphrodites (having both female and male reproductive capacities), but the group leader never told the group this. Because sexism and gender stereotyping are so pervasive in our culture, even when families raise their children in an egalitarian and supportive home, it is no guarantee that children can escape or undo negative social attitudes and practices toward females, or rigid male role models. As Nicole and Talia get older, I see further proof of this.

Nicole: Mom, kings are royaler than queens.

Me: Why?

Nicole: Because on "Mister Rogers" when the trolley stops at the King and the Queen, the King answers the questions the most.

≋

Nicole: Shira [her female music teacher] could be a conductor of a band, but usually they're boys.

Me: There are women conductors, too.

Nicole: I know, but all the ones *I* saw are boys (i.e. men).

Our three-year-old daughter, Talia, was playing with two Fisher Price toys: a female figure and a tractor. I had put the figure into the tractor.

Talia: No, she doesn't go there.

Me: Why?

Talia: Because she's the sister.

Me: Then who goes there?

Talia: The daddy.

Thus do our language and our cultural images teach us about gender whether we want them to or not. The question I am currently struggling with is how parents, friends, relatives, child educators, and advocates can stop the perpetuation of female invisibility that is communicated through language and that is already at work on the next generation. I know that it can be done.

Mary is one of Talia's child-care providers. She told me about a weekend trip to a lake that she took with her parents, her significant other, and his thirteen-year-old son. The boy was talking about fishermen, and Mary pointed out, rather matter-of-factly, that it wasn't really fair to talk about fisher*men* because women also like to fish. Mary's mother then mentioned a few such famous women that she knew about. Mary's father suggested that they use *angler* instead of *fisherman*. This is a change that five speakers of English consciously made. They chose to use a word to describe an activity in a way that is not demeaning to women, for to be invisible is a way of being demeaned. Their choice allows the listener to create images of *both* women and men fishing. It affected the way three generations in that family think about and use English. In addition, I'm sure that the boy, who didn't understand what the problem was initially, learned something valuable about what kind of choices people have in life. We are even free to change the way we use language.

Taking an active role in changing our language must become one of everyone's nonsexist child-raising techniques. My three-year-old daughter helped *me* out a few days ago. As we were waiting in a restaurant, she said, "where's our server?" That word immediately found a place in my mental dictionary, bumping out the awkward attempt to neutralize *waiter* with *waitron* that has become part of our local restaurant scene. For me, leaving my daughters with caregivers and educators who are sensitive to the biased messages that can be found in language, and who are working to change those messages so that they don't exclude half of the world's population, has become a priority.

I wish I could see that become a part of the job descriptions of all the people who serve children. I was certainly uncomfortable with the experience that my daughters had with their dental hygienist a few weeks ago. She probably thought that she was finessing the dental procedure by talking to them at what she imagined was the generic three-year-old and six-year-old conversational level. She called the overhead dental lamp "Mr. Sunshine" and the vacuum pipe that they put in your mouth "Mr. Thirsty." I gathered my courage and asked her whether or not there were any "Miss" anythings in her office. For my efforts I got a blank stare and the reply, "We've *always* called them Mr. Sunshine and Mr. Thirsty." Clearly she did not understand the problem.

I admit, language is an abstract thing. It's hard sometimes to see it as part of the problem. It's not an issue that is dramatic and life-threatening, but it is fundamental to the problem of how our culture construes women and how women interpret their lives. It is thus one of the social institutions that must also change. As I raise my two little girls, these everyday experiences show me a small, but perhaps representative, slice of how they are learning the culturally accepted ways of being women and men in this society. Some of the ways I fundamentally disagree with. The more I see, the more I feel the need for us to take an even closer look at influences on children's lives in order to see what they are learning about growing up female and male. How much of what they are learning are behaviors and attitudes that we want adults to *drop* when they get to be adults? Finally, I have another, rather selfish, reason for asking people to say "stop" and to find alternatives to sexist language: I don't want to feel so alone at places like my daughters' dental office when I speak up.

Shelter

Linda Hogan

Tonight the walls are only thin, dead trees
of a felled world that stands again
between this body and the stars.

Downstairs, my daughter sleeps.
There is only a thin, closed eyelid
between her and all the rest.
A dream
I am to her.
She doesn't know my sorrows or passion.
I am just large and dark,
the woman who feeds her,
but now, her body grows beyond her
and wants to make life of its own,
to let new worlds fall from her
like dark water through a tribal hand.

She believes she is safe
in the shadows of this house
and what's above us both.
Once I told her about my cousin.
On a rainy day

a man took him to a cave
in order to hurt him.
She did not believe me,
she is such a dreamer,
and she doesn't believe in god.

At the shore
there is a quiet bird.
It stands on one leg.
Blue fish hover in its shadow
believing they are safe
in dark shade
that will bend and swallow them.

SYLVIA

Nicole Hollander

Black and Blue

Jane Lazarre

---

*"What did I do
To be so black and blue?"*
—*Louis Armstrong*

Each time, he thinks of his father never finishing high school, then remembers his own crumbling, poorly equipped schoolhouse. Each time, she thinks of her father leaving school in the fifth grade to learn the skills of a weaver.

Red and grey stone buildings border a shady quad. A winding path leads to the playing fields. It is late October and the numerous trees are heavy with purple and yellow leaves. Each time they come here for a parents' meeting, one of them says, I'm glad we sent them here. Even though we had to sacrifice. Even though it compromises our principles. At least they can see the seasons change. At least they are safe here. At least there are other black kids in this private school.

But often in class, Anthony or Daniel will tell them, there is no other black kid. And that can be hard, Anthony once said. How? she asked, fully attentive. How exactly?

—Well, take my English class this week, he answered. We were discussing whether novels can be racist, and all the other kids said they can't because art just shows how the world is and doesn't take a position. And besides, if the book is a great one for lots of reasons, why talk about its racism? So I told them about that line I found in Hemingway, and even Whitman slips once and calls us "the heavy lipped slave." Anthony's eyelids close slightly as they do when he is in pain. —But this writer, Penn Warren, keeps using *nigger* and *nigger woman* and his black characters are always saying shit like "Lawd God, hit's a-nudder one done done hit." Well, I definitely think it's racist. But when I say that the whole class is against me. They laugh at me, a kind of scornful laugh. And the teacher too.

—The teacher too?

—Well, she doesn't laugh but she says it's not relevant that these writers can seem racist today. It was normal for their times.

Daniel snorts. Bruce says, shit. Julia says, Normal for who?

In his English class this semester there are no other black kids besides Daniel. And so on Parents' Day when mothers and fathers crowd the classrooms to observe, Daniel and Bruce are the only black people in the room. The class is reading the novel *Invisible Man,* and the teacher, a man Julia trusts, smiles at them all with a trickster face, about to lead them through labyrinths and around edges of pits they cannot yet imagine. His blue eyes twinkle. He leans against the blackboard and puts his hands in his pockets. He begins to talk about the color imagery in the novel, black and white mixing, colliding, contrasting. Red splashing over white, even in the first few pages, the red liquid of sloe gin dripping over the white mound of ice cream. The students realize right away it's blood imagery. Then they talk about color, how they see color in their lives, how they see color on other skin. Daniel is silent. Bruce smiles slightly with one side of his mouth. He twists his pencil around and around in his hand.

They have all read the "Prologue" in which the nameless narrator asserts his invisibility, curses and claims it, then describes hundreds of lights he has hung in his stolen basement room, lighting up his world, his face, as he listens to music.

—Let's talk a bit, then I'll play you the song he's listening to in this chapter, says Mr. Sonelle with an impish grin.

There is a tape player on one of the empty front desks. Slowly, Mr. Sonelle inserts the tape but doesn't turn it on. Julia herself has just taught this novel to her college class. She has taught it because of the intricacies of its imagery, because of its place in American history, because it reminds her so intensely of how it is to feel invisible. She elbows Bruce who hasn't read the novel in ten years and has forgotten—she can see by his quizzical look—what is coming next. Daniel, she thinks, has never heard the song. He looks down at his notebook, tracing doodles with his pen. He has completed over half the book already, ahead of the class, but he is the only black student in the room, and he looks down, doodling.

Julia feels the familiar dislocation of her now lifelong double consciousness. She remembers twenty years before, the first time she was sent out to get a cab for Bruce with a white woman's confidence, he appearing only after the cab had come to a full stop. She hears Daniel's four-year-old voice coming in from play, asking —what's a nigger, Mom? She is black inside, she thinks with an ironic smile which Mr. Sonelle notices and returns. He is about to undermine the illusions of these well-meaning white children who would say, if asked, that there is no difference, we are all the same, what matters is what you are inside.

Which she too would have said (and would still say) as she was raised by radical, immigrant Jews to believe that, "Negroes are the same as everyone else." But the sentence never reads the other way around.

She has also learned with her children's developing consciousness that black people know it is never the same. And so, the other night, Saturday, when she and Bruce were alone in the house (Anthony sleeping over at a friend's, Daniel out for the evening) and he told her what his administrative assistant, a young white man, asked him the other day, she knew his answer before he finished the story. But she wanted him to tell her, so she remained silent. Anyway, they have three hours to wait in the unsatisfying half-sleep of Saturday nights, the restless dozing to which they have become accustomed since Daniel began staying out well past midnight. She is afraid of muggers, of cabs passing him by until streets are deserted, that he will drink too much. And now Bruce has taught her to fear the police who will see not *Daniel* but a black boy out for a night on the town.

They set the clock for two, but she tries to remain awake anyway, because she is afraid that she will wake up to the alarm, find Daniel not home and be frightened out of her mind. To avoid that possible moment of fear, which is unrealistic since Daniel is always on time, she keeps her eyes opened and tries, through extending conversation any way she can, to keep Bruce awake too. He tries to stay awake with her because he knows she wants him to but he resents it because if left to his own desires he would certainly go to sleep. Daniel is seventeen. He will be leaving home soon. Even Anthony will begin going out at night by the end of the year. What's he supposed to do? Never get any sleep on Saturday night? Every time his eyelids droop, he jerks himself awake and sees her watching him.

—Then let's sit up and read, he says, annoyed. I hate this inbetween shit.

It is incomprehensible to him, her need to keep a pointless vigil. As if her consciousness will somehow protect them from the harm of the streets.

The television is on, a low background noise. They are reading the Sunday papers. She lies in bed. He sits in the old armchair from her father's house, its white linen cover beginning to tear. Underneath the slip-cover, Julia has patched the torn upholstery with layers of carpet tape which is partially visible, silver and frayed. The house is weirdly and pleasantly quiet when the boys aren't home. Since he has to stay up, he might as well tell her the story of how Phil, his administrative assistant, asked him that question the other day. She will like the story because she likes him to tell her about his life, which he rarely does, and because the end of the story is how he suddenly, unexpectedly cried. She will like that he cried.

—I had this experience yesterday, he says, lifting his eyes from *The News of The Week in Review,* and she instantly takes off her glasses, excited, a child-like attention which still, after all these years, charms him.

—You know Phil? My assistant? We were sitting in the office and it was a slow day. We were talking about politics and all of a sudden he says to me: what was the hardest thing about growing up black in the south during segregation?

Bruce is fond of Phil, but he is no closer to him than he is to most people. Not *close* as she meant the word. Not in the sense that he'd bring him home for dinner. He almost never brings his friends home for dinner, Daniel reminds him, accusingly. It's hard for him to understand Julia's and Daniel's need for friends. One of them is always on the phone with someone, talking for hours, planning or getting ready for or returning from "dates."

—Can't he ever be by himself? Bruce complained to Julia one night after they'd recovered from the usual ten or twelve calls.

—They're his friends, she answered defensively, as if he had criticized her. He needs to talk to them. You wouldn't understand.

Along with their ardent attachment to each other there is this stream of never-ending conflict. Her wanting him to be something he never can be. He feels bruised by all the years of it. And recently, she had said, pleased with her beloved double meanings, Oh, I'm just sore from it all Bruce. Don't talk to me about anything. That'll be just fine.

But he sees the fairness of her need for a sort of companionship he finds hard to provide. His solitariness gets in the way. It has been with him always. He has never known himself to be any other way.

He remembers sitting on the porch at home, the town quiet, nothing happening by seven o'clock in the evening and all day Saturday and Sunday, quiet as death. In this idea of *nothing happening* he includes the visits of neighbors, always talking about the same things, his family incessantly arguing. On the other hand, one was always subject to the most annoying intrusions. Everyone thought they knew you, that they had a right to tell you who you were. And there must have been other things which made him hate the memory of that town, the sorts of things he might not mention to his black friends fearing they would misunderstand. They would accuse him of undervaluing his blackness, question his commitment. He had started his working life as a neighborhood organizer, then as a lawyer and government official in the human services (which always meant services for those humans too poor to buy them). Still, people are uncomfortable when you are different from them. He remembers sitting on the porch, smelling whatever his mother was cooking for dinner, nodding politely to whichever visitors were coming to talk, watching his older brother signifying and hand-slapping with the other guys, and he would think: I am going to get out of here. He had thought it since he was about six years old: the small-townness of it; the repetitiveness, like slow motion movements in a dull, predictable dance. The way people were always in your business, thought they knew you, thought they had the right to tell you who you were.

—But you seem pretty happy whenever we go down there, Julia told him, enjoying the opportunity of pointing out layers of contradiction Bruce preferred to ignore. —Yeah, how about that time with Anthony and the puppies? Daniel piped up. Lately, he and Anthony had been wanting to go south more often, for holidays and vacations. It's our heritage, Dad, Anthony said to him recently. Bruce sighed.

When Phil asked him the question, Bruce thought about it seriously, laying his pen down.

Good or bad, almost all of his childhood memories are connected to race in a way that white people's memories never would be. He remembers the black project he lived in, the black school he attended, the white swimming pool he could not swim in even though he was black state champion.

—So what did you say? she asks, sitting up in bed. She already knows what he will say, something about the artificial limits on his life, perceived so young, the lack of possibilities.

At times he feels as if he can hear her thoughts, and it was not only the twenty years of living together that made it so. He'd felt it from the beginning, that somehow he knew what she was feeling because she was who he might have been if he had been someone else. Which does not mean he always likes what he sees. He worries about Anthony, who is overly sensitive. Until his tenth year he played with dolls, then hid them when friends came over to the house. Every other week he had something wrong with his stomach or his head ached. Until he was thirteen, she kept a mattress in their room for him since he had night-mares nearly every night and couldn't get back to sleep alone. —Isn't he a little old for this, Bruce would hiss at her in the dark. —At least we can all go to sleep, she'd say, hiding her own happiness in providing this comfort for Anthony. Julia told Bruce once that he should be able to understand, once he must have been like that, was therefore still like that down deep. —Maybe I was long ago, he'd told her sadly, but not now. It's long gone. Believe me.

—What about that time last June when we heard the Vietnamese woman talk about her experience being a boat person, Julia countered, wanting him to identify with Anthony. You were crying, remember? Not everyone was, but you were.

—It was early in the morning, he had told her. I always cry if some-thing sad happens early in the morning.

—There's nothing wrong with indulging them a little, she'd said, insisting on the mattress for Anthony.

She could never understand, he had thought, the distance he'd travelled, his own sort of boat-person life, moving from one world to another of a completely different kind. When she expressed every feel-ing that crossed her brain, it frightened him. It seems right to him, what he learned as a child—that you have to harden yourself to some degree. There has to be some calloused, numb part. When he ignores her feelings, or criticizes her for the intensity of her reactions, or for paying too much attention to Anthony's, it is not that he does not, "will never as long as he lives and breathes" (she says) understand. It is that he feels angered by what he sees. She senses this and accuses him of coldness. But the word is wrong, and once, when he was feeling apologetic and ashamed, he gave her the right word: callous. I can be callous, he warned her, looking sadly into her eyes.

In Daniel's English class, Mr. Sonelle is asking the students what they make of the violence of the "Prologue": *I pulled his chin down sharp upon the crown of my head, butting him as I had seen the West Indians do and I felt the flesh tear and blood gush out . . . I kicked him repeatedly in a frenzy . . . and in my outrage I got out my knife and prepared to slit his throat . . .* The teacher reads the words aloud slowly. Is this rage extreme? he asks.

—It sure seems extreme to me, a girl says.

—It's not extreme, someone else argues. The guy called him a nigger, or we're made to believe he did. He's probably heard it all his life. He just exploded. He lives in this dark world where no one really sees him.

—But if the guy called him a nigger, he saw him, didn't he? So why does he keep saying he's invisible? Mr. Sonelle asks.

The week before, Julia had attended a poetry reading in her school given by ten students, six white, four black. The white students wrote about lots of things, she told Anthony the next evening as he rummaged through the refrigerator looking for snacks. But all four black students wrote about being black. Why is that?

—For them, everything is related to race, her son told her.

—Is it for you, she asked. And for some reason, said it again —Is it for you?

—Well, yes, he said. I know it's the first thing people see about me wherever I go. White people, I mean. They don't think, there's a boy. They think, there's a black boy. I'm very aware of that. I'm always black so they never see *me*. He strikes his chest hard with a fist which she feels against her temple, then, as if to take her breath away, against her heart.

Mr. Sonelle is waiting for someone to answer his question. He leans against the blackboard, looks at the ceiling, contented with the nervous silence in the room. Finally Daniel says —Because they don't see him. They only see his blackness. But he keeps his eyes on his notebook where he continues doodling. Now Bruce is looking down too, and Julia feels her skin is scorched by their blackness, like a branding iron would scorch her skin. Her skin seems to go up in smoke from a body that is hot, wounded.

Mr. Sonelle nods at Daniel, then looks at the rest of the students, eyebrows raised. She is wondering, as she has at other times like this—

somewhere at the edge of her mind there is a sense of turmoil—if Bruce ever regrets being married to her, a white woman.

But he thinks of her more as a Jewish woman than simply a white woman. Not that the Jews in the town where he grew up were that much better than other whites, but once he moved to New York it was obvious that some Jews maintained an assiduous sensitivity to any oppression. Her father had been such a Jew, an immigrant from a small town in Roumania, and Bruce had come to love him. He spent one summer nursing him back to health after a heart attack. Julia, pregnant with Daniel and in graduate school, was away from the apartment at dinner time when the anxiety and loneliness that brought on her father's heart attack in the first place threatened to engulf him with the coming of the dark. Bruce wasn't sure what he made of such psychosomatic interpretations—his father-in-law had nothing but disdain for them—but Julia believed in them thoroughly at the time. Sam smoked two packs of cigarettes a day. Like most Jews of his generation, physical exercise was, to him, something admirable and slightly incomprehensible, something gentile. A heart attack was a heart attack, Bruce tended to believe along with his father-in-law. But even the doctor had suggested a psychological element in this case.

During the summer, Bruce would return from his job at 5:30 and begin to make dinner for the two of them. He didn't know how to cook, but between Sam's haphazard instructions and Julia's detailed recipes, he learned. And he discovered a surprising pleasure in food preparation—cutting vegetables, learning about spices and the wonderful variety of mustards, an even greater pleasure in serving food to an appreciative diner, in this case one whose life depended on it— especially if Julia and the doctor's theory was to be believed. It was the pleasure of these activities that converted Bruce, as much as the obvious fairness of the arguments of the then-incipient women's movement, to become a highly competent housekeeper. Even now, twenty years later when Sam was fifteen years dead, Bruce could hear his voice praising him almost every evening at dinner: *Excellent, son, excellent.* Or, *Not as good as last night,* Sam told him once, *but not bad.* Bruce enjoyed the honest evaluations, being called Son, the silent knowledge between them of travelling from one sort of world to another, what you lost along the way.

Mr. Sonelle is trying to get the white students to hear what Daniel has said to them, to comprehend it so they will understand the novel and the terrible lyrics of the song Louis Armstrong is about to sing.

How can you get people who have never experienced such things to understand that the world can twist the self, spin it into hideous distortions until it turns around to punish the world? How do you crack the sense of entitlement wide enough to teach that behind and within every fiction is the story of a real life? —Why read this book? Mr. Sonelle asks. —Why read any book?

—So tell me, she insists again, wanting to hear the story about Phil exactly as it happened. But just then the cat jumps onto the bed and stretches on Bruce's pillow. Bruce sneezes. —We have to get rid of this damn cat, he says. I hate this cat. —You're afraid of it, admit it, Anthony had shouted at him. But Bruce himself had gone with Anthony to Bide-A-Wee to get the cat nearly eight years before. —I should never have done it, he says now.

—Why did you? she asks. Why didn't you say no?

—Everyone wanted it, Bruce says. You all made me feel so guilty.

She remembers other times when Bruce's failure to insist on what he wants makes him angry at them for weeks. —You think you were being kind, she accuses.

—Not kind, he says. It's that I don't have any right.

—What did you say to Phil? she asks again. You didn't finish your story.

—Well, I tried to remember, he says, leaning back in the old chair. —It all started coming back to me, how I felt growing up there, and how happy I was when I came to New York. He points his toes toward each other, chews on the frame of his glasses, smiles when he thinks of the city. Even now, with the housing crisis, the mental-health crisis, the employment crisis, the crime crisis, even though they sit home every Saturday night after midnight and wait anxiously for Daniel and soon Anthony —(if Julia weren't there, he'd probably remain half-awake, keeping an eye on the clock until two), —still, he can walk through the city streets and feel the excitement of first arriving here twenty-five years before. It was a new world, and even after all these years parts of it remain new, unknown to him. It fills him with a sense of possibility, there being always something unknown. He likes what is distinct from his own life—new foods, new places, new sorts of people. It was Julia's difference he was drawn to, that she wasn't numbed (though he wishes she were at times), that she was a writer (though now she hasn't written in years).

—I hated that town, he says. But it wasn't only the town itself, of course. So I said to Phil, the hardest thing was the sense of restricted possibility, that from so young an age, maybe five or six, you knew you would never be all you could be.

But certainly he has told her this before, he worries now. His answer can't come as anything new to her. Then he sees real excitement in her eyes, some hidden pleasure he doesn't understand.

—"Only let her be more than this dress on the ironing board, helpless before the iron," she says.

His brows knit in confusion.

—It's a line from Tillie Olsen, she tells him. The last line of a famous story. That's what the story's about, what you just said. "So everything within her will not bloom. In how many does it?"

He nods and smiles, feeling her happiness as their worlds meet. Here they were, she would be thinking now, exactly the same feeling at exactly the same moment, so rare for them.

In the release this feeling provides she remembers old wounds, the insecurities of her childhood and his. Legacies of slavery and Eastern European poverty, generations of hardship coming to rest in their life, the first generation of precarious comfort, a startling expectation of safety she can suddenly feel. She remembers her father's chronic depression infiltrating every day of her childhood until she felt she carried it around in her flesh. The house always in disrepair, beyond his ability to cope, drawers clamped shut by garbage no one had gone through in years, cracked and useless dishes kept for decades under newer ones of plastic bought in a corner hardware store on sale. The paradox of his ability to inspire a union meeting to belief and action and his lifelong sense of strangeness in the world. "I need a comfortable chair," he had called them once to say. "What should I do?" Bruce had taken him to a furniture store two blocks away. She thinks of Bruce's mother who fights for every inch of what is owed to her, her children, her grandchildren, who plots with the brilliance of a fanatic and plans with the fastidiousness of a lawyer each time it seems the world may do her in. In her apartment are Xerox copies of enough bills, letters and memos to stock a paper warehouse, along with every piece of furniture, sheet, and towel she has ever owned, cluttering up the small space in case any member of the family, not yet on his or her feet, may get an apartment and need something. She is thinking of Daniel's conviction and belief in himself—how he would talk to anyone on the street when he was three years old, asking questions, expecting their interest. Of Anthony, weeping about the misery in the world yet whispering to her in the dark of burning self-confidence that somehow he will help to change things. *Warring races divided / yet inside of me / the two races beautifully united,* he has written in a recent poem. This belief in their power and goodness it took generations to make.

She leans back against the pillows. What has drawn us together? she is thinking: some reparation of old mistrust? of lack of faith? He had known the meaning of faith for the first time when he was in jail during the Civil Rights movement. It was only one night, he often says, but it was jail! Maybe we were singing, but it was jail! But in that night he felt something new. Not certainty of victory, nor fearlessness. But faith that something good existed. She had known the meaning first when she completed her first novel—the idea that she could do it; or it was when the children were born, after all that pain, Daniel and Anthony. But no, before that, it was Bruce. He sees that he is what she first knew of faith, his body, maternal, promising even what may be false to assuage the harshness of the moment, answering her whisper that yes, he will hold her when she is dying, he will forgive her her rages, her betrayals, her sadness, he will watch the clock with her. He remembers himself as a boy, surrounded by light (it seems to him now when he thinks of it) while visitors and even his family float transparently around him. He is sitting alone on the front porch until he has her, and Daniel, and Anthony.

—And before I knew what was happening, he says to her, I began to cry.

He had let so long a silence pass after she quoted him the lines from Tillie Olsen, she had returned to her paper, put her glasses back on. Perhaps he hadn't planned to tell her, or had forgotten, but now he wants her to know. She takes her glasses off again. Tears come to her eyes.

—Yes, he says, right there in front of Phil, a man I hardly know. I cried. I had to pretend I had to go to the bathroom so I could get away.

They are quiet together. She touches the soft curls of his hair.

—Do you ever regret that you married someone white, she says.

—Oh my god, he says. You're white?

The darkest, wordless interior of Armstrong's blues open to her, resonates through the room, through their bodies. Daniel says, *Yeah!* nods his head emphatically, raises his eyes to Mr. Sonelle's giving him the thumbs-up sign. He looks back at his parents and sees her crying. He lowers his brows anxiously, shakes his finger at her, warning against any too obvious display of emotion. She shades her eyes with her hand since she can't control her tears. The lyrics sear into her. *I'm white inside, but that don't help my case. Cause I can't hide what is in my face.* Bruce winces—all the white people in the room who might misunderstand—brutal and poignant words fifty years ago that would never be used today. But the twisted meanings linger, layer into the sound of the trumpet, the dark heart of the blues not shrinking from the horror of this history, what I am not is good, what I am is bad, their terms, my terms, *wish'd I was dead.* Body shapes and flesh tones spin around her. As the music comes to a stop Bruce is tapping his pencil on the table to the final notes, and in the silence another tap, two, three. Then Mr. Sonelle's voice reading to them from the last pages of the novel: *but then I remind myself that true darkness lies within my own mind. . . . Still the passion persists. Sometimes I feel the need to reaffirm all of it, the whole unhappy territory and all the things loved and unlovable in it, for all of it is a part of me. Till now, however, this is as far as I've gotten, for all life seen from the hole of invisibility is absurd. So why do I write, torturing myself to put it down?*

She is thinking of generations of struggle for goodness, of Bruce's mother's mother, half-white like Daniel and Anthony. Really? Anthony said smiling broadly when he first heard this piece of his history. Really? He was so young, they didn't have the heart to tell him about the rapist great-grandfather, how that half-white daughter must have felt inside. She was like me, Anthony said. Her skin smokes, burns. *My only sin is in my skin.* She has silenced her own story with shame it cannot be too hard to name, not when she thinks of what others have named before. She is across a wide gulf speaking in a thundering whisper that is almost a shout, trying to bridge their differences with her voice.

Motherhood: The First Step on the Road to Recovery

Sheila Fay Braithwaite

I was born into a family of strong black women who worked hard, educated themselves and their children, and tried to make the world a better place. They were proud of their African heritage when life would have been easier if they had denied it and passed for white; and they were also proud of their European heritage when that was not a popular position among black people. My family had been more fortunate than many, but they always remembered they were oppressed as long as other blacks were oppressed, and they worked to end that oppression. This was part of my legacy, and I felt an obligation to pass it on to my children.

If I had had a son first, I might have rationalized that he had his father as a role model, but because my first child was a daughter I felt an extra responsibility. I knew, however, that if I wanted this mighty heritage for her, I would have to change my life. Thus, I had to reexamine my attitude toward drugs.

It took quite a few years for me to understand what a drug addict was, and by the time I understood, I also realized that I was one. After flunking out of college I took a year off, then transferred to a larger university, where I majored in drug use, with special emphasis on marijuana. I minored in drug sales and took a few classes on the side. (According to the university, I was a secondary education and history major.) I married a man I met in college, with whom I had a lot in common: jazz, Spanish, rock music, humor, and drugs.

At first Mike and I were happy. We both had jobs, money for a few luxuries, and plenty of "smoke." Somewhere I knew that I wasn't acting responsibly, but I had the idea that at the age of thirty I would magically grow up. I'd stop running all over town to buy reefer and other mood-altering substances because I wouldn't want to escape from reality any longer. It didn't happen, of course: the big three-oh came and went and I was still smoking, toking, and occasionally snorting.

Preparation for motherhood, the nine months when both you and the baby share your body, began to raise my consciousness about drugs and led me to question what I was doing—smoking cigarettes and two or three joints a day (more on special occasions) and boosting my high with alcohol. Preparing for motherhood by attempting to cleanse my body was a big change for me.

Most women try to take care of themselves during pregnancy, but it presents special problems for a woman who is addicted to drugs. During both pregnancies and nursing periods I cut way down on my use of marijuana, alcohol, and tobacco, but being an addict I could not stop completely. While nursing my son, I would try to get slightly high, enough to feel it yet not enough to harm him. When he was four months old and I stopped nursing, I felt free to get high without guilt. I did not have to fight the urge to get wasted; I could go back to being me.

My daughter and son were born close together, and while they were both babies my scheme worked—for a while. One day my daughter found a little piece of paper and pretended to roll a joint, "just like Mommy." I was horrified, not by the lessons I had apparently been teaching her, but by the consequences for me if she were to do that in public. Then I found her playing in my boxtop—the sifter that cleans seeds out of marijuana. Aged two and a half, she was mimicking one of Mommy and Daddy's behaviors. I had not realized how my actions made an impression on her, and when I did, I began to sneak.

Sneaking, I think now, was the beginning of my realization that my all-important pastime of getting high was not a healthy one. I started going to the basement to smoke marijuana, sitting on a ragged chair amid cobwebs and dustballs, outgrown clothes and toys, lawnmowers and garden rakes. Later, when cocaine became an important part of my life (shared by my husband and my closest friends), the basement was my cocaine parlor.

I never thought I would question the use of what I believed were recreational drugs, but mothering was starting to make me introspective. I believed cocaine and marijuana were harmless mind-expanders, a widely shared belief in the late 1970s and early 1980s. But as I sat in the basement getting high among piles of dirty laundry, I began to wonder why I was there. If smoking marijuana was okay, why did I want to hide it from my children? They were going to come to me, looking for answers to their questions about life.

I thought of myself as a feminist; I wanted both of my children to know they were people with rights and power, in a world that would like to deny them both. They would have to fight racism, sexism, and elitism, and maybe injustices I had not yet faced. Could I prepare them if I were intoxicated? Wasn't I running away, not just from my personal problems but also from my responsibilities?

I began to remember other things—times when my own mother drank too much, and her judgment was impaired. Once I had fallen off a bicycle downhill while we were visiting friends. My mother had had quite a few drinks, and she decided my bloody knee could wait for attention until we got home, but we had a flat tire on the way and my infected knee puffed up dramatically. Of course, that was only one of many skinned knees, and I survived with only a small scar—but we were lucky. It could have been a worse accident. How many children were killed or seriously injured by parents under the influence of drugs? Would my children be among them?

To understand my motivation to recover from addiction, you must understand why I began using drugs. I began to smoke marijuana when I was about eighteen years old. The euphoria I felt gave me relief from the crushing blow of my mother's death.

Mommy and I were close. She divorced my father when I was a baby, and she and I lived with her parents until I was three. My granddaddy was sometimes a warm and loving man who cuddled and played with me and told me stories, but when he drank he turned into a verbally abusive tyrant. He would rant and rave and "cuss like a sailor," as my grandmother said. I remember approaching him cautiously, never knowing whether he would be the man or the monster. Granddaddy always drank for purposes of celebration: New Year's Eve, birthdays, paydays, rainy days, sunny days. He never seemed to enjoy being drunk, and I always wondered why he celebrated with booze.

Then my mother remarried and we moved into our own home, with the stepfather I have always thought of as my father. I continued to see quite a bit of my grandparents, and Granddaddy often gave me sips of his drink. I remember having menstrual cramps when I was about twelve, and he made me one of his drinks, bourbon and ginger ale. He always poured the bourbon freely and measured the ginger ale. As I drank, I felt fire going down my throat and then a warm blanket that relaxed the cramps. I had learned that alcohol made the pain go away.

Granddaddy sometimes came home drunk and yelled at my grandmother. If my brother and I were there, playing a game with Nana, he would scream at us too, for no reason I could see, and in the worst language I've ever heard curse all of us for being no good and on his back all the time. Nana would yell at him about swearing in front of us, but then she would get him into the bedroom and close the door on him. I have an unforgettable picture of Granddaddy lying on the bed shouting profanities at the demons who were out to get him. I'd be afraid the demons might get me, too.

We would go on with our game, pretending things were normal—after all, this happened often enough. Granddaddy showed me that when you were drunk you could act crazy and everyone would ignore it, and the rest of the family taught me to pretend that a problem was not there. To acknowledge the problem would require some action.

My mother first became ill with breast cancer when I was five and my brother was two. She had a long remission, but the cancer struck again when I was sixteen. As a dutiful first child, I played the role of assistant mother when it was necessary, and it was necessary much of that year. Mommy had a serious operation from which she never recovered fully, and my senior year of high school mingled SATs, parties, dates, a boyfriend, and the senior prom with grocery shopping and other household responsibilities as well as frequent trips to the hospital for my mother's chemotherapy and radiation therapy.

My mother died that summer, while I was away at a college orientation program—exactly one year after her father died from a combination of colon cancer and alcoholism. I felt as though my insides had been ripped out, leaving me in pain yet empty. I wanted to cry from the pain, but my emptiness had no tears.

During my first year of college I did what had to be done, without much thought or passion, stuffing all the feelings that tried to invade the emptiness. I cursed God, for He had betrayed me. He had taken away the person who understood me in times of confusion, and now I was at my most confused. I did not want to talk to my father, because he too had suffered her loss; I tried to protect him from my pain and grief. I know now that talking would have helped us both, but the only person I opened up to was my boyfriend, and he could not handle the pressure. His response was to turn away from me, which left me even more alone.

My addictions first appeared in the months after my mother's death. I was angry that she had left me, and I felt guilty for my anger. I had no one and nowhere to turn. I began to eat uncontrollably, trying to fill my emptiness with food, and gained about thirty pounds in nine months. I had miserable vascular headaches all the time I was awake, so I slept twelve to fourteen hours a day. Sleep also allowed the painful feelings that were beginning to emerge to remain buried.

Now I know that my doctor—the same doctor who had treated my mother during her second bout of cancer, and who was well aware of the strain on our family—should have recommended counseling. Instead, he did what doctors are trained to do: he prescribed drugs. I was given two medications, one for headache and the other, a mild amphetamine, to keep me awake, and told to take them daily. By the end of the first year I realized that the amphetamines would keep me awake longer if I took double or triple the prescribed dose, and I used them to stay awake and cram for exams.

That summer vacation, our house echoed with loneliness. I kept away from my father and brother, thinking that I had to be strong for them, that if they got too close, they would see the cracks in my facade. I couldn't wait to leave the empty shell of the house, the table set with only three plates, the fourth chair that stayed vacant. I returned to college fat, lonely, and in pain, and my first act of rebellion was to start smoking cigarettes.

All during freshman year, several friends had tried to get me to smoke marijuana, telling me what a harmless drug it was, not a real drug like heroin, and what fun. So my second act of rebellion was to smoke marijuana. The fears I had had, of doing something horrible to myself by using drugs, no longer mattered—as I no longer mattered. I really did not want to live any more. Besides, there seemed to be some distinct benefits: all my friends who got high were enjoying life. Like alcohol, marijuana gave them a feeling of having no pain, without the side-effects of hangovers, puking, or headache. Most important, while my friends were high they felt good about themselves. They felt life was beautiful and they were beautiful. Maybe with reefer I could not only look happy but *I could be happy.*

I had to learn to smoke reefer, to contend with watery eyes, burned fingers, sore throat, and coughing fits, but I was determined to master the art of getting high, and once I learned the nuances, I excelled at it. Marijuana made me feel normal and happy, so I smoked it every chance I got. Then, when I wanted to get high, I used alcohol, speed, prescription drugs, and cocaine. I once said I would try any drug except heroin, because I knew heroin was addictive and I certainly didn't want to risk becoming an addict ...

All mothers have dreams and aspirations for their children, especially mothers who belong to segments of society that have known the burden of oppression. My mother had worked to get the vote for the citizens of Washington, D.C., who had been denied that right because of their skin color. Others before her had fought to end slavery, to end discrimination, for equal education and employment. My children were needed to carry on the progress of the civil rights movement. What was I teaching them that they could pass on to benefit future generations—how to roll a joint?

The African-American community does not need any more people who are good at being drug addicts; we have more than our share of people with that talent. What our community needs is people who can help us out of the despair of drugs. Children hate to admit it, but unless we work hard against it, we tend to walk in our parents' footsteps. I was choosing the footsteps of my alcoholic grandfather, and if I did not want my children to follow me, I would have to figure out a way to get out of the cycle of depression and drug use in which I was caught.

While coming to grips with my addiction, I changed jobs several times. When I quit using, I was working as a salesperson in a large insurance firm, making more money than I ever had. The position offered flexibility but required me to work several evenings a week and sometimes on weekends, and I needed a lot of cooperation from my husband. He agreed to help, but soon began to resent spending extra time with the children as well as the fact that the house was not as orderly as before. If I made sure the children were fed, diapered, bathed, and ready for bed, he did not mind "babysitting."

Mike felt that it was his job to work, to pay for the house and the bills associated with its functioning. According to him, it was my job to do everything else. I paid for all the children's clothes as well as my own, and I cleaned the house, cooked our meals, shopped for groceries, did the laundry, dropped the children off at daycare and picked them up, and changed all the diapers. He did pay for most of the drugs, a considerable chunk of the family budget. I had to face the fact that my marriage was not supportive, nor did it provide the family environment I wanted for our children.

Mike did not want to get involved in any of the family activities. The children and I went swimming every Friday night, but Mike never joined us: it was always either too cold outside (when the pool was almost empty) or too crowded in the pool (when the weather was warmer). He seldom joined us for church, and even today he doesn't know what the children and I do on Christmas Eve. Our daughter and son took swimming lessons every Saturday, and not once did their father come to see them show off their skills. If he was not sleeping or doing errands, he was out with his friends.

I was not happy in my work, having been underemployed for most of the twelve years since I left college. Trained as a teacher, I lacked the confidence to get a teaching job until the very last and worst stages of my drug addiction, when I knew I was worth more than what I had. I was afraid of failure, but sitting in the basement smoking dope I knew the future held more for me if I could only give myself a chance. Glimpses of reality began to flash in my mind, and I tried to eradicate each one with a cloud of euphoric smoke. They flashed longer and brighter, and the marijuana began to lose its effect. Then it completely lost its power to make me feel good, when I had so much to feel unhappy about.

By the time that realization came, I was hooked on cocaine, really in the middle of triple drug abuse: cocaine, alcohol, and marijuana. Coke speeds up a person's heart rate and breathing. The mind speeds up, too. If one uses coke, as I did at the time, several times a day for four or five days in a row, one doesn't eat or sleep much. Normally I need to sleep seven to nine hours at night, but after four or five days of use, with four hours or so of sleep each night, I'd crash on the weekends, sleeping ten or twelve hours and still feeling groggy when I woke.

I worked full time, leaving the house around seven a.m. and arriving home about four p.m. every day. I had two young children, aged one and three, whose care was solely my responsibility. My husband contributed a small amount of help if I nagged or begged him or went nuts, and then only after an argument. I was working at my first teaching job, a forty-five-minute commute each way, and bringing home large amounts of paperwork. Almost all of the housekeeping as well as the child-rearing responsibilities fell on me, along with the stresses of insufficient sleep and a poor diet because cocaine robs the appetite, which many women find desirable. I was also obsessed with the need to be perfect, often a problem among addicts: each of my three thousand and twelve daily chores must be done on time and perfectly.

One evening as I rushed to get the children ready for bed, some small thing irritated me. I don't even remember what it was, just that my reaction was crazed: I picked up the closest object, a mirror, and threw it—not at anyone, just on the floor, where it shattered. Fortunately I didn't hurt anyone, but my cocaine-induced rage could have seriously harmed one of the children. I was shaken. What if I were high on cocaine and became angry at them? What if I became an abusive mother—or already was one? Through the overwhelming relief I felt that I had not hurt anyone I glimpsed the possibility that I had been an emotionally abusive mother for some time.

Even with a teaching job, I did not do my best that first year but simply plowed through the day so I could run home and escape with drugs. I had been an avid reader but being high made it hard to follow the lines of print, so I gave up reading for pleasure. I had always been a quick learner but noticed that ability fading with each year of drug use. I had even been a health nut, eating whole grains and no meat while poisoning my body with drugs. Mothering caused me to look at these problems, as well as others.

I had nursed my two beautiful children because I wanted to give them the best start. I made their baby food at home, from the best ingredients, and I diapered them in cloth—less convenient for me but better for them. I made sure they had the best possible day care. Shouldn't I give them the best possible mother? Through a process of recovery that took many months, with the aid of a wonderful therapist, that question became: Shouldn't I give myself the best possible life?

Yes, I wanted to be a better person; not perfect, just the best I could be. I wanted to try to reach the potential I had within me, to be a person in my own right. I needed to feel good about who I was and what I could accomplish, not merely to supplement the family income. I wanted a career that would use the intelligence I had too long camouflaged with drugs, and I wanted to make a difference in my own life, and the lives of others.

My newfound self-esteem led me to active feminism. I became active in local politics, in the church, and in the twelve-step program of Narcotics Anonymous, and the gulf widened between my husband and me. I wondered why parenthood didn't have the same impact on Mike as it did on me, though I saw that society allows a man to place his own personal needs and wants above the needs of his children and family.

Our marriage did not work for several reasons, and I believe one of them had to do with the removal of drugs. Drugs had been an important link in our relationship; we bought and sold them, used them for sport and recreation, experimented with different types and even tried to grow our own. Shared interests are the center of a couple's life, and when we removed the drugs, there was a huge gap between us that we were unable to fill.

As I look back on my ten years or more of active addiction, I see that having children pointed me in the direction of the road to recovery. Unhappiness, low self-esteem, and pain led me to abuse drugs, but I am grateful for the many people who helped me when drugs could no longer numb my pain. They led me toward recovery, sometimes carrying me when I could not walk. The journey would not have been possible without the help and encouragement of members of the twelve-step fellowship of Narcotics Anonymous, who are still cheering me down the road by sharing their strength, hope, and experience. I'm grateful that as a recovering woman I now have the power to choose the positive aspects of my family legacy and let go of the rest. And I'm grateful for my Higher Power, who makes all things possible.

Three Sonnets for Iva

Marilyn Hacker

He tips his boy baby's hands in an icy
stream from the mountaintop. The velvet cheek
of sky is like a child's in a backpack
carrier. Then wrote his anthology
piece, began it while she changed the Pamper
full of mustardy shit. Again rage
blisters my wet forehead as the page
stays blank, and you tug my jeans knee, whimper
"I *want* you!" I want you, too. In the child-
sized rowboat in Regent's Park, sick with a man,
and I hadn't spoken to another
grown-up for two days, I played Amazon
Queen and Princess with you. You splashed pond water
outside my fantasy, nineteen months old.

The bathroom tiles are very pink and new.
Out the window, a sixty-foot willow
tree forks, droops. Planted eighteen years ago,
its huge roots choke the drains. The very blue
sky is impenetrable. I hear you
whine outside the locked door. You're going to cry.
If I open the door, I'll slap you. I've
hit you six times this morning. I threw
you on the rug and smacked your bottom. Slapped
your face. Slapped your hands. I sit on the floor.
We're both scared. I picked you up, held you, loving your cheek's curve. Yelled, shook you. I want to stop
this day. I cringe on the warm pink tiles of
a strange house. We cry on both sides of the door.

Chip took you to your grandmother's today.
You scoop sand-cakes from your orange-and-blue
dump truck, while he reads *The Times Book Review*
on a hot slatted bench four feet away.
Solitary for work, I pay bills, spray
the roaches' climbing party on the flank
of students' dittoed manuscripts and bank
statements. Myself as four-year-old, I play
with your clean clothes, open my closet, finger
old lives' skirts dependent on plastic hangers.
You ask for dresses now, and I demur,
then buy you a crisp shift, blue with white cats,
which I just once have offered you to wear.
I love you most when you are what I'm not.

Childbirth With Fear

Kathryn S. March

When we talk about reproduction, our language, especially as feminists, is about "choice": the freedom to parent, or not to parent. My own experiences have been more constrained. I have struggled to find the words to talk about them, without much success. These are things we do not talk about. Clinically, they are called "childbearing losses"—infertility, miscarriage, stillbirth, and neonatal death, among others. These losses touch many more people than any of us believe. Still, we are collectively silent.

I am a professional anthropologist and an amateur mother. I write, research and teach on gender beliefs and the relative positioning of the sexes around the world. My career has hardly been tidy: it seems to be as much in keeping with Webster's definition, "to go at top speed, esp. in a headlong manner," as to be that "for which one trains and which is undertaken as a permanent calling." But for all my professional adventures and misadventures, work has provided a clearer sense of productive direction than have my efforts at reproduction.

I began to see life through my cervix darkly, when, in 1971, I was among the first to get a Dalkon Shield IUD. As happened to so many others,[1] an infection nearly cost me my life. As young women concerned about *not* getting pregnant then, few of us realized that the very device we chose to get control over our bodies could take it away further. Each woman's experiences vary but, for most of us, "control" was lost with those first embarrassing unpredictable menses. For those of us who live in women's bodies, the issue of control is not the same issue it is for those who do not. If anything, pregnancy and childbearing are the prototype for absence of control.

I had a tubal pregnancy in 1973, followed by four laparotomies and numberless other infertility treatments between 1979 and 1981. Major surgery in 1982 tried to fix the then-remaining tube, and was followed by increasingly aggressive hormonal interventions. We went into an *in vitro* program in 1985, but I found myself pregnant, in a nontreatment cycle, only to lose that child, starting with placental separation and hypoxia at his birth and then in daily medical and legal machinations for the six months of his sadly compromised nonlife. A second *in vitro* program in 1986 was disrupted when again I was pregnant; it was in and destroyed the other tube. More recent attempts in 1988-89 at *in vitro* progressed farther, but there were no more babies.[2] I spent all my early adult years, then, alternately enjoying the wider vistas of child-freeness and obsessed with my ever more constricting childlessness.

Instead of loss of "control," however, what I felt was failure. I was schooled early in responsibility: first, as the oldest and only girl child; then, later, as a feminist eager to chart my own life course. Perhaps because in most respects I have been successful, my inability even to foresee, let alone forestall, my varied reproductive disasters was an unexpected insult. Never, and in no other matter, have I felt so worthless. Especially having cast the issue of mothering as a "choice," I had no

1. Including at least the 330,000 who have filed a class action suit against A.H. Robins, manufacturers of the Dalkon Shield IUD.
2. Lest this tale seem one of unremitting woe, I must also say that, after the long dying of our birth son, and with support of family and friends, I travelled abroad as soon as I reasonably could, both to complete some research that had been started long ago and to pursue adoption. Our son was almost four when he came to us and is now an energetic, courageous eight-year old. A year and a half after he made us a family again, we went abroad in search of a second child. Our daughter was seventeen months when she came to us. She and her story are completely different from her brother's, but today she charges through life with all the physical and verbal gusto that should mark any four-year-old. She and her brother have very different personalities and, undoubtedly, possibilities, but together they bring us the joy and chaos that we had been seeking. And more. I don't include them in this story more fully only because this paper is about how we come to terms with childbearing sorrows, not the pleasures in parenting—which they are.

shelter from the double blow of neither being a mother, nor having chosen *not* to be one.

I always knew I wanted children. But I wanted many other things as well: a loving partner and a job I loved. I resented the polarity presented by popular wisdom and my mother—that you had to choose between having children and having meaningful work if you were a woman. Even though I tried to be realistic about my inadequacies as a superwoman, I hoped that, especially if you had a partner who shared your desires and if, together, you were willing to make endless compromises, it didn't have to be an either-or decision. Imagine my consternation: I thought the problem in redefining mothering was juggling family and work without too much personal or professional damage; instead, *not* having a family extracted a devastating toll on both counts.

But the terrible irony of all my efforts to understand what had happened to my body, and why willpower couldn't make babies, or make them whole, or how to move beyond my grief and anger is this: there is often nothing there to understand. It is, all too often, a gratuitous lesson in bad luck. Slowly, I am coming to accept that there is no sense to be extracted from the senseless. To be unlucky is, however, unfashionable, in this era of planned pregnancies and a woman's right to decide. As an explanation, it helped assuage the guilt and blame, but not the feelings of failure, anger, jealousy or fear. I was at loss again, buffeted by unfamiliar political currents. We—feminists and not, alike—are encouraged to think of childbearing as the most natural thing in the world. Childbirth without fear is the idiom of our generation. It is not mine: my births and non-births have been all wrong; mine is very much childbearing with fear.

Uneasily, I have tried to set my fears aside. And I tried to return to my work as an anthropologist of women's worlds and gender. I have been working on a book based on women's life stories and songs from the other side of the world, in Nepal. Childbearing figured importantly in the telling of their lives, but their tales were not at all like those of women I knew here.

Most of the birth stories I'd heard in the U.S. danced around a maypole of joyful images. Joyce Maynard, in her ninth month pregnant with her third child, once wrote in the "Hers" section of the *New York Times*:

> ... It's an odd state to be in.... Unexplainable tears.... I have known plenty of women to dread the birth, and afterward to

curse the agony they went through. For myself, I look forward
to the event with the anticipation of a passionate surfer.... still
I thought this was death my body was registering, not birth....
I think of my children's births—carry them around with me—
every day of my life.... I love riding the wave of childbirth—
love even how hard it is....

We've all heard accounts like this, even though few women's actual
birthing experiences lived up to expectations. Many women lament the
years of "trying," that end in a caesarian section, or drug-assisted birth.
Some seem to regret the birth being too short, some too long, some
homey, some clinical. But all are oriented and understood in relation to
some mythically "natural" birth. Even the women who feel their childbearing was utterly unremarkable know to preface their own stories
with a "Mine was never like ..." Still, women often believe in the myth
of a positive, "natural" birth.

Not so the accounts from women I met in the course of my anthro-
pological work in Nepal. They expected to face suffering and death in
birth. One life history I recorded came from a woman, also in her ninth
month with her third:

It's a personal plague, this illness, this childbearing. . . . Some
others have no trouble; I, I have a lot. . . . a lot of hardship.
That's all you can think about. You know you are pregnant and
then as soon as you are pregnant, that's all you can think about
. . . hardship. All night long, worry and suffering come to
mind. You try to sleep, but you can't.

[She began to cry softly, but held tightly to my hand and continued talking.] You try to do your work, but you can't. Others
speak to you sharply; they scold you. You think about it and
only anguish comes into your mind. It's your own personal
anguish. It's very hard....

[Very deliberately] I wonder how it will be for me: if what's
inside me is a source of grief and trouble, how will I survive?
What might happen? That's what comes to me now. I don't
think about anything before now, or anything that might come
after. At any other time, it wouldn't bother me, but when I'm
this way and can't do anything.... When I'm this way and can't
do anything and get scolded, my heart-and-mind is pained; I

feel like crying. I feel like crying, and I cry. I even cry when it comes time to go to sleep. . . .

[Pausing] Maybe I'll die. Or maybe I'll live. How will it be? What will happen to me? That's what comes to me now; that's what's in this heart-and-mind of mine. . . . My heart-and-mind hurts! I hurt and a crying need overcomes me and then I cry. I cry.

The similarities between these two narratives are stunning. Both women are overtaken by their childbearing, at least for the moment. Both recognize it as a distinctive state. Both cry, but say they wouldn't if they weren't pregnant. Both know that they're in for something big. Both think of death. And both know that the range in women's experiences of birth is very wide. But the difference between the two women's orientations is equally striking: according to the one, "as soon as you are pregnant, that's all you can think about . . . hardship" and the other, "I love riding the wave of childbirth—love even how hard it is."

The difference between these two accounts is not statistical. Or at least it is not just that. Infant and maternal mortality are high in countries like Nepal, but they have not vanished from the medical landscape in the U.S. In the U.S., for example, one in six to one in five couples are infertile. Perhaps as many as two in ten conceptions result in miscarriage. Six in a thousand to almost two in a hundred pregnancies are ectopic.[3] One in as few as eighty term deliveries are stillborn. One in one hundred and ten infants die in the first twenty-eight days of life. "Every year," according to Panuthos and Romeo, "those who have suffered a childbearing loss [in the United States] are joined by millions of new mourners: 600,000 to 800,000 who miscarry, 60,000 with ectopic pregnancy, the parents of almost 250,000 victims of perinatal death, 15,000 SIDS [Sudden Infant Death Syndrome] parents, 1.5 million women who abort, and over 3 million who cannot conceive.[4]

It is not just, then, that other women are more likely to suffer childbearing losses than their American counterparts are.[5] It is that,

---

3. These figures are the most divergent of all, perhaps because there has been such a rapid rise in the incidence of ectopic (or tubal) pregnancy: from 18,000 in 1970 to 61,000 in 1981.
4. Claudia Panuthos and Catherine Romeo, *Ended Beginnings: Healing Childbearing Losses* (South Hadley, Mass.: Bergin and Garvey, 1984) is one of the most comprehensive, personal, and constructive of the emergent literature on the subject.
5. The statistics show that poor women even in the U.S. are more likely to have bad pregnancy outcomes. Perhaps they know better than the privileged sectors in which I largely live how to talk about such losses.

regardless of the individual experiences of women in either country, my overseas friends (however counterproductive it may sound to us), surround their contemplation of childbearing with shared and loudly voiced expressions of fear. We, on the other hand, collectively want to think of childbearing without fear so we surround ourselves with a discourse of joy. We can presume (although, of course, never know) that women everywhere experience about the same range of pains and pleasure coming from childbearing, children and mothering. What we clearly do differently to express that range. What they talk about easily, we cannot. And vice versa.

American expectant parents arm themselves with lollipops for labor, worry about whether there will be enough light in the delivery room for their cameras, and stock up "baby on board" signs almost as soon as they set aside their diaphragms. Our newspapers discreetly withhold announcements of births that are, or are soon to be, deaths. Miscarriages are mentioned only in whispers. And infertility is not mentioned at all.

Quite conversely, the women and their families that I came to know through my field research publicly bewail infertility, repeat miscarriages, hard births, and deaths in and near birth. They are, in many respects, collectively unable to give voice to the joys that are potentially there for them, too. Where they are distressed by the ways in which their childbearing fears loom so large culturally, we have been deceived by our shared faith that chosen childbearing is always happy.

Nowhere are we so deceived as in our own childbirth education. I never got to take my "birthing kit" with me when I rushed to the hospital spouting blood, but its irrelevance was waiting for me—lollipops, camera, warm socks, focal point, and all—when I came home. Two of the couples in our childbirth education class lost babies, ourselves to placental abruption and another to prematurity with fatal birth defects. All that we had learned in class seemed to me afterwards like so much disinformation. Nothing had ever been said about babies born dead. Or dying. Or unformed for life.

When our childbirth educator came to see me sometime after the delivery, I asked why all the "birth reports" she had shared with us had been without trauma. Where were the thousands of stillbirths, birth defects, and neonatal deaths? She—a bright, blond, long-legged mother of three handsome births—agreed there was a problem: she worried what effect the news of our disasters would have on the remaining members of the class. I worry more what the effect of such classes is on those of us whose experiences do not fulfill their cheery expectations.

And so I feel betrayed. Not just by my barrenness, but by the inarticulateness pressed upon me by our collective silence. I still find it hard to talk about my childbearing fears. They are not what people want to hear in talking about mothering. My anger at my body's failures, my jealousy at others' successes, my fear of the very intensity of those sentiments, my guilt at not being able to control if not events at least my reactions to them, and my anxiety about all these continuing inadequacies—all are heightened by their very absence in our everyday language and thought.

I have, I think, come to accept the senselessness of all that has happened to me, but I still seek meaning in some shared validation, or at least mutual recognition, of what happened. I am no longer obsessed to know how or why these things happened to me. Nor do I expect to be assured they will not happen again. But it is important to acknowledge that they *do* happen.

Seeing the difference in how childbearing losses and fears are expressed in different cultures has been, for me, almost a revelation. In the U.S., I have many good, deep and dear friends. Family, too, is always there in support and love. Indeed, without their encouragement and affection, I surely could not be writing as I do. But talk—the kind that shares knowledge, validates experience, and understands the struggle to heal—is missing. People "don't know what to say." The few who come forward to talk about the ordinary and the terrifying without melodrama are cherished. The irony, of course, is that our general silence binds each new victim in its ever-widening conspiratorial circles.

When I returned to my original fieldwork in Nepal, I found a completely different interplay of talk, experience and emotion. In America, for example, ask anyone how many children they have and you will hear about Liz, who's eleven, and Johnny, who's five. About living children, in other words. When women talk at parties about their pregnancies, difficulties are only a vaguely humorous subtext on successful outcomes. The words of the women of my work re-count their children very differently: they include all births, near births, still births, and deaths. "Seven children have come to me," said one friend, "the eldest daughter I still have today; the two sons born after her died, one was born dead and the other died after he was big; then came the son I still have who is now grown; last are my two little daughters I still have, but in between them was the 'half-trail'[6] baby I lost."

Hearing these women talk, I came to recognize some of the characteristics of my situation: the night sweats, the forgetting to breathe, the inability to complete sentences, the fatigue, the anger, the increased (not lessened) desire for more children, my monochrome vision and the general two-dimensional flatness to the world, the sense that time had stopped still, the fear that my own ill fortune could be contagious, the need for physical contact.

Their discussions of infertility, childbearing trauma and death, however, did not extend to understanding the special ironies of cosmopolitan medical practice with regard to our birth son's death or our many infertility treatments. They talked about death and infertility openly, but they could not know how uneasy American medicine is about death and unbirth—each in its own way ultimately beyond the scope of the miracles of modern science.

It was among these Nepalese friends that I was fortunate to learn answers to the many questions I didn't even know how or whom to ask at home: how long would my breasts continue to produce milk? why do I fall asleep only to wake up violently three hours later? how long was it before you stopped crying every day? what did you do when others got angry with you? how did you keep from hurting your other children? how did you interact with others and their children, especially those who are the age yours would be?

Women I knew in Nepal talked about loss and fear in mothering frankly and openly. Not because such issues are any the less painful for them, but because they are part of "mothers' talk." I try to think of analogies to demonstrate the difference. In the U.S. we know only too well the stereotype of what mothers talk about: the consuming details of raising children. Parenting is communicated in American discussions of coping with nighttime fears, with separation anxieties, with school bullies and buddies, and with a host of other issues of genuine concern and bewilderment. In the conversations I know from my work in Nepal, such talk extends to include even those child-caring difficulties —like terminal illness, death and recovering from deaths—that we censor.

I chuckle to imagine how these women's stories would chill American conversations. Cocktail party question: 'When did you say that the new highway was built?' or 'When was it that the old barn burned?'

6. That is, 'miscarried.'

Answer: 'Just before Mary was born,' or 'When I was pregnant with Ted,' but not 'Oh, that was the summer I had my third miscarriage,' or 'When my only son was dying.' Those of us who have lost pregnancies or children tell time by them, too; but we have learned to keep them to ourselves. To bring them up would redefine any conversation as a highly-charged encounter session. Even people who have experienced similar losses share only the general fact that they, too, have felt a similar pain. We do not talk about specifics. And we definitely do not talk about them over breakfast, on airplanes, or at parties.

They can be discussed, but only if they are given the entire conversational and emotional floor. For many of us that means we end up having to pay someone for that therapeutic space. Or we rediscover our clergy. I wrote lots and lots of sad and angry and bad poetry,[7] as well as tried to use my more "academic" writing skills in essays such as this one. But we neglect daily activities because the effort to keep our own preoccupations are too great. Our needs are so raw that we may not even know them. We certainly don't need only, alternately, to replay and to silence them as it suits other people's comfort. We need everyday contexts in which we can consider the complexities of our emotions without having them either reassume their most horrific outsized proportions or be compressed into impenetrably rock-hard and diminished lumps.

Our individual and collective denial of the place of fear in childbearing puts us all at a dreadfilled risk. Put bluntly, it seems obvious: how could we ever have imagined that reproductive choice, self-confidence, or freedom from fear would conceive children and deliver them up whole? For those of us whose fears are not realized (who maybe birthed healthy children, more or less easily), even the ghost of fearfulness is cast aside because it was "wrong" in not accurately foretelling disaster. For those whose attempts to overcome our fears still did not see good results, the realized fear that others continue to deny leaves us horribly alone, confused and unable to reach out even for solace.

It is not, however, the fears themselves that we need to set aside, but our fear of talking about fear. In childbearing, whether from the charged perspective of modern professional womanhood or from distant rural lifeways, bad things will happen to many of us, whether or not we are brave. To silence our fears denies the special poignancy and

---

7. Marion Deutsche Cohen has collected a set of such poems—although many of these are angry and sad and good—in her *The Limits of Miracles: Poems about the Loss of Babies* (South Hadley, Mass.: Bergin and Garvey, 1985).

very human vulnerability of childbearing, in which happy endings are separated from sad ones by chance as much as will.

Section III

The Politics of Mothering

Nancy Spero

Section III

The Politics of Mothering

———————

Judith Arcana's "Abortion is a Motherhood Issue," which opens this section, powerfully positions abortion as a motherhood issue and, like *all* aspects of motherhood, a political issue as well. Alicia Ostriker's "Cambodia" tells how the biological fact of mothering changes women's social relations. As mothers, writers in this section became acutely aware of how society devalues mothers and children, from lack of a federal family policy to the U.S. government's bias for weapons and war against health and welfare. Restriction of choices in women's lives—choice of dwelling, livelihood, partner, sexuality, motherhood itself—assumes new importance when mothers try to view the world as though it could be made a fit place for their children.

Some writers, like Sherry Lee, have known the cyclical struggles of a single mother, "working poor," which she describes in "The Best Mom in the World." Barbara Schapiro ("Mothering . . . 'without any irritable reaching after fact and reason'"), like many women, has frantically juggled job, marriage, and motherhood. For political activists like Martha Boesing, mothering is central to a commitment to social change. As she makes clear in her "Statement to the Court," Boesing's work in the peace movement was undertaken in part as a legacy to coming generations, her own children included.

Greta Hofmann Nemiroff talks straight from the shoulder in "Reflections of Motherhood" about real family values in the real world, and "Linda's" story in Judith Lermer Crawley's text and photograph vividly illustrates this real world.

Minnie Bruce Pratt's poem focuses on the predations of homophobia in lesbian mothers' lives. "All the Women Caught in Flaring Light" helps readers to understand that bringing political realities into consciousness makes mothers angry. Feminist activism provides many examples of anger productively transformed. More women than ever now run for and hold elective office; mothers and potential mothers bring their knowledge and concerns to the running of civil societies. We believe that feminist mothers can use their power to change the world, so that women, children, and men will face an array of good choices when they come to make them. Nicole Hollander's Sylvia leavens this section on how the power relations of the world affect women's most private maternal selves.

Abortion is a Motherhood Issue

Judith Arcana

Before I write about the relationship between abortion and mothering, I will first offer a brief history of my uterus and myself—our credentials, so to speak, in terms of that relationship. I came to woman's consciousness through my body, through coming to know and appreciate what my mother and aunts had often called, in the years of my growing up, "female plumbing."

I can picture my youthful cervix as I write. I remember when it was not yet thirty, still smooth and shiny pink all the time, a relatively innocent little volcano, periodically discharging the bloody contents of my uterus, or slowly oozing the thick clear mucus of ovulation. Occasionally it might erupt in some nasty raw eversions or erosions; as it got older, once or twice it stuck out the tiny red tongue of a polyp in the face of my flashlit plastic speculum.

But now, at fifty, it's one of the cauliflower ears of the cervical world, battered by our mutual experience. It's not such a rosy pink these days;

it's on the pale side, showing a bit of blue vein on occasion, and that slick cone has gone all bumpy. Motherhood has left its mark on my cervix, just as it has on the rest of me. I can't see into the uterus, but I know it too has altered over the years, and is in the process of making the big change. It doesn't realize its fallopian tubes have been short circuited by sterilization, so it's still doing its periodic building—however erratically—making thick wet red nests, only to drain them away into cotton pads.

Motherhood has left its mark on more of me than just my cervix. I've published two books about the subject (*Our Mothers' Daughters* and *Every Mother's Son*), along with various articles, some essays, and a few poems. I've led dozens of workshops and made many speeches about mothering, from the points of view of both daughter and mother. I've taught classes about the mother/daughter and mother/son relationships, and have carried on from a variety of pulpits about the culture-wide practice of mother-blaming in our time. Then too, I spent twenty years raising my son. I have given a great deal of thought to motherhood issues.

Abortion is a motherhood issue. Abortion is neither a separate subject, nor a subject in a different category. What I mean to emphasize here is that abortion, along with contraception and sometimes even miscarriage and adoption—including both the giving out and taking in of children—to say nothing of sterilization and current reproductive technology, are all usually separated from discussions of mothering, even when those discussions are carried on in the voices and writings of women of consciousness.

Sometimes that separation is a matter of convenience, because we just can't talk about everything all at once. Sometimes the separation is deliberately—that is, strategically—used by pro-abortion people to fend off attacks from right-to-lifers, who make the same separation in some ways but not in others, and do so out of their own strategic choices as well as their ignorance or closed-mindedness. Sometimes, though, the separation occurs because we have lost sight of the fact that abortion is not only about women getting pregnant, but also about babies growing inside of women's bodies. When that happens, we forget that abortion is, in the ordinary motherhood-type way, the concern of women who are taking responsibility for the lives of their children.

Conception *is* the beginning of maternity, no matter what the religious leaders, legislators, lawyers, or scientists and doctors, might decide. Women have always known this. When the pregnancy is deliberate, or accepted, the child is called a baby. When the pregnancy is an accident, or rejected, the child is called a fetus, or an embryo, or a mass of cells and tissue. We have sometimes allowed ourselves to be cajoled or forced into accepting a priest's or a government's ruling about "quickening" or, these days, "viability"; and when we've been on the defensive against those who would deny us the right to make this choice for ourselves and our children, we have sometimes been quiet about the semantics of embryos and fetuses—but we never didn't know that being pregnant meant having a baby growing inside of our bodies.

Choosing to abort a child is like choosing to send it to one school and not another, choosing whether or not to allow it to sleep with you in your bed, choosing whether—or when—to tell it you are a lesbian, choosing whether or not to send it to Hebrew school, to catechism, to meeting; in magnitude, perhaps this choice is most similar to choosing whether to have it institutionalized or keep it at home when its retardation or physical disability is an enormous burden; certainly, deciding whether or not to give it to adoptive parents, an orphanage, or foster care is a similar decision for a mother. Choosing to abort a child is a profoundly made life choice for that child, a choice made by a woman or girl who is already a mother, no matter how ignorant, angry, sad, hopeful or frightened she may be. And whatever our religious teachings and spiritual commitments, we have never not known that choosing to abort our babies is a dreadful responsibility. We have accepted that responsibility—many of us have even accepted eternal damnation—because we believe that the choice we were making was the best one for ourselves and our babies.

I began to think this way when I was a medic in an abortion clinic. I helped women abort in the same period in which I became a mother. In fact, in one five-year period of my life, from when I was twenty-seven to when I was thirty-two, I racked up almost all of my major uterine experiences, with menarche and menopause the only outstanding exceptions thus far. In those five years, I learned and practiced abortion with a small group of women, got pregnant, gave birth to a child, nursed it for fourteen months, got pregnant and had a miscarriage, got pregnant and had an abortion, and then had myself sterilized. In those times, I was a young woman being empowered and enlightened by the second wave of twentieth-century women's movement in the United States, and my education about motherhood is born of that extraordinary good fortune. Abortion work was the crucible of much of my consciousness as a woman, and many of my choices as a mother.

My education took place in the Abortion Counseling Service of the Chicago Women's Liberation Union, now called "Jane" in the oral and written history of the women's health movement in the U.S.A. The abortion service worked with over eleven thousand women in less than four years. I learned then that abortion is a simple procedure, especially when done early, in an atmosphere of comfort, by women who care for and about the health and emotional well-being of pregnant women—just like home birth. Through the service, I knew literally thousands of women, the youngest eleven years old, the oldest over fifty, who made the choice to abort. These women were of various races and classes, of many religious and philosophical persuasions. Not one of them—even those who were themselves children—made the decision lightly or carelessly. Every woman who chooses to abort a pregnancy is justified in her decision. Every woman who has an abortion knows what it means, and lives in that meaning the best way she can. Abortion is a matter of life and death, we used to say in the Service; we all knew that.

Long ago and far away, time out of mind, all the peoples of the earth understood that matters of life and death belonged in the hands of the mothers. Mothers gave life and death as their wisdom decreed; this was as it should be. Mawu in Africa, Kali in India, Sussistanako in North America, the Morrigan in the British Isles, Asherah in the Middle East, Pele in the Pacific islands—all the Great Mothers were respected in their choices, decisions made for the good of the child, the mother, the clan, the tribe, the nation. The Great Mothers of song and ritual and the human mothers all wept for the deaths of their children born and unborn—wept for the grief of their loss—though they understood well that death, like birth, is part of life.

Women, supported by the custom of their societies, took responsibility for their choices, accepting the necessity of the decision to end a just-begun life. They considered the conditions surrounding the mother, and the probability of her child's life being a strong one, including joy, good work, health, maturity, and usefulness. In their considerations then, as now, women sometimes judged that that probability was too slight, uncertain, or simply absent. Their choices, like our own when we abort, were never made in a vacuum; even in our time, in this woman-hating, mother-blaming society, there is always the decision made on balance, weighing both the potential years of the child's life and the mother's struggle to nurture it against great odds.

Surely we too need rituals, songs and dreams and talking in the women's circle, so that we can tell our babies, and ourselves, that this is not their time, that they would not flourish if they came to us now, that we cannot do right, cannot do enough for them, cannot mother them as they deserve to be mothered. We need to speak of our abortions, not in an atmosphere of guilt and shame as a result of the spiritual terrorism of contemporary anti-abortionists, but in open recognition of our regret or loss or joy or relief—even of mourning—and in acceptance of the responsibility of our choice.

Cambodia

Alicia Ostriker

———————

My son Gabriel was born on May 14, 1970, during the Vietnam War, a few days after the United States invaded Cambodia, and a few days after four students had been shot by National Guardsmen at Kent State University in Ohio during a protest demonstration.

On May 1, President Nixon announced Operation Total Victory, sending 5,000 American troops into Cambodia to destroy North Vietnamese military sanctuaries, in a test of "our will and character," so that America would not seem "a pitiful helpless giant" or "accept the first defeat in its proud 190-year history."

He wanted his own war.

> The boy students stand in line
> at Ohio State
> each faces a Guardsman in gasmask
> each a bayonet point at his throat

U.S. air cavalry thrusts into Kompong Cham Province, seeking bunkers. Helicopters descend on "The Parrot's Beak." B-52's heavily bomb Red sanctuaries. Body count! Body count high! In the hundreds. The President has explained, and explains again, that this is not an invasion.

Monday, May 4, at Kent State, laughing demonstrators and rock-throwers on a lawn spotted with dandelions. It was after a weekend of beer-drinking. Outnumbered Guardsmen, partially encircled and out of tear gas, begin to retreat uphill, turn, kneel, in unison aim their guns. Four students lie dead, seventeen wounded. Four hundred forty-one colleges and universities strike; many shut down.

The President says: "When dissent turns to violence, it invites tragedy."

A veteran of Khe Sanh says: "I saw enough violence, blood and death, and I vowed never again, never again . . . Now I must protest. I'm not a leftist but I can't go any further. I'll do damn near anything to stop the war now."

A man in work clothes tries to seize an American flag from a student. "That's my flag! I fought for it! You have no right to it! . . . To hell with your movement. We're fed up with your movement. You're forcing us into it. We'll have to kill you." An ad salesman in Chicago: "I'm getting to feel like I'd actually enjoy going out and shooting some of these people, I'm so goddamn mad."

One, two, three, four, we don't want! your fucking war!

They gathered around the monument, on the wet grass, Dionysiac, beaded, flinging their clothes away. New England, Midwest, Southwest, cupfuls of innocents leave the city and buy farmland. At the end of the frontier, their backs to the briny Pacific, buses of tourists gape at the acid-dropping children in the San Francisco streets. A firebomb flares. An electric guitar bleeds.

Camus: "I would like to be able to love my country and still love justice."

Some years earlier, my two daughters were born, one in Wisconsin at a progressive university hospital where doctors and staff behaved affectionately, one in England where the midwife was a practical woman who held onto my feet and when she became impatient with me said: PUSH, Mother. Therefore I thought I knew what childbirth was supposed to be: a woman *gives birth* to a *child,* and the medical folk assist her.

But in the winter of 1970 I had arrived five months pregnant in Pasadena, had difficulty finding an obstetrician who would take me, and so was now tasting normal American medical care. It tasted like money. During my intitial visit to his ranch-style offices on a street where the palm trees lifted their crowns into the smog like a row of fine mulatto ladies, Dr. Keensmile called me "Alicia" repeatedly, brightly, benignly, as if I were a child or a servant. I hated him right away. I hated his suntan. I knew he was untrue to his wife. I was sure he played golf. The routine delivery anesthetic for him and his group was a spinal block, he said. I explained that I would not need a spinal since I had got by before on a couple of cervical shots, assumed that deliveries were progressively easier, and wanted to decide about drugs myself when the time came. He smiled tolerantly at the ceiling. I remarked that I liked childbirth. I remarked that childbirth gave a woman an opportunity for supreme pleasure and heroism. He smiled again. They teach them, in medical school, that pregnancy and birth are diseases. He twinkled. Besides, it was evident that he hated women. Perhaps that was why he became an obstetrician. Just be sure and watch your weight, Alicia. Smile and twinkle.

I toyed, swelling and bulging like a watermelon, with the idea of driving out into the Mohave to have the baby. I continued my visits to Dr. Keensmile. I did not talk to Dr. Keensmile about Cambodia. I did not talk about Kent State. *Sauve qui peut.* You want a child of life, stay away from psychic poison. In the waiting room I found pamphlets which said that a newborn baby must be fed on a strict schedule, as it needed the discipline, and that one must not be moved by the fact that it would cry at first, as this was good for it, to start it out on the right foot. And my daughters were laughing at me for having difficulty buckling their sandals.

In labor, I discovered that I could have an enjoyable time if I squatted on the bed, rocked a little while doing my breathing exercises, and sang songs in my head. The bed had muslin curtains drawn around it; nobody would be embarrassed by me. So I had settled into a melody and had been travelling downstream with it for some distance, when a nurse came through the curtains, stork white, to ask if I was ready for my shot. Since the pains were becoming strong and I felt unsure about keeping control through the transitional stage of labor, which is the hardest, I said fine, expecting a local of Novocain which would temporarily alleviate the pain of the fast-stretching cervix, leaving other muscles free.

Of course it was a sedative, the first in my life. I grew furry. They laid me down. I was eight fingers dilated, only five or seven minutes away from the final stage of labor, where a woman needs no drugs because she becomes a goddess. Then Dr. Keensmile appeared to ask if I was ready for my spinal. A faint flare of "no" passed like a moonbeam. Because of the Demerol, if they had asked me if I was ready to have my head severed, I probably would have said yes. Drool ran from my mouth. Yes, I said.

When they wheeled me to the delivery room, I fought to maintain wakeful consciousness despite the Demerol, and I fought to push, with my own body, myself, to give birth to my child myself, despite the fact that I could feel nothing—nothing at all—below the waist, as if I did not exist there, as if I had been cut in half and bandaged.

A stainless place. I am conscious, only my joy is cut off. I feel the stainless will of everyone. Nothing red in the room. I am sweating. I feel like death.

The black-haired head, followed by the supple limbs, emerges in the mirror. The doctor says it is a boy. Three thoughts fall, like file cards. One: Hooray! We made it! Finito! Two: YOU SONOFABITCHING BASTARD, NEXT TIME I'M GOING TO DO THIS RIGHT. Three: What next time?

Our bodies and our minds shoot into joy, like trees into leaves. Playfulness as children, sex, work with muscles, work with brains. Some bits survive, where we are lucky, or clever, or we fight. The world will amputate what it can, wanting us cripples. Cut off from joy, how many women conceive? Cut off, how many bear? And cut, how many give birth to their children? Now I am one of them. I did not fight. Beginning a day after my son's birth, and continuing for a week, I have swordlike headaches, which I attribute to the spinal. I am thirty-three. In the fall I will be back at work, back East. My husband and I have two daughters, both all right so far, and now the son for whom we were hoping. There will never be a next time.

What does this have to do with Cambodia?

The Best Mom in the World

Sherry Lee

———————

I t is often the crises in our lives that strengthen us and give us determination. A time of crisis for me was when I became a single parent.

I tried not to panic. I had a college education and a job. Still, my income was not enough to pay for everything, even though it was too much to get any financial assistance. I checked out all available resources to no avail. There was no child support from my children's father. I assessed my situation:

> *I don't know how to live poor*
> *how to let the telephone ring*
> *put the creditors on hold.*
>
> *I can't cut up*
> *my credit cards/*
> *when I'm tired of crying*
> *tired of trying . . .*

I buy myself a moment's peace
which I pay for later
with high interest

a new dress
a pair of shoes
Clinique/to cover up
my disposition.

On pay day
my kids and I
eat
out
order pizza
and a pitcher of Coke
before
we calculate the checkbook
(pretend we're not broke).

We celebrate/surviving
another two weeks.
We might even go to a movie.

I don't know how to manage money.

If I have it/I spend it.
If I don't have it/I spend it.

I don't know how to manage money.

Someone set guidelines for poverty.

For a family of three
we are not disadvantaged.

$1,000 a year
above
low-income

we can't get free lunches,
subsidized housing,
or food stamps.

We can pay the rent
    but we can't pay the car insurance;
We can buy food
    but the student loan is in default;

The car needs tires,
    the kids need clothes,
        it's someone's birthday
            someone's wedding
                I have to buy a beer, once in a while.

I don't know how to live poor.

We should get a roommate
    but we don't have an extra room
    and we like our privacy;

We should move to a smaller space
    but they only allow two
    in a one-bedroom apartment;

We should sell the car
    but how do we get
    to parent-teacher conferences,
    the doctor when someone is sick,
    or to inconveniently located
        affordable grocery stores?

We should eat less
    but a bag of food
    costs $25.00
    doesn't last a week
        and bread and milk are a constant.

My friends say:
    "I wish I could help."

But so many Americans are distressed—
    even two-income families can't
        afford child care.

We don't know how to live poor.

Billboards beckon us,
    tempt us,
        arouse us.

TV sitcoms portray us
    as doctors and lawyers
        living well/
            they make us laugh.

We laugh.

We don't take seriously
    the
    politics
    running
    America
    running
    the
    economy
    down
    deeper
    and
    deeper
    beneath
    consciousness.

We don't know how to live poor/in America.

We don't know we are poor/in America.

We don't deserve to be poor/in America.

My mother raised five children on her own. We were poor, but we survived. However, we lacked the advantages that money could buy (not necessities because Mom was very creative as far as stretching the food dollar and sewing clothes). There was never enough money for us to belong to Girl Scouts or participate in church activities, and there was never anything for Mom. Challenged by being a single parent, I wasn't sure if I could provide even the basics for my children and myself. Yet, I knew I wanted more. I didn't want the lack of money to keep my sons from participating in sports or going to camp or me from going to a play or taking a writing class—and we all wanted a computer!

So seriously reflecting on my dilemma, the choice I made was to apply for a second job:

> *I almost worked*
> > *in a funeral home,*
> > *answering death calls*
>
> *women and children die/slowly*
>
> > > *poverty kills*
> > > *hungry spirits.*
>
> *I almost worked*
> > *in a funeral home,*
> > *answering death calls*
> > > *eight hours every Sunday*
> > > *four hundred sixteen hours a year.*

"Crisis Intervention," I named it.

> *$150.00 per month:*
>
> > *—could pay the car payment*
> > *—could pay the utility bills*
> > *—could pay the student loan servicing center*
>
> > *but couldn't equalize*
> > *the debits and the credits!*

"Crisis Annihilation," I defined it.

> *A second job:*
>
> > *—would surely maim me*
> > *—would possibly kill me*
> > *—would kill me so another single parent*
> > > *could answer death calls.*

Death calls.

> *Women and children are hungry.*

Women and children are homeless.

Working women are poor.
Children of working women live in poverty.

"I make too much money
to get free lunches for my boys.

I don't make enough money
to pay the rent.

But I will pay the rent.
I will put food on the table."

Love is more than $ bills.
Love is more than extended work weeks.
Love is more than death.

Love is maternal; Love is eternal.

I kiss my son on the cheek,
tousle his hair; we care
about each other.

Death calls.

We don't answer.

I was hired to replace another single mother who needed to work two jobs to place food on the table. But I couldn't do it. I wouldn't do it. I needed the time for my kids, time for myself, time to clean our house and wash our clothes. I decided there must be other options.

My sons agreed a second job was not the answer. Their solution was "just write a check, Mom." It was difficult for them to comprehend that to write a check you have to have money in the bank!

Both children, Michael and David, did what they could to help. David (age fourteen) was quite the entrepreneur. He bought candy and sold it at school for twice the amount. He invested his money in baseball cards, sold some, and saved the best for equity in his college education. Michael (age ten), a poet, could only envy his brother's business charisma, but he was quite endearing and helped by telling me "Mom, you're the best mom in the world and I really love you." When we went grocery shopping, he encouraged me to buy generic.

But children, although they are probably more resilient than adults, do experience the effects of poverty. Peer pressure is relentless. Even poor kids don't want to shop at Kmart. Fortunately, even though my children wanted quality brand-name clothes, they didn't expect quantity. When my overextended credit cards allowed me to buy them one pair of brand-name jeans and one pair of brand-name tennis shoes, they were ecstatic. But even more than clothes, they wanted skateboards and hockey equipment. Poor kids can't participate in most sports or extracurricular activities, let alone eat well or have a decent place to live.

Poverty is not pleasant. Personally, the times I have been most depressed/most stressed were when I was financially devastated, when I didn't know how I was going to pay the rent or buy groceries. When I felt powerless to take care of our family I would often cry, trying to avoid my children so they wouldn't be upset, too. But they were usually aware when our economic situation was intolerable. Sometimes, to cheer me, they'd make me breakfast in bed.

There were times when I would just have to get away, get out, hear some good blues music, and drink a lot of cheap brandy. There were times when I was so tired and so angry, I would scream at anyone about anything. And there were times when I just wanted to take time out for "mental health"—but I knew my health insurance only covered eighty percent of a hospital stay. Even a visit to a psychiatrist needed a ten-dollar co-payment. Sick days had to be saved for when the children had strep throat or the flu.

Several months into my crisis, I met a man I liked. Our courtship eased my financial burden. He took us out to eat, bought groceries, paid my car insurance, took us bowling and to the movies, even took us on vacation. However, even though I was in love with him, it was difficult for me to accept his generosity graciously, without feeling guilty—without feeling I owed him something. It was also difficult, after spending time at his recently purchased townhome and driving around in his Cadillac, to return to and accept our crowded living quarters, our limited income, our not being able to make it comfortably on our own.

My new boyfriend wanted a relationship with a woman who was independent and could take care of herself. I guess he thought I was, and could, despite my financial constraints. Perhaps it wasn't how much money I earned but how well I survived on what I did make.

≈≈≈

Eventually, I chose to get married—a choice not every poor mother has/or even wants. I was fortunate, my choice was financially advantageous for my family.

My husband's daughters seem pleased about the marriage. I think they want and expect me to *take care of Dad* and *make him happy* (in a historical sense of *wife*—a term I hope to redefine for them).

My sons were more ambivalent about my new commitment. For them, I think, it means another authority figure in their lives who might threaten their autonomy. (I prefer to visualize my husband as a role model and positive influence on two boys who seldom see or talk to their dad.)

And for me, our marriage presents a challenge to live with and love someone else without allowing him to subtly deny/or manipulate me to deny any of my multifarious identity: Asian/Black American, mother, feminist, writer, et al. It means I will have to come to terms with compromising some of my independence in order to share leisure time and responsibilities with my husband, hopefully without becoming dependent, controlled—or losing sight of my spontaneity, creativity, intuitions, and wildest dreams. And it also means not feeling guilty or privileged because I will be experiencing a higher economic standard of living, but to remain empathetic to those of us who have experienced, are now experiencing, or may in the future experience being poor/in America.

Mothering . . .

"without any irritable reaching after fact and reason"[*]

Barbara Schapiro

A s I sit down to write this, my two-and-a-half year old daughter is raging in the other room. She's just woken from a nap and is furious that Mommy is not there with her. Daddy's "on duty" and I hear him valiantly offering up the usual repertoire— "Juice?" "Read a book?" "Bubble bath?" "Cookie?" She rages on. I stare at the screen of my word processor and the usual repertoire of feelings runs through me: guilt, desire to run down and comfort her, pleasure that I don't have to run down and comfort her but can sit here in my room and write, anger (why does she need me so much?), love (she needs me so much).

---

*John Keats to George and Tom Keats, 21-27 December 1817, *The Letters of John Keats 1814-1821,* ed. Hyder Edward Rollins. (Cambridge, Mass.: Harvard University Press, 1958), vol. 1, 192.

Mothering has taught me not only to understand, but to tolerate living, what Keats describes in one of his letters as "negative capability"—the capability "of being in uncertainties, Mysteries, doubts, without any irritable reaching after fact and reason." In other words, our familiar frameworks and categories are negated in this state. We merely remain open to a reality that defies our usual rational and logical structures. Uncertainties and doubts, mysterious paradoxes and ambivalences, were born right along with my children, and I've indeed found it fruitless to reach after any facts or objective truths, any rational resolutions—the irritability part I'm still working on.

I entered a state of negative capability, in fact, with even the first thought of motherhood and the attempt to become a mother. For five years my husband and I struggled with infertility, which for me became a bitter, paradoxical battle between my head saying yes and my body saying no. Then there was the advice from doctors, nurses, and everybody else who knew of our problem that I simply needed to relax. This advice I tried to heed while counting the days of each month, taking my temperature each morning, marking on an elaborate graph our prescribed schedule of sexual intercourse, and then discovering my period each month (often late). I was so tense from trying to relax through all this that I found myself breaking into uncontrollable tears at inappropriate times. Once I broke into sobs at the aquarium (crying at fish—there seemed no reaching after fact or reason there).

When I thought about it, the fact that I was having trouble conceiving did not actually surprise me, even after the supposed source of the problem, some scarring from an IUD, was surgically removed. Deep down I suspected that my body was not so much at war with my head as it was very likely carrying out its subtle orders. Was I ambivalent about motherhood? Was it a coincidence that I'd written a scholarly book about ambivalence towards the mother in Romantic poetry? At the first meeting with my infertility specialist I was eager to talk about this, to probe my history and my psyche as well as my body. My doctor, however, a superb surgeon and renowned in his field, was not interested. He focused solely on my body as a malfunctioning reproductive machine. My feminism, I believe, made me especially sensitive to this sort of objectification of my body, as well as to the infantilizing view that I was incapable of being a responsible or active agent in the medical process of healing my body.

I recall one afternoon in the doctor's office when I ventured a suggestion in regard to my treatment. Since nothing in our present methods seemed to be working, why not try, I hazarded, artificial insemination with my husband's sperm? This suggestion aroused a look of unconcealed disdain: "What are you talking about? Where do you people get such ideas?" Always before, my doctor's brisk and efficient manner seemed singularly emotionless, but now he was clearly furious. "Nothing," he scolded, his voice rising and his neck turning red, "nothing is better than the penis!" How dare I suggest, I realized, that anything might be superior? As he continued to berate me, angrily extolling the incomparable virtues of the penis, the nurse and I, for one brief second, exchanged a look—a single, quick smile with our eyes— that I shall always savor as a particularly sweet moment of sisterhood.

My relationship with my doctor, however, was not without its contradictory feelings. I was, and still am, extremely grateful to him for having made it physically possible for me to conceive. He also succeeded in defying my "irritable" attempts to label or define him. I remember one office visit, over a year after the surgery, when we had run through all the batteries of tests and there seemed nothing left to do. He looked at me at one point and sighed, "Maybe it's just not God's will." I was stunned. This materialist-minded physician, this hard-nosed man of science—"not God's will"?

Negative capability demands a sense of humor. The contradictory or irreconcilable perspectives one must hold in the mind at once create the very conditions for irony and a sense of the absurd. The chronic pain of infertility for both my husband and me was sporadically relieved by a keen recognition of ridiculousness. One of the tests we had to take, for instance, required that I be examined within an hour of having had sexual intercourse. As we lived more than an hour out of town, this was not a simple matter. I had to ask a friend if I might borrow her apartment, and her bed, for an afternoon tryst with my husband. Even trickier was how my husband would explain having to take the afternoon off work: the truth, that he had to drive into Boston to make love to his wife in her girlfriend's apartment, might not be considered a legitimate excuse.

Most wonderfully ludicrous, however, was my husband Scotty's ordeal with submitting his sperm sample. This test posed the same problem for us as the other one: the sperm needed to be examined while still fresh and perky (i.e., less than an hour old). As Scotty could not bring himself to ask my girlfriend if he might borrow her apartment for this purpose, he would have to produce in one of the sterile bathrooms of the Harvard Community Health Center. I offered to buy him a *Playboy* or *Penthouse,* but my husband, a feminist's dream, said that he honestly did not find those magazines a turn-on. He would have to rely on his imagination, he said.

When he returned home late that afternoon, he looked decidedly frazzled. He had locked himself into one of the ungendered, single lavatories that are scattered throughout the building, he explained, and had gone to work. White enamel and stainless steel were not particularly conducive to erotic fantasy, however, and he was having more trouble than he had anticipated. Contributing to the problem was the fact that at regular intervals people would come by and try to use the lav. They would jiggle the handle or knock on the door. Finally, after about twenty-five minutes, just as he felt that something at last was about to happen, the doorhandle jiggled and an angry voice sounded outside the door. As a result, Scotty said, he felt his "product" was embarrassingly small.

Starting all over again, however, was not an option. There was nothing left to do but turn the sample into the lab. Several people were standing in front of the reception desk, he reported, and as he wanted to avoid any public scrutiny of his offering, he decided to wait till things cleared out a little. About thirty minutes later there were still a few people standing at the front, but he couldn't put it off any longer. He handed the container to the nurse behind the desk and mumbled his name. "WHAT KIND OF SPECIMEN IS IT?" The nurse apparently had the voice of Ethel Merman. "WHAT? . . . OH, SPERM. WHEN DID YOU PRODUCE IT?" At that point, Scotty reported, everyone seated in the waiting area, including those in the back rows, was waiting for his answer. The clincher is that a few days later I got a call from the lab. They were terribly sorry but a lab technician had seen my name on the sperm sample (I am the policy-holder and also have a different last name from my husband), thought it was a mix-up or mistake, and threw it out. Scotty would need to give another sample.

One of the old saws, again a paradox, that infertility patients often hear is that if they stop trying, if they give up, they'll get pregnant. Surrender, believe that you'll never conceive, and you'll conceive. This is an infuriating thing to hear when you're desperate for a child, but from one perspective, it is what happened with us. From another angle, though, I believe that our experience proved something quite the opposite. The most therapeutic treatment of my infertilty, besides the surgery, began with our becoming involved in the adoption process. With the decision to adopt, both Scotty and I ceased concentrating on physical conception. As we became more immersed in the adoption process, however, we began to feel pregnant—we carried the idea of our coming child within us. It was not that I gave up on or rejected pregnancy before it could happen, but, contrarily, that I actually had to be pregnant in mind before I could become pregnant in body. As our assignment date drew near and the certainty of our soon having a child became real, I was able imaginatively to conceive of and accept myself as a mother. For me, I think it was that deeply internal conception of myself as with-child, an identification of myself as a mother on a level I had not achieved before, that was the key.

A few weeks before we were due to be assigned a Korean child, I discovered I was pregnant. The phenomenon of a pregnancy occurring upon or soon after an adoption is well-known and documented. It is, again, probably one of those mysteries I shouldn't reach irritably to explain. Nevertheless, my intuition about it, at least in my case, is that it has to do with some sort of unconscious acceptance of one's own motherliness. If in one's internal world there is unresolved anger bound up with issues of nurture or mothering, that unacknowledged anger, and the unconscious fear of it, could be pregnancy-inhibiting factors. (This assumes, as I believe in my bones, a holistic mind-body connection.) Once one becomes a mother, however, it is profoundly liberating to discover that one's rage does not destroy baby or self, or more pointedly, does not destroy one's ability to love. The experience of that discovery, furthermore, need not be conscious in order to be effective.

My pregnancy, despite having to lumber around with an extra forty-seven pounds, was a purely unambivalent, joyful experience, as was the birth, despite the pain, of our ten-pound, two-ounce son. Scotty and I were fortunate enough to be able to afford my taking off work for a year, and so I was able to surrender completely to that enthralling, fiercely "in-love" experience of caring for a newborn. Friends with children had told us of the exhaustion, the anxieties, and also the love that we would experience as parents, but they hadn't mentioned how much sheer, plain fun having a baby could be. We couldn't get over that—the fun. Still, ambivalence, I've discovered, will eventually have its say, and when my son was about a month old, I began to have a recurring dream.

I would be in some pleasant setting typical of my pre-motherhood days—having lunch with a friend in a small cafe, browsing in a Harvard Square bookstore—when all of a sudden I would have a flash of my baby alone in his crib: "OH MY GOD!" I'd realize, "I'd completely forgotten him! He's been there for hours, maybe days!" I would wake up in a panicky sweat. Such abandonment dreams, I've since learned, are not uncommon among new mothers. Recently I came across a letter in the "Confidential Chat" column of the Boston *Globe* by a mother who felt disturbed by her "baby-abandonment dreams," as she called them. A few weeks later she wrote back to thank all the other mothers who had written to share their baby-abandonment dreams with her.

While I was certainly distraught in these dreams, when I thought about them, I was less disturbed than wryly amused. Mothering this baby was all-consuming, the responsibility overwhelming, and of course I needed some relief, even if just subconsciously. I knew I simply needed to accept the ambivalence and the irony. In other words, the need for negative capability had called again. Another version: I'm sitting in an airplane on my way, I believe, to Sanibel Island. I've just unfastened my seatbelt and am asking the flight attendant for a Diet Coke, when . . . "OH MY GOD!" . . .

A year after the birth of our son, Scotty and I reapplied to adopt. The termination of our original proceedings had felt like an aborted pregnancy, and we were still emotionally committed to adopting a child. We videotaped our daughter's delivery—as wondrous a birth as our son's: the anxious waiting and pacing at Logan airport, the low moaning of the plane as it pulled to a halt at the gate, and then the view down the long tunneled ramp as we watched our baby being carried towards us. Not coming straight from the blissful womb, however, Mira brought with her three months' worth of infant-anxiety and rage. She looked angelic when she arrived, deep in a tranquil sleep, but when her escort handed her to us, he chuckled disconcertingly: "She's yours, huh? Heh heh. Good luck!" It seems she had screamed for close to the full twenty-four-hour trip—even those in the back smoking section of the plane were astounded by the lung power and sheer stamina this tiny baby possessed. According to the escort, she finally collapsed into oblivion the moment the plane touched down in Boston.

Our daughter had been cared for in Korea exclusively by women, and as a result, she bonded immediately and exclusively to me. She was so terrified of separation that I had trouble even leaving the room to go to the bathroom. Though the first three months were especially exhausting, Scotty and I survived for over two years without an uninterrupted night of sleep. Our bonding with her, consequently, was slower and more difficult than that with our son. Nevertheless, the attachment ultimately became just as powerful. Watching her learn to trust and relax, not to mention sleep, was wonderfully gratifying. I believe another feeling, too, infuses our connection with her. Because she came to us as a "lost" child, whatever feelings of loss Scotty and I each carry, whatever of the lost child that still resides within us, resonates with her and richens our love for her. The bond with our adopted child, though different than that with our birth child, feels no less deep.

When Mira was about six months old, I returned to work full time, and Scotty, feeling burnt out on teaching, decided to take on the job of full-time child care. This arrangement has continued to work well for us, which is not to say that it has always been smooth or easy. I often still find myself leaving for work in the morning in that discomfitting state of negative capability, troubled by doubt and contradictory feelings. Pulling out of the driveway, I admit a feeling of unmistakable glee, though there's also some sadness. I feel buoyant relief, yet also anxiety. My children could not be in more capable hands than those of their loving dad, yet still I wonder guiltily if I'm doing the right thing.

One other contradiction or paradox that I've discovered as a working mother is that children, despite having obviously curtailed my freedom, have also brought me a new freedom that I hadn't anticipated. They've liberated me from the sorts of petty career or work anxieties that formerly were capable of obsessing me, especially the need for approval from those in authority. No anxieties compare to those of having children; and as a mother, I've experienced my own authority, tied in with my own self-worth, so strongly through loving and being loved by my children that it can't be easily undermined. Though I was certainly more tied down, I returned to work feeling freer than I ever had before.

Luckily my husband's sense of self-worth is also quite strong, else he would never have survived his role as what others are fond of calling "Mr. Mom." While he has always been perfectly at ease in this role, other people, we've noticed, often seem distinctly uncomfortable with it. On the golf course, for instance, he is typically asked what he does for a living by the others in his foursome. Scotty unhesitantly replies, "Househusband. I take care of our two kids while my wife's at work." The response of the other men, Scotty says, is invariably hearty, often exaggeratedly so: "HO HO, how'd ya' manage that?" "That's GREAT! Wish I could wangle that!" "You've got it made, huh?" The implication is clearly that he's in early retirement. These men either don't know what taking care of children full time means (I know one other couple who tried our arrangement; the husband lasted exactly one week), or they don't mean what they're saying, their hearty enthusiasm only covering their real feelings of embarrassment.

I find similar reactions when men ask me what my husband does. When I told one former colleague, a man in his fifties, his discomfort was so palpable that I found myself adding, "Well, he also does some freelance writing, and he's active in a couple community organizations, and he does a lot of work with his computer." This man grabbed onto that word "computer" as if it were a life raft: "Oh yes, computers, computers, he's into computers!" Taking care of children, it seems, is emasculating. Taking care of computers obviously is not.

Scotty has mothered our two children, has been as passionately involved in their nurturing as I have. Nevertheless, his role in relation to them is still not the same as, nor interchangeable with, mine. My daughter's wailing that accompanied the beginning of this piece, for instance, was finally quelled only when Scotty brought her up to me and I held and talked to her for ten minutes. On the other hand, Mira is more quick to anger and to fall into a full-blown tantrum with me than she is when her father is caring for her. It may be that that intense and intricate negotiation of connection and separateness, of helplessness and power, needs to be played out first and primarily with one other person. The gender of that one person, however, might not be significant: it seems entirely possible that a baby could bond first and primarily to a male caretaker. This was not the case with our family, as I had the primary nursing relationship with our son for the first year, and our daughter, due to her history, bonded to me as a woman first.

Though our children act out their separation and power struggles with both of us, those negotiations are more acute and volatile with me. Sometimes I'll return home from work and the kids will immediately begin whining and fussing about something or other. Scotty will look at me, shrug, and declare, "I don't get it. They were great all day, till you got home!" I'll glare back at him, angry and jealous that he has an easier time with them. Nevertheless, true to the contradictory nature of negative capability, I know I'd also feel angry or jealous if that bond with my children was less intense—and therefore less problematical— than it is.

Mothering has not only forcibly thrust me into a state of negative capability, but to some extent I have also deliberately chosen and cultivated it. As a psychoanalytically inclined literary critic, my habit is to probe for unconscious dynamics and patterns in a text. In one class I taught on psychoanalysis and literature, a student timidly raised her hand, then dared to ask, "Do you, um, do this sort of thing on your own kids?" "Heavens, no!" I replied, and we all broke into relieved laughter. The thought of analyzing one's own children in this way, of prying into their unconscious lives, is indeed a disturbing notion. Not only is it invasive, but it also strikes me as potentially oppressive to the mother as well as the child.

Sometimes, though, my kids will present such a stunning manifestation of a psychoanalytic concept that I can only shake my head and acknowledge it. There was, for instance, the time I returned home from work after teaching a class in which we had discussed Freud's overemphasis of the penis. I had also pooh-poohed his notion of the phallic woman. That night Owen woke crying from a bad dream. "Mommy," he sobbed, "I dreamed you turned into an elephant, and your nose grew into this lo-o-ong trunk!" Well, sometimes an elephant trunk is just an elephant trunk, but still. . . . In any case, I generally try not to probe too deeply or insistently into my children's inner lives.

Keats introduces the concept of negative capability in the context of a discussion of Shakespeare, who, he believes, achieves this quality in his work. Unlike Coleridge, Shakespeare, Keats claims, can remain "content with half knowledge." He does not inflict reasons, neat answers, or categorical structures on his work. This is not to say that critics can't fruitfully analyze or determine orders and categories in Shakespeare's texts, only that the writer himself did not think this way in his writing. Shakespeare trusted in his creative unconscious, in its irrationality, and in all of its mysterious paradoxes; he simply let them be.

Mothering, too, is an essentially creative, not a critical, activity. So as a mother, I willingly shove my usual analytic and critical mode of thinking to the background. Imposing too much "fact and reason" on my children's behavior—analyzing and interpreting their every predilection or move—would be a violation of their being, of their freedom simply to "be." Like the artist, a mother, I believe, has to trust in her creative unconscious, has to have faith in herself and her ability to act intuitively and spontaneously in relation to her children. She needs to respond to who they are at any given moment, not to her own definitions, fixed ideas, or interpretations of who they are.

The irony of the fact that I am at this moment analyzing and imposing definition on the act of mothering does not escape me. That I as a mother cannot completely rid myself of this irritable need is just another paradox that I'm forced to accept. The negative capability of mothering, finally, is not a serene or comfortable state. The paradoxes, ambivalences, and uncertainties are not always easy to bear. Still, there's often the comic relief that those contradictory perspectives allow. Sometimes the laughter in mothering is the recognition of the ironies and absurdities. Sometimes, though, it's just pure, unthinking delight.

Statement to the Court

Martha Boesing

_____

Martha Boesing delivered this statement to the court at her trial for criminal trespass, on Feb. 21, 1983. As a member of the Honeywell Project, Boesing had blocked access to Honeywell Corporation headquarters in November, 1982; at this trial, she and thirty-three co-defendants were found guilty and sentenced to twenty hours of community service. In April, 1983, Boesing was again arrested in a civil-disobedience action at Honeywell headquarters. In June, a jury found her and thirty-five others not guilty.

My name is Martha Boesing. I am a playwright and the artistic director of At the Foot of the Mountain, a Minneapolis-based women's theater. My most recent play, *Ashes, Ashes, We All Fall Down*, a ritual drama about nuclear war and the denial of death, was the result of years of research on the economics and politics of militarism and the weapons industry. I have spent most of my adult life trying to effect change through democratic channels and through my work as a theater artist. I am forty-seven years old. I speak here today as a woman and a mother of three children.

As a mother I am often confused about how to help my children make wise decisions for themselves. One day I extol the virtues of a free and open education and the next I tell them they can't watch TV until they finish their homework. One day I tell them to eat what they like, their bodies know intuitively what they need; and the next I say, "Okay, that's it—no more junk food in this house!" I flounder like this because I have no training and very little support for this work and there are days when I'm the one who needs the parenting, even more than they do.

But I do try not to lie to them. I try to tell them the truth as I see it at any given moment. I cannot tell them that they are growing up into a benign world where they will be given an equal opportunity to succeed at whatever they wish to do with their lives, when the television, the newspapers, and their own nightmares belie this reality. They want to know whether there is even going to be a world for them. They want to know why they should prepare themselves for a life that cannot be lived, a life that is doomed from the start.

I have asked my children since they were very little not to use violence. No punching each other out, no toy guns inside the house, no hitting. You work things out by talking them over, or you go to your room until everyone cools out a little. That's the rule. I cannot therefore turn around and support the rights of one nation to murder another, with my votes and my tax money. And I cannot tacitly agree that it's all right for Honeywell, a major industry in my neighborhood, to build cluster bombs which are right now killing hundreds of people in Lebanon and Southeast Asia. Which standard are they supposed to believe? And I cannot say, "What those other guys do is none of our business," because it is the business of all of us. It is our own lives we are talking about and the lives of our own children.

I believe that Honeywell and the thousands of other corporations who make profits from wars, such as Control Data, Sperry Univac, and FMC Corporation, are run by men who have lost touch with reality. They have clogged up their imaginations, so that they no longer see the faces of the people whom these bombs are killing today, so that they no longer see the faces of their own children whom these bombs will kill tomorrow.

And I believe it is the women, because we are the ones who give birth and because for the most part we are the ones who are asked to raise and nurture the children, who understand the connections and the bonding each one of us has with all living creatures. It is up to us, and to our brothers who are willing to share in this terrifying task of nurturing a new generation of life on the planet, to educate those whose creative intelligence has been stifled.

We live on a precipice. It is not a tolerable place to live, to breathe, to work, to die, to raise children. We must say no to those who are pushing us nearer and nearer to the edge.

And so I sit on Honeywell's doorstep—and since they are determining the fate of all of us, it is no longer a private doorstep—hoping to wake them up and bring them to their senses. Raising children gives one a certain kind of patience. I am willing to sit on this doorstep over and over again, for as long as it takes for them to hear our passionate plea for life.

I have three very beautiful, intelligent children. I have been deeply blessed. They bring enormous joy into my life. I do this for them, and for your children, and for all their friends both known and unknown to them and to us. I pray for a world that is sane and safe for them all to grow up in.

Reflections on Motherhood

Greta Hofmann Nemiroff

I have been "made" into a mother three times over; I have *lived* motherhood for more than half my life. Not only have I had difficult times with each of my children, but also with myself-as-mother. When I first experienced motherhood in the 1950s, I was repeatedly made aware of the "shameful" discrepancy between my own experience of and feelings about motherhood and the "convenient social virtues" ascribed to motherhood by the predominantly male sages who infiltrated my life as experts through the print, radio, film and television media.

Like many women of my generation who had our children early, I am furious at how the medical profession appropriated my experience of childbirth both by mystifying it to the point where I no longer knew my own body, and by imbuing it with a punitive chill and hysterical sterility. I rage at my inability as a conscientious mother ever to achieve the level of "performance" so assiduously prescribed by those "experts" validated by the patriarchy.

My last child was born in 1971, too early for me to benefit from the feminist reassessment of childbirth. However, since then, I have felt empowered by each piece of feminist scholarship, art or expression which repossessed childbearing and mothering as women-defined experiences. Despite this, I have never regretted choosing to become a mother to my children; I am thankful at having been able to initiate these most gratifying if often frustrating lifelong relationships. Since the experience of motherhood has still to be fully described, I find myself a fortunate participant in the redefinition of the experience, of the subtraction from it of all those definitions created through the nostalgic or fearful fantasies and projections of men. It has been only within my lifetime that some women in the world have been able to take control of our own fertility; women's economic dependence on men in the past enforced our collective acceptance of the male criteria for "successful" motherhood. Through a massive global feminist movement, women are beginning to understand and express the view that these male criteria never did work to the interest of women and children.

While I would like to focus on the positive aspects of mothering, I also want to make it clear that I speak in full wakefulness, mindful of all its difficulties and frustrations from the moment of conception onwards. Pregnancy can bring with it discomfort, illness, apprehensiveness and the difficulty of redefining one's corporeal identity. Childbirth can bring with it variable pain and disappointment. Postpartum depression of varying degrees of intensity and length is not uncommon, and even breast-feeding can cause pain and anxiety as well as the sobering realization of the child's absolute dependence on the mother. Being a parent requires toleration of frustration, deferment of gratification, ability to withstand discomfort and sleep deprivation, not only with neonates but with small children and recalcitrant adolescents. For most people, having children imposes financial burdens of long duration, limitation of mobility, time and concentration. Because of our socially constructed role, mothers are especially susceptible to bouts of guilt and feelings of inadequacy, often based on our unconscious assumption that we can and must protect our children from all pain and difficulty.

Since Canadian mothers, like mothers elsewhere in the "developed" world, are usually the primary care-takers of children, they are in the constantly beleaguered condition of trying to find appropriate and affordable child care in a country which does not value the well-being of its most important resource . . . its future citizens . . . sufficiently to come up with a workable, fair and affordable child care programme. Most mothers who work outside of the home do so because they must; yet they are often treated as a "secondary labour force," to be put to work or relegated to the home at the convenience of the economy and the needs of men who benefit the most from it. Mothering is considered a low-status occupation unless there are expedient reasons for its public exaltation . . . such as creating jobs for war veterans by sending the women home. The woman who works full time in the home often lives a life of boredom, of isolation from stimulation and other adults with an increasing drop of self-esteem. The complex organisational and inter-personal skills she may be perfecting are never considered marketable or valid when she chooses to enter or return to the paid labour force.

Contemporary feminist theorists have coined the term "motherwork" to cover only *part* of what women do in the family. The average full-time married "housewife" has three jobs: motherwork, housework, and wife/partner work.[1] Though these categories are not hermetically sealed off from one another, they are a useful tool for establishing which and how many tasks absolutely *must* be done by the mother. Single mothers living with only their children may not have wifework, but frequently they have other primary relationships whether heterosexual or lesbian. "Work" in these relationships may involve resolving the inevitable divided loyalties between lover and children.

Mothers in the paid labour force add that fourth job to their roster. Many women work at lonely jobs, only to return to prepare and have dinner with their children and ready them for bed at the most difficult time of the day. Without time to "gear down" from one world to another, they often rush from work to day care, and thence home to their second job. This routine can be both stressful and boring for mothers full-time at home as well. "I hate coming home and facing a meal alone with the three kids, which I do regularly. You know that five-to-seven blah, I just hate that time," says Arlene,[2] who is kept very busy with a toddler and twins. Very often the three- and four-job mother has very little time, energy or money left for nourishing her

---

1. While this conceptualization has been articulated by several writers, I am here indebted to *Through the Kitchen Window: The Politics of Home and Family,* by Meg Luxton and Harriet Rosenberg, (Toronto: Garamond Press, 1986).

2. Comments about Arlene, Linda and Marsha refer to mothers represented in a photographic essay book, *Giving Birth Is Just the Beginning: Women Speak about Mothering,* by Judith Lermer Crawley. (Montreal: Book Project, 1987).

own life while struggling to provide for her children. "This mother occasionally needs to get high," says Linda,[3] caught by the camera mid-air above a trampoline. [See page 203 of *Mother Journeys*] A rather modest wish with only "occasional" fulfillment requested.

Traditionally the father's role has been to "bring home the bacon," to materialise at ceremonial occasions requiring his presence, and occasionally to contribute to the socialization of his sons. Despite ample historical evidence that many men have been dynamic influences on their children, prescriptive behaviour for fathering has not been as clearly delineated in our culture as that for mothering. The father's obligation to support his family financially has traditionally been given the *imprimatur* of the patriarchy, yet there are few sanctions when the father does not fulfill this role. Consider the staggering percentage of child-support payments awarded by Canadian courts to women for child care which is never paid. It is more than timely for men to reflect and research what fathering means to them and what their appropriate contribution should be as the criteria for mothering are defined by women.

"Sometimes when the kids are asleep, I feel overwhelmed by all the responsibility. I think to myself: I am the Atlas, I'm holding up the whole world," says Marsha,[4] and her feelings are confirmed by the realities of mothering across the globe. According to a United Nations Study on the status of women in the world in 1980, women comprise fifty-one percent of the world's population but do about seventy-five percent of the work for ten percent of the pay. Evidently there has been no overall improvement of these statistics in the interim. Moreover, many of the tasks included in this shocking statistic have to do with mothering; indeed, mothers do hold up the world, but we must also sadly recognize that from the most privileged to the most oppressed mothers, the essential tasks associated with child care are accorded low status and often trap women in a never-ending cycle of hard work which can never be completely done.

Most synonymns for "woman" describe her in relation to men: she is a virgin, a wife, a widow, a divorcee, a mother, a spinster, etc. There is, however, no noun for the woman who chooses not to have a child but who is not celibate. The option *not* to have children must also be examined. Many women exercise the choice not to have children for a

---

3. Crawley, *Giving Birth Is Just the Beginning*.
4. Ibid.

multitude of reasons. Some have placed their priority on projects which require their undivided attention. In considering the difficulties of rearing children and concentrating on other matters, writers often invoke as examples Virginia Woolf and Simone de Beauvoir. In their time, however, the experience of motherhood was still awaiting a feminist interpretation, a project which is just beginning. In contemporary Western society, children are increasingly viewed as depriving us of satisfying our media-managed ambitions and consumer "needs" to their fullest potential. With birth control and a shift in values from the familial to the individual, bearing and rearing children can be perceived as a liability. Some women choose to defer their decision until it will not interfere with more immediate needs such as career moves which will increase job rewards and satisfaction, status, wealth and equity, and access to consumer goods. Often they reason that they want to be able to offer their children "everything." Nothing is to be gained by the mother, the child or the society through encouraging the dubious to have children. Choosing not to bear or raise children should not result from the definitions honed by men through centuries of rule, but through the same process of sorting and reflection accorded the defining of motherhood.

The bearing and rearing of children over an extended period of time is unique to the human experience, which in itself is characterized by relationships of long duration. While it may be true that one doesn't have to experience *everything* in life, most women do have the potentiality for bearing children; even more have the opportunity for rearing them through adoption, or of participating in their rearing through other familial attachments. Active feminists must ask ourselves for whom we are struggling if we do not think the bearing and rearing of children a viable choice. Because of urbanism with its emphasis on the nuclear family in Western society, increasing numbers of adults live in isolation from children, deprived of participating fully in the human experience of the age continuum still visible in most parts of the world. There is much to be gained in sharing one's life with children.

Children bring us a sense of intimacy which cannot be replicated in adult relationships. An adult discussing her bowel movements, hunger, or discomfort will at the least be considered a bore; at the most pathological. Yet such subjects are the very material from which all lives are made. Being attentive to physical comfort, hurt feelings, the ability to play with total concentration and joy . . . the nakedness of childhood preoccupations helps us to keep in touch with ourselves, with the child imprisoned within each adult. This consciousness-rebuilding through the care of children is essential to us in facing our own aging processes. It is too easy for the healthy and ambitious to forget how much we depend on the maintenance of our physical and affective functions in order to share fully in the world. If we lose touch with these matters, we risk becoming rigid and traumatized when we face the inevitable changes in our own life cycles.

Adults in our society have an elaborate etiquette regarding physical contact; our attitudes to tactile communication often verge on the phobic. Indeed, to our own detriment we often confuse our needs for tactility with sexual urges. There is ample evidence in the health and social sciences that humans need caring physical contact throughout our lives . . . especially into old age. We desperately need to link to others by touch, by that bodily warmth which is repressed by our constricted cultural notions about private space. Children provide us with occasions of spontaneous and uncritical tactility, keeping us in touch with our human needs.

That children link us with the future is hardly news. Yet we live in a social order which represses the facts of aging and death, and which separates the generations through the formation of mutually exclusive consumer patterns and life-styles. The threat of nuclear and/or ecological extinction hangs over us all; I do not believe our only fear is for our individual mortality. The vision of a universe without the world and its people only reinforces our respect for human life in its state of flux and generational sequence. When we participate in the growth of children, a sense of wonder must take hold of us, providing for us a sense of future. Without the intimation of concrete individual futures, it is hardly worth bothering with social change and improvement.

Some time ago I was visited at home by a group of Women's Studies students from my class at a community college, The New School of Dawson College. While we sat and talked the afternoon away, my five-year-old daughter, Rebecca, sat nearby on the floor drawing. We were discussing the option of having children; it emerged that not one young woman in the group intended ever to rear children. The discussion flowered with mutual reinforcement until Rebecca's voice piped up: "You're all wrong," she said firmly, "us kids are the best."

These words best sum up my view as well. Our children reflect back to us visions of ourselves and our reality unhampered by our "official stories" and rationalizations. The relationships enjoyed as mothers are unique in lives often holding other sources for love, affection, and fulfillment: lovers and partners, relatives, colleagues, friends and especially women friends, causes, vocations, work. This uniqueness is the focus of an article in which Dorothy Lee, the anthropologist, explains that the Wintun Indians have no equivalent to our notion of "having a child." Rather, the children refer to their mother as "She-whom-I-made-into-a-mother." This expression counters the European concept of children as possessions, an attitude which has tragically become the standard rationale for the brutalization of children through every means from extreme parental control to battering and incest. Through their language, the Wintun emphasize the dynamic and unique relationship of mother and child. Lee describes it this way: "When I make a decision *to be,* to be a mother, I make, at the same time, in the same act, the decision that a child is to be. Maternity is a relationship. So also, when I decide that a new life is to come into being, I make a decision for myself . . . to be a *mother* and not just a mother. I may think of myself as a mother already; I 'have' other children. So actually my decision is not 'to be a mother' but to be a mother-to-this-child."[5]

By declining to experience this reciprocity, we might be saving ourselves from discomfort, expense, worry, the curtailing of spontaneity, and the reduction of day-to-day choices. We may also deprive ourselves of a unique opportunity for intimacy, for knowing facets of ourselves visible only when mirrored back by our children, and for living in the first person the one corner of each person's experience that has truly universal potentiality.

---

5. Dorothy D. Lee, "To Be or Not to Be: Notes on the Meaning of Maternity," in *The Challenge to Women*. Ed. S.M. Farber and Rozen (New York: Basic Books, 1966), 51.

Mothering, like trampolining, requires stamina, balance, patience, fearlessness, consistency and endurance, all merely to sustain the business of bouncing up and down on the same spot, repeating again and again the patterns necessary for the maintenance and development of these wild young beasts—my kids!

But another me is suspended in mid-air, free of all attachments. I remain an independent life on temporary hold. This mother occasionally needs to get high!

Linda

Judith Lermer Crawley, 1987

All the Women Caught in Flaring Light

Minnie Bruce Pratt

———————————

1.

A grey day, drenched, humid, the sun-
flowers bowed with rain. I walk aimless
to think about this poem. Clear water runs
as if in a streambed, middle of the alley,
a ripple over bricks and sandy residue,
for a few feet pristine as a little creek
in some bottomland, but then I corner
into the dumped trash, mattresses, a stew
of old clothes. I pull out a wooden fold-up
chair, red vinyl seat, useful for my room,
while water seeps into my shoes. A day to
be inside, cozy. Well, let's pick a room:
Imagine a big room of women doing anything,
playing cards, having a meeting, the rattle
of paper or coffee cups or chairs pushed back,

the loud and quiet murmur of their voices,
women leaning their heads together. If we
leaned in at the door and I said, *Those women
are mothers,* you wouldn't be surprised, except
at me for pointing out the obvious fact.

Women *are* mothers, aren't they? So obvious.

Say we walked around to 8th or 11th Street
to drop in on a roomful of women, smiling, intense,
playing pool, the green baize like moss. One
lights another's cigarette, oblique glance.
Others dance by twos under twirling silver moons
that rain light down in glittering drops.
If I said in your ear, through metallic guitars,
These women are mothers, you wouldn't believe me,
would you? Not really, not even if you had come
to be one of the women in that room. You'd say:
Well, maybe, one or two, a few. It's what we say.

Here, we hardly call our children's names out loud.
We've lost them once, or fear we may. We're careful
what we say. In the clanging silence, pain falls
on our hearts, year in and out, like water cutting
a groove in stone, seeking a channel, a way out,
pain running like water through the glittering room.

2.

I often think of a poem as a door that opens
into a room where I want to go. But to go in

here is to enter where my own suffering exists
as an almost unheard low note in the music,
amplified, almost unbearable, by the presence
of us all, reverberant pain, circular, endless,

which we speak of hardly at all, unless a woman
in the dim privacy tells me a story of her child
lost, now or twenty years ago, her words sliding
like a snapshot out of her billfold, faded outline
glanced at and away from, the story elliptic, oblique
to avoid the dangers of grief. The flashes of story
brilliant and grim as strobe lights in the dark,
the dance shown as grimace, head thrown back in pain.

Edie's hands, tendons tense as wire, spread, beseeched,
how she'd raised them, seven years, and now not even
a visit, Martha said she'd never see the baby again,
her skinny brown arms folded against her flat breasts,
flat-assed in blue jeans, a dyke looking hard as a hammer:
And who would call her a mother?

                                             Or tall pale Connie,
rainbow skirts twirling, her sailing-away plans, islands,
women plaiting straw with shells: Who would have known
until the night, head down on my shoulder, she cried out
for her children shoved behind the father, shadows
who heard him curse her from the door, hell's fire
as she waited for them in the shriveled yard?

All the women caught in flaring light, glimpsed
in mystery: The red-lipped, red-fingertipped woman
who dances by, sparkling like fire, is she here on the sly,
four girls and a husband she'll never leave from fear?
The butch in black denim, elegant as ashes, her son
perhaps sent back, a winter of no heat, a woman's salary.
The quiet woman drinking gin, thinking of being sixteen,
the baby wrinkled as wet clothes, seen once, never again.

Loud music, hard to talk, and we're careful what we say.
A few words, some gesture of our hands, some bit of story
cryptic as the mark gleaming on our hands, the ink
tattoo, the sign that admits us to this room, iridescent
in certain kinds of light, then vanishing, invisible.

MOTHER JOURNEYS

3.

If suffering were no more than a song's refrain
played through four times with its sad lyric,
only half-heard in the noisy room, then done with,
I could write the poem I imagined: All the women
here see their lost children come into the dim room,
the lights brighten, we are in the happy ending,
no more hiding, we are ourselves and they are here
with us, a reconciliation, a commotion of voices.

I've seen it happen. I have stories from Carla,
Wanda. I have my own: the hammering at authority,
the years of driving round and round for a glimpse,
for anything, and finally the child, big, awkward,
comes with you, to walk somewhere arm in arm.

But things have been done to us that can never be
undone. The woman in the corner smiling at friends,
the one with black hair glinting white, remembers
the brown baby girl's weight relaxed into her lap,
the bottle in her right hand, cigarette in her left,
the older blonde girl pressed tense at her shoulder,
the waves' slap on the rowboat, the way she squinted
as the other woman, her lover, took some snapshots,
the baby sucking and grunting rhythmic as the water.

The brown-eyed baby who flirted before she talked,
taken and sent away twenty years ago, no recourse,
to a tidy man-and-wife to serve as daughter.
If she stood in the door, the woman would not know her,
and the child would have no memory of the woman,
not of lying on her knees nor at her breast, leaving
a hidden mark, pain grooved and etched on the heart.

The woman's told her friends about the baby. They
keep forgetting. Her story drifts away like smoke,

like vague words in a song, a paper scrap in the water.
When they talk about mothers, they never think of her.

No easy ending to this pain. At midnight we go home
to silent houses, or perhaps to clamorous rooms full
of those who are now our family. Perhaps we sit alone,
heavy with the past, and there are tears running bitter
and steady as rain in the night. Mostly we just go on.

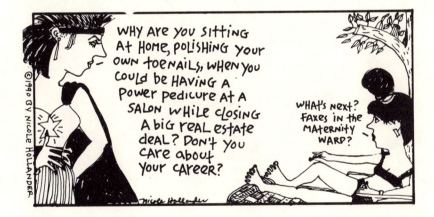

SYLVIA

Nicole Hollander

Section IV

Nancy Spero

Continuity with Our Own Mothers

Section IV

Continuity with Our Own Mothers

————————

Humanity's earliest gods were female. Feminist scholars have found that much of Western civilization, beginning with the Bible, is a reaction against the worship of female fertility and the substitution of one patriarchal deity for the multiple capricious spirits that earlier religions feared and worshipped. These chthonic powers—the angry mothers—are real forces in all human lives. Nothing is so terrible as the mother's wrath, and all children experience it.

The classical tradition of Western civilization reflects the subjugation of the mothers, but contemporary feminist scholars of religion have breathed new life into the concept of the Goddess, the creative power that is a source of women's vitality and dignity, not shame. Feminists could understand part of what comes from the-Mother-as-a-vital-force as well as from the-Mother-our-physical-parent when they chose whether or not to become mothers themselves.

Mothers are keepers of ceremonies, makers of sacrifices, guardians of tradition, experimenters with madness, victims of the nuclear family, dragons of cruelty. Several contributors chafed against their mothers' strictures and struggled to free themselves in order to create a choice of whether or not to follow their mothers' examples. Diane McPherson, in "Making Do," describes some of the lessons she learned growing up in a working-class family and coming from "a long line of mothers." From mothers, women learned destructive lessons as well as good ones, self-hatred and danger as well as love. In "Night Song for the Journey: A Self-Critical Prelude to Feminist Mothering," Rose Stone examines some of these conflicting lessons as she considers her own reluctance to mother.

Linnea Johnson's "Blood Chant" continues this section's exploration of maternal power—nourishing, destructive, sometimes both. Judy Remington in "The Reconstruction" creates a hopeful vision of possibility, where family members of different sexes and sexualities can celebrate together at their children's weddings.

Jewelle Gomez's lovely poem, "A Mother," speaks to motherhood and women's friendships. In Maxine Kumin's short story, "Beginning with Gussie," a family of strong women support one another as single parents. For Genny Lim, differentiation from the mother involves a history of immigration; packed into her family story is the shattering experience of alien cultural encounter. Molly Hite's "Mother Underground" is both hilarious and sad as it tells of how a mother's mute rebellion against conventional family life educates her daughter in sorrow and acceptance.

Carolee Schneemann writes about her decision not to mother in "Anti-Demeter." Schneemann saw that she could not live as an artist if she were to accept her mother's experience as a model for her own.

Rita Dove's "Missing" looks at the mother who "can never/die" from the perspective of the lost child grown up into maternity herself, and her two "Persephone" poems extend this image. Molly Layton, in "The Mother Journey"—the essay that inspired our title for this collection— turns the tools of social psychology on herself and provides a sort of natural history of mothering, reminding us that loss and grief are as intrinsic to the condition as fulfillment and joy.

Making Do

Diane McPherson

I am descended from a long line of mothers. I don't mean this to be funny; on both sides of my family, the women call themselves mothers before claiming any other identity. They are strong, opinionated women; smart, resourceful, and ingenious at what they call "making do with what you have," which for several generations has been next to nothing. I cannot say that any woman in my family called herself a feminist, before I came along. My mother, my grandmothers, my aunts, my sisters—each is traditional, conservative, her sense of self entangled in her relations with her children and her husband. When you work hard at menial jobs and still live in poverty, or near it, as most of the women in my family have, you have little energy left for politics.

There have been individual acts, though, particularly things my mother and grandmother did when they were younger, to which I can trace the beginnings of my own feminist identity, acts that taught me to respect female strength, to feel that secret pride at being a woman out of which feminism can arise, and does, given time, given education, given the luxury to think about something besides your husband, your children, the daily necessity to make do.

My mother's mother, aged eighty-nine, died this past spring of cancer. I guess I loved her when I was a child, although not as much as I loved my other grandmother, she always claimed. I was her first grandchild. I liked to visit the small apartment where she lived with my youngest aunt. I was her reclamation project, a disappointment to her: she wanted Shirley Temple, not the gawky precocious intellectual she got. On Saturday nights she tried to curl my hair with rags. She threw my shamefully tattered underpants into the rag-bag and bought me new ones from Woolworth's. On Sundays she took me to mass. She had set herself the goal of converting at least one of us to the Catholic Church, from which my mother had been excommunicated for marrying my father.

I learned to avoid my grandmother as I grew older. Years of drinking too much and being dissatisfied with her life, her children, her grandchildren, had made her critical and often unexpectedly mean. Sometimes she made fun of us, and she pulled our hair when she insisted on hugging us and we tried to get away.

She died during the busiest part of the semester. I decided I couldn't attend her funeral, but that was all right. She was survived by a brother who is over a hundred, three daughters, one of two sons, their husbands and wife, at least eighteen grandchildren, at least fourteen great-grandchildren. Despite her meanness her daughters cared for her at home until she was able to let go of life. They were enlisted to make this significant sacrifice, not only because of her threats to damn them to hell if they put her in a home, but also because they loved her. She was their mother.

The death of someone who often willfully causes pain, and who has undergone too much of it herself, isn't really sad, but I felt guilty that I couldn't mourn my grandmother, and I began to try to remember the things I had admired about her. She was a smart woman who somehow managed to attend Normal School and become a teacher, at least for a while; she worked at something all her life. She was not a feminist, but she was sometimes courageous and independent in a way that I found admirable. She did not learn to drive until her early sixties, when she could finally afford her first car, a little Opel she named Bluebird. The first time I rode with her, I could sense her terror of the more confident drivers who all seemed to be rushing toward her from behind and menacing her from front and sides, and the relief with which she reached her destination—as if she had not been quite convinced she would survive the journey. She was terrified to drive, but she made herself drive every day.

My mother once told me a story about my grandmother. In the late 1930s, when my mother was in high school, her father died after a long illness, leaving my grandmother with five children and no income. In her grief she started drinking, and for a time she neglected her children. My two aunts, my mother's little sisters, were still in primary school, and someone, some childless woman with money, asked my grandmother to let her adopt the girls. I think she even tried to intimidate my grandmother into agreeing by hinting that the girls might be taken away from her anyway, that she wasn't a fit mother.

My grandmother refused. Somehow she turned back from her own grief to attend to her children, because, as my mother said when she told me this story, she wouldn't have been able to live with herself if she lost her kids. Somehow (I never knew where the money came from) she started a business, a small convenience store that brought in enough income to support her family. This is a tradition for us, the women of our family: we take care of our kids, no matter what.

I think about my grandmother's story now when I think about the accusation of unfitness that is used so often to force us to behave. It is an accusation used almost exclusively against women, who currently constitute three-fifths of the Americans living in poverty; I suspect that poverty *is* our real unfitness. I know it was the basis of the two custody cases my ex-husband raised against me, a charge far more serious than the official accusations he made, that I had abandoned him, that I had "cohabited with several men," that I tried to undermine my son's gender identity by once sending him to school in a pink hat. The history of my family, the fact that my mother's mother was an alcoholic, that my father is also an alcoholic, that my family could not be of financial help to me in an emergency, that I never remarried, as my ex-husband had, so that my small stipend as a graduate student, supplemented by student loans, was all I had to get by on—all of these details were used against me twice, in family court, while I tried to finish graduate school. Against my husband's respectable and comfortably well-off parents, his second marriage to a woman who could, once he had finished graduate school, stay at home and care for his son, I could offer only an immaterial asset, my inheritance from the women of my family: I know how to make do with what I have. I learned about making do from my mother, when I was a child. She taught me how to stretch a pound or so of hamburger to feed a family of ten, twelve, thirteen. She taught me how to substitute items in recipes, when you just didn't have an egg, or cream, or sugar, or butter; she taught me how to make bread, how the same recipe could turn into pizza dough, how to sew, mend, cut hair, conceal a culinary disaster and make it seem like a wonderful new recipe. What to say to creditors when I couldn't pay their bills.

My mother learned these things in her own childhood; as the oldest girl, she was expected to take charge of the house while her mother was working. In the small Maine town where we lived, no one found anything unusual about expecting children to do the work of adults. My mother was expected to do this, and so was I; from the age of ten, I was left in charge, responsible for the house and the care of my brothers and sisters. Like my mother, I was capable, vigilant and very good. Like my mother, I did not think to disobey, or question the expectations of me, until later in my life, when I was in my thirties. It is only now that I can trace my ingenuity, and the origins of my courage to rebel, to my mother's acts of disobedience.

When my mother announced that she intended to learn to drive, Dad put his foot down. The world, he said, did not need another woman driver. That was that, end of discussion. Ordinarily my mother accepted this kind of ultimatum; Dad had a way of being intolerable when he didn't get his way. But now she developed a new strategy: what he didn't know wouldn't hurt him. She had a bit of money saved, in a secret place only I knew about. This paid for eight hours of driving instruction from the Safety First Driving School, represented by a cadaverous man with unusually long grey hair and shaking hands, probably a result of his dangerous occupation.

Two days a week, after my father went to work, Chuck the Safety First man came and gave my mother her lessons. We all lined up on the steps to watch. My mother, looking disturbingly small and vulnerable, slid herself forward in the driver's seat, fussed with the rear view mirror, and painstakingly backed down our long rutted driveway. This was a hazardous route in reverse; on the right was a drainage ditch that was often filled with murky water, and on the left the open cesspool was hidden behind a luxurious swampy tangle of weeds. We had invented the story that this was a bottomless pit, and also that alligators lived in it; now we all believed the story was true. I was worried my mother would lose control of the driving education car, back straight through the cattails, and be eaten by the alligators lurking under the stinking green surface of the water.

At the time I didn't realize this, but my mother was still a young woman, only twenty-nine; she had reached that age at which a woman either resigns herself to her life, or makes changes. My mother made changes. When she had survived eight hours of lessons, she was not ready to take the test for her license, but she had no more money to pay for instruction either. She didn't want to admit this. Instead, she told Chuck that her brother-in-law would now take her out to practice every day.

This was a lie. She had five brothers-in-law (and also her own two brothers) who would gladly have taken a turn or two, but my father had expressly forbidden her to learn to drive, so she couldn't really ask them. She had another plan in mind.

At that time, my father worked winters driving the school bus for the city. His job didn't pay very well, and he also worked for his own father most summers, mowing and raking fields and baling hay. It was hot, exhausting work, and having grown up on a dairy farm, my father hated farming. But we needed the money and the milk he brought home.

His parents lived on the same road we did; their farm was just over a hill about a mile and a half away, but hidden from view. To save wear and tear on the tires, Dad claimed, and to convince my mother that the car wasn't safe for her to drive either (one of his arguments), he drove back and forth in one of the farm vehicles, an old Model-T with a wooden platform built in where the back seats would have been. Our car, a turquoise Studebaker station wagon with big silver nostrils, sat conveniently in the driveway every day, the keys dangling from the ignition, when just after my father left in the mornings, my mother marched out to the car to give herself her daily lesson.

The first day she just sat in the driver's seat. She adjusted the rear-view mirror, she looked over the instrument panel, she fiddled with the stick shift. The car was old when we got it, and my father did not take good care of machines. He was also a large and heavy man, and the front seat was permanently adjusted to his height, and couldn't be slid forward. After trying to do this, climbing in and out of the car, and even greasing the seat slider with Crisco, my mother gave up. She carried the Sears catalogue out to the car and sat on that. It lifted her too high off the seat; her feet barely reached the pedals. But at least she could see out the windshield that way.

Her next lesson was to turn the key and start the engine. She practiced this for two days, getting into the car, adjusting the mirror (which
she had to return to its original adjustment when she left the car so that
my father would not guess what was going on), and looking carefully
over her left shoulder. I had the job of keeping track of my brothers and
sisters, making sure that while my mother was practicing, they were
safely out of her way on the front steps; she was terrified that she might
back over one of us on her way down the driveway.

The first time she shifted gears she forgot to use the clutch, and the
engine gave such a terrible shriek that she had to get out of the car and
smoke a cigarette on the steps. But she kept going back, growing bolder
each time she approached the car. During her first death-defying
descent of the driveway I held my breath the entire way, until she made
her wobbly progress to the turn-around beyond the cesspool and
rolled back up to the exact spot where the car had rested before (she
marked the place by drawing lines in the dirt, in case my father
happened to remember where he had parked). After that day, she
began going all the way to the end of the driveway, to where it joined
the paved road we lived on. There she shifted into reverse and backed
toward the turn-around, often stopping to maneuver the car onto the
driveway again when it slid off into the weeds.

She spent a few days at this stage before she dared to drive out onto
the road. But one morning, just after the mail-car had passed, when the
coast was clear, she suddenly astonished us by nosing tentatively out
onto the road and disappearing beyond the line of trees that blocked
her from our sight. We knew (she had told us) that you were allowed to
drive without a license as long as you stayed on your own property.
And I think we believed that by driving up and down the driveway
enough times, she could learn all she needed to know about driving, or
at least enough to pass the test. But my mother, like a bird grown too
large for the nest, could no longer bear the containment of the driveway, and she wobbled off beyond our reach, at first just going a little
way out of sight, turning around in a driveway just beyond the first
crossroads, and returning, honking gleefully when she came back into
our view. We were still sitting lined up on the steps, stunned that she
dared to break the law so boldly.

Soon even this short trip became too confining to her. Announcing
to us each time that she was just going for a little spin, she began to
drive farther and farther away, staying out of our sight for longer and
longer intervals, until my brothers grew restless and left the steps to

play in their sand pile, or ran to the top of the hill beside our house to see if they could see her returning. She was severely limited in direction. If she went left, the road eventually led to town, where she might be recognized and where traffic was less predictable and more difficult to maneuver through. And just a mile beyond us to the right were the houses of our aunts and uncles on my father's side. Several of them lived between our house and my grandparents' house; anyone who happened to be looking out a window would recognize the car and might tell my father what was going on. So she couldn't drive that way either.

While I sat on the steps with the baby, keeping an eye on my brothers and sisters and waiting for her to return, I began to think about my mother's life. For the first time it occurred to me that she was a person in her own right, not merely someone who belonged to us and who would always be where we expected her to be. Although she was not yet thirty years old, her life had shrunk to the very small circle of places she could see, or walk to, or drive to now in the stolen car. To go to the grocery store or the doctor's office, she depended on my father, or occasionally one of his sisters, who all drove and who loved to know other people's business. She had seven small children, all under the age of ten, and, pregnant with the eighth, she would soon have trouble getting around at all.

And she couldn't even attend the church of her choice. Dad, who declared himself a heathen, refused to go to church at all. Her own family was Catholic; my father's family had been Baptist, but for mysterious reasons they one by one joined the Congregational church. Their liberality did not extend as far as Catholics; my mother could get a ride to church on Sunday, but only for the 10:45 Congregational services.

Watching my mother, who suddenly looked so foreign and daring behind the wheel, disappearing for longer and longer periods and then suddenly coming back into view smiling and waving and honking the horn at us, I realized I was afraid, each time she went away for a little spin. She might never come back; there might be nothing at home to really interest her any longer. That was what driving meant: it was a way to escape from us. At the same time, I realized that like my brothers and sisters, I had betrayed her by not being like her. Although she had thick black hair and hazel eyes, every one of us children was blonde, with blue eyes and large teeth, like my father's side of the family. Now it seemed terrible to me that I had been proud not to look like my mother. Slipping away for a moment into the bathroom, I posed and shifted in front of the mirror, looking for resemblances to her, but I could see none.

While I was at it, I felt guilty for disliking the Catholic church. But I couldn't understand the Latin, and I was afraid to look at the bloody statues of Jesus that hung on every dark wall, and because (as my grandmother often reminded me) I had never been confirmed, I was never sure which of the ritual kneelings and crossings I was allowed to do. I preferred going with my cousins to the Congo church, where there was a kindly attitude toward children. Each summer, a smiling black man named Mr. Sam came from Africa for something called One Great Hour of Sharing. In bible school we collected pennies and glued them onto a big rainbow stretching across the map from Maine to Africa; when the rainbow was filled we pried the pennies off again and used the money to buy milk powder for the children in Mr. Sam's village. I loved doing this, but now I couldn't imagine how such silliness could ever have appealed to me.

My mother later told me she had almost run out of gas on the road. Several miles away from our house, on a road no one in my father's family used, there was a small general store that sold gas, but she wasn't sure she could maneuver close enough to the pump, so she didn't dare drive in. Instead she came up with the scheme of leaving the car on the side of the road, just out of sight of the store, and walking there as if she had run out of gas. While the owner filled her gas can, she told him she had left her children in the car, and he was so taken with the idea of her running out of gas with seven children in the car that he gave her a box of popsicles for what he called the little nippers.

From the beginning of her driving lessons, my brothers begged my mother to take them with her on one of her little spins. She consistently refused, even when they complained bitterly that they never got to go anywhere. This was almost true. Sometimes, as the month of July grew hotter and hotter, my father took us swimming at a place we called the Second Res, short for the second reservoir. The First Res was a shallow natural basin that collected spring runoff; it was a smelly mud hole by mid-summer. But the Second Res never dried up. It was a man-made pond, created when a granite quarrying operation had uncovered a natural spring. The water was clean and very cold, even in the hottest part of the summer, and unlike the swampy First Res, the Second Res had a long narrow ledge of granite, opening onto a deeper pool where someone had floated a raft on old truck inner tubes. We weren't allowed to swim out to the raft where the water was deepest, but we loved splashing around on the ledge. We played a game called Christies, named after the most poor and grimy family in our town. The point of the game was to get wet, coat ourselves thoroughly with mud, and then chase each other around screaming "Christies are coming!" before running into the water to wash off again.

My mother always kept her promises to us, but my father forgot promises as easily as he made them, so if he told us in the morning that he would take us swimming at the Second Res that afternoon, he had usually forgotten his promise by the time he finished haying at the end of the day. My brothers did not forget, however many times Dad broke his promises; they lined up on the steps, holding their towels, every sunny afternoon, waiting for him to come home from work.

But haying depends on weather. Dad's workday sometimes didn't end until dusk, especially if thunderstorms were predicted for the next day and there were bales to get in. And other times he didn't come home, but went to town and drank beer with his friends; he claimed beer was the only good thing to wash the chaff out of a man's throat. My mother had no way of knowing, when he didn't show up, whether he was working late or didn't intend to come home at all. So one interminable July afternoon, when she got tired of watching my brothers, one by one, run around to the sunny side of the house to see if Dad was coming every time they heard a car, she offered to take us to the Second Res herself. She seemed to be convincing herself as she convinced us, when we were astounded that she would finally take us with her in the car.

"Why not?" she said in a new outlaw's voice. It sounded to me like she was talking to our father when she said it, but like my brothers, I raced to the car and jumped in.

Riding with my mother felt surprisingly different, like the car had been transformed into another vehicle altogether. My father, drunk or sober, drove fast, and wove constantly from one side of the road to the other; he claimed the car had bad shocks. My mother drove very slowly so she wouldn't need to shift, creeping ahead with small lurching bumps because she couldn't manage to keep her foot at a steady pressure on the gas. She gripped the steering wheel with both hands at the top, in order to pull herself forward enough to reach the gas pedal and brake with her toes, and she whispered to herself tensely as she drove. I found riding with her so unnerving that I sat holding the baby around the waist with both arms and stretched my own toes to reach the floor so I could brace myself each time we needed to stop.

When we reached the gravel parking area at the Second Res and the car stopped, we all sat there silently for a moment, grateful to be alive. Then my mother smiled brightly at me and said, "There! I bet you didn't think we'd make it." We all got out of the car and headed for the water.

The Res was not supposed to be a swimming area; the old quarrying machinery was still submerged in the deepest end, where you could see it after a long dry hot spell. Mostly adults swam there, and sometimes there were broken beer bottles on the rocks, or unfamiliar men drinking and tossing away burning cigarette butts, or other hazards to children, so I was expected to keep an eye on the younger kids and not really swim myself. But that day the Res was nearly deserted. My mother, in her faded brown maternity bathing suit, sat on the rock ledge submerged up to her waist, and kept the baby with her. That meant I could practice my dog paddle in the deep water just before the drop off, for what seemed like a long while, until my brothers' lips turned purple and they couldn't stand still without shivering. Then we made a wide wobbling circle in the empty parking lot and started home.

To this day I cannot guess what possessed my mother to stop at my grandparents' farm on the way back. Perhaps she thought they would be astonished that she had learned to drive, and they would help her persuade my father to let her get a license. Perhaps she thought my father had gone drinking instead of coming home, and she hoped my grandparents (who disapproved of drinking) would give him a lecture. Perhaps she even wanted to be caught, to expose herself as an outlaw once and for all. At any rate, she took us on a different route home from the Res, a road that led down a long curving hill. At the bottom of the hill was my grandparents' farm, and as we wobbled into sight of it she said, "Let's stop and visit Gram and Gramps." At nearly the next moment, my mother, who had not yet mastered making sharp right turns, tried to turn into my grandparents' driveway, missed completely, and drove over the top of a culvert into the shallow stream that ran along the side of the road.

Luckily I was still clutching the baby, now squirming and unhappy at being in the hot car after the cool water, tightly around the shoulders and waist with both arms. We slid into the stream with exceeding slowness, like disasters happen in bad dreams. I had time to brace myself before impact, which threw the baby's head backwards, hitting me sharply in one temple, and forward again just short of the dashboard. She began to shriek. My brothers had been riding all the way in the luggage compartment of the car; they flew into the back seat and landed behind my sisters, who had been thrown against the padded back of the front seat. My mother had braced herself on the steering wheel. So although everyone was yelling and thrashing around in the back seat like a lively catch of fish, no one was hurt, and one by one we climbed down out of the passenger side doors and ran up the driveway to our grandparents' house.

My father, as it turned out, was not in town drinking after all. He was standing in the open window of the barn stacking bales as they came off the conveyor belt, and he watched us slide into the stream. For a long while his mouth hung open in surprise. Then, although he was not allowed to swear in front of his parents, he began to work his way through every curse he had learned in the Marines, beginning with "Holy old jumped-up Jesus," getting wound up as he went through the list, which started softly and ended in an irate bellow. Everyone else in the yard, my brothers and two of my uncles who were helping with the haying, began to yell at my mother as well. My grandmother heard the noise and came running out of the house, drying her hands on her apron, to see if anyone was hurt. My grandfather, at the bottom of the conveyor belt, watched us climb out of the car; scratching his head, he muttered his own favorite curse: "Judas Priest."

She appeared to be completely in the wrong, but my mother was remarkably calm for a pregnant woman in a wet bathing suit who has just crashed a car with seven children aboard into a stream. Straightening her back, as she always did when she was mad, she marched up under the window where my father was swearing at her. "This is your fault, Harry," she told him. "You're the one who keeps leaving me at home all the time with all these kids and no one to talk to. You should have taught me to drive yourself."

I was right behind her, carrying the baby, who had suddenly stopped crying and was struggling to get down into the dirt to chase the chickens. Before anyone else could yell at my mother, I jumped in to defend her. "She's a good driver," I lied, "she just needs a little practice."

Years after this, when I had left home forever, I had a dream about our car crash. In my dream, only my mother and I were in the car, and she was taking me for a ride to show me how much her driving had improved. Without warning, she turned to take a shortcut through a hayfield near our house. The car bumped down over a log hidden in the high grass, and I was thrown forward; my face hit the dashboard and my top front teeth were knocked out.

While we collected ourselves after the accident, my mother apologized to me for knocking out my teeth. I put the teeth into a little pocket on the front of my bathing suit and assured her that the dentist could put them back later. Then I forgot all about them. Later in the dream I was shocked to realize I had waited too long; my teeth were dead and could never be replaced. Now I think these teeth represented the part of myself that belonged to my father's family, the part I chose to give up in defending my mother. And just after our crash, although I continued to resemble Dad's side of the family, people began to notice for the first time that I also looked like my mother.

On January 30, 1994, my son and only child turned eighteen. As one of my women friends reminds me, he is now a white man. I have no daughter who will carry on the family tradition of making do, who will rebel against her mother, who will leave home and discover later what she most admires about me. And yet I have managed to pass on to my son something else of importance: at eighteen, he is one of those rare, sweet creatures, a man who loves his mother. He has lived with me for much of his life, full-time during the four years he was in high school; that is, he has lived with me and my partner. One of the things I celebrated, on his eighteenth birthday, was the end of my fear that he could be taken away from me by his father. That I would again be accused of being an unfit mother because I am now a lesbian, and because I grew up in poverty. Because I am still poor and in debt from years of graduate school, and sometimes can't afford to send him to the dentist when the check-up card comes. Because he attends college on financial aid, as I did. Because I come from a family of alcoholics and have been unable to provide him with positive male role models. Because, as a woman, I supposedly cannot teach him what it means to be a man.

None of the dire predictions of the custody suits has come true. Entering adulthood, he is tall, handsome, bright, hardworking, inventive, dependable, messy, musical, sentimental, secretive. Cheerful in the mornings. Able to do his own laundry. Able to be a friend to women as well as a lover.

This is my most precious memory of my son: he is still an infant, not yet walking or talking beyond occasional word-like babbles, but already in day-care at the home of a woman a few blocks from where I work. In the middle of one night I come down with intestinal flu, and spend a long night feverish and vomiting. The baby screams beside me on the cold bathroom floor, angry that his feeding is interrupted, but safe. The next day I take one of my precious sick days to recover. My husband wants to take him to day-care so I can sleep (as he did, all the night before, deaf to the baby's crying) but I refuse; I have so little time to spend with him as it is. There is a spare bed in the baby's room, so I barricade the door and put him on the floor with his toys, and lie down to rest.

Sometime during the afternoon I drift awake; soft hands are patting my face. Something solid slides across my matted hair. My son has found a small comb among his things, and is tottering along the edge of the bed, stroking my face and combing my hair as I sleep. Still only a baby, he has discovered the pleasure of mothering someone else.

Another memory: He starts elementary school. He already knows how to read; I taught him when he was two, because he wanted to learn. I taught myself, at three; early reading is a family trait. Because I know that, already reading and doing math, he will be bored and perhaps ostracized in a public school, I arrange for him to attend a Montessori school. His father reluctantly agrees to pay some of the tuition, and I earn the rest teaching art at the school.

It's a good school, a good place for a child who loves to learn. Most of the teachers are women; they do their best to use non-sexist language, to treat boys and girls equally. But sometimes, on the play-ground, uglier ideas creep out, things the children have learned at home or among their friends. One day several of the boys decide to exclude from their play a girl who is my son's friend. She's a girl, they say; girls can't play this. Girls are stupid; girls can't do anything. My son, alone, rises to the defense of girls: Maria Montessori is a girl, he reminds them, and so are your mothers.

Night Song for the Journey:
A Self-Critical Prelude to
Feminist Mothering

Rose Stone

———————————

As an incest survivor whose multiple perpetrators include my mother—a seemingly strong, independent, professional woman whose exterior corresponded neatly to both the early second-wave feminist profile of superwoman and the '50s profile of Super-mom—as well as my paternal grandfather, my only male cousin and possibly my father and maternal grandfather—the term "feminist mothering" evokes in me tremendous and dynamic feelings of conflict. As a child I thought my mother defined the term feminist: I loved her brilliance, I loved it that she was professional when many of my school-mates' mothers weren't, I thought the contempt she showed my father, painful as it was for me to witness, was a mark of the self-assertion whose absence she loudly noted in other women.

———————————

This essay owes much to conversations with and feedback from Katie Cadigan, Joanna O'Connell, Judith Raiskin, Martha Roth and Stacey Vallas.

As I matured, the claustrophobic bond I had felt with her, the prisonhouse of love and exploitation I grew up in, came to define my relationships with powerful women; I saw their frustration and anger as signs that they were special beings whose gifts had gone unrecognized by the world (and so they were, many of them); I joined their campaigns for vengeance, justice or recognition without getting that *I* deserved justice, recognition; that *my* desires for revenge—against my mother, among others—deserved a hearing.

In the following essay, I want to examine the legacy of mother-daughter incest in my relationship to feminism, and my re-understanding of feminist mothering as a process of self-empowerment rather than as an attempt to live up to certain political ideals. In the process, I want to show how this has evolved away from my earlier, skewed vision of motherhood and my attempt to pass this vision off as "feminist," and I want to juxtapose the dangers of the women's movement's duplicating incestuous situations with some redemptive possibilities for women survivors in a feminist context.

Current public attention to healing from the devastation of incest owes much to feminist insistence on the personal as political, and on the relationship between horrors in the domestic sphere and wider socio-dynamics. However, when I started looking for information on my particular circumstance, I realized that the politically pro-women roots of incest-awareness have helped to maintain an overwhelming denial of mother-daughter incest, or its dismissal as less severe (because less common) than father-daughter incest, and have deflected focus away from the former as ultimately a result of "the patriarchy" anyway. In other words, female initiators have not been held accountable as fully responsible agents to the extent that male initiators have been. When Ellen Bass's and Laura Davis's landmark five-hundred-page treatise on incest recovery, *The Courage to Heal,* came out, a friend warned me: despite their courage to speak the unspoken on most counts, the authors relegate mother-daughter incest to a footnote [pp. 96-97] explaining it away, even though a fair number of personal testimonies in the book designate mothers as primary perpetrators.

Although one of the editors of *Voices in the Night: Women Speaking About Incest* specifies her mother as a perpetrator of what is now known as "emotional incest," the sole paragraph in which this information is mentioned gets swallowed up in the whole of the preface, which analyzes incest as a "training ground for female children to regard themselves as inferior objects to be used by men," pre-emptively criticizes hypothetical "male" and "male-oriented" critics who will find themselves implicitly indicted by the book's contents, and urges victims to understand how they were trained for a life of abusive relationships by "fathers, brothers, uncles, grandfathers, more distant relatives." Moreover, some woman- or feminist-identified therapists who specialize in incest recovery, using the common paradigm of father = abuser and mother = silent partner, often go to great lengths to exonerate the silent partner from any kind of responsibility.

At the level of popular culture, this displacement of responsibility occurs in a slightly different way in the book *Sybil. Sybil* is the book that first apprised me, at an intuitive register, of my own abuse, though it would be years before I knew to use the term "incest" for what happened: home from college on vacation in the early '70s, I sat in my mother's dining room flipping through the women's magazine in which the story first appeared in serialized and abridged form. My eyes fell on a detail about something Sybil's mother did to her, and a charged current of shame and recognition passed through me. I put the magazine aside. "This is contraband information in this house," I thought. "I'm not supposed to know this here." And that, for many years, was that.

Over ten years later, in an incest recovery group where the book was available to members as part of the group's literature, I read *Sybil* in its entirety. In this best-selling real-life story of mother-daughter sexual abuse, the terms "incest" or even "sexual abuse" are never used in the heavily psychotherapeutic content of the book, nor were those terms a part of the popular discourse surrounding the book or its made-for-TV dramatization. Instead, it's a sensationalistic tale featuring a spectacularly extreme disorder resulting from spectacularly extreme abuse— but, God forbid, not "sexual" abuse, although Sybil's reproductive system was so mutilated that she would not have been able to bear children even had she been able to sustain a relationship which would have allowed her to entertain such a project as a reality. The media gives us a "crazy" (multiple-personality) daughter coming from a "crazy" (schizophrenic) mother—a monster, we are told, not really a woman.

The book's huge public acclaim has, I think, to do with its silence about the specifically "sexual" nature of the abuse along with the heightened demonic characterization of the mother. Both distortions are misogynistic: the former denies that women have the power to *sexually* abuse each other, the latter reinforces the terror, so charged in the popular imagination, of the preternaturally omnipotent Mother who is to blame for all domestic tragedies (a Momism of the '70s). The mystification of the mother's sadism forecloses the possibility of our saying, "Yes, this is incest, a common practice, a widespread social injustice." I believe that if Sibyl's perpetrator had been a man, the "sexual" and incestuous aspect of the parent-child relationship would have been so overwhelmingly obvious that the book could not have been published or at least would not have received the same kind of reception. In fact many of the abuses Sibyl suffers at the hands of her mother are common elements of mother-daughter incest (as well as other incestuous relationships), as are the psychological results: multiple personalities, dissociation, depersonalization, "splitting."

In the foregoing paragraph, I put "sexual" in quotation marks to acknowledge the controversy over the meaning of the adjective in the term "sexual abuse." The common analogy used to refute the sexuality of sex crimes is: "If someone walked up to you on the street and hit you with a frying pan, would you call that cooking?" This is confusing. On the one hand, possibly what is implied is that "sexuality" is co-extensive with "pleasure," "intimacy," "reproduction," so that sexual contact that is either unwanted or intended to inflict pain is perforce not "sexual." On the other hand, it is the specifically sexual nature of crimes like rape, incest, and child sexual abuse that marks these crimes with an order of violation that groups them together. Only slowly are the links between sexual and other forms of child abuse being acknowledged—which is leading to a healthy breakdown of polarized gender-typing of victims and perpetrators. The strategy behind the frying-pan analogy is, of course, to de-exoticize the crime and make it possible to talk about: "Everyone knows you can't talk about sex, so let's say this isn't sex so we can talk about it." However, its use in circles that traditionally silence woman/woman sexual abuse indicates that sex and/or gender does indeed play into conceptions of what constitutes sexual abuse.

During the year when I had identified myself as a survivor and my mother as a perpetrator, but well before I had gotten into any formal recovery work focused on this subject, an academic advisor, innocent of my personal history, wanted to give my career a boost by having me organize a conference panel on "Anne Sexton and Incest." Two of the papers focused on the father/daughter incest encoded in Sexton's poetry; the third examined her play *45 Mercy Street,* which treats both father/daughter incest and great-aunt/grandniece incest. The presenter pointed out that critics had chosen to overlook the latter aspect of the unpublished drama, in spite of clear evidence; she quoted the mother in the play: "It makes me shiver the way Aunt Amy keeps touching you and stroking you . . . Women don't touch women that way," and the father, who initiates his incestuous scenario with: "Lie back now, and I'll give you a back rub the way Aunt Amy does." But my panelist characterized this incest as "daughter-daughter" incest, infantilizing and exonerating the adult female perpetrator by ascribing her motives to a "pre-Oedipal" connection to female sexuality.

As I sat on the podium with these three well-meaning, committed academic feminists—potentially my professional mother-mentor figures—I felt exposed, ashamed, infantile: abused not necessarily by them but by the discourse they were deploying—quite innocently—to talk about my secret. (I have now used the word "innocent" twice instead of "unconscious," as if my consciousness implicates me in my own victimization. I am "guilty" of what happened to me, and those who don't understand are "innocent.") Let me tell you what this feeling means: I felt genitally violated as I sat there; my clothes felt awkward as in certain recurrent dreams; I felt humiliated. I think I was rude to the big name on the panel, a woman I experienced as motherly in an earthy, gutsy kind of way, and hence resented.

A final aside about Daisy, the girl in Sexton's play: when she breaks down as an adult, her language imitates the rapturous, self-mutilating, quasi-religious language of her female violator, thus suggesting the extremely complicated, painful, and characteristic identification of the abused girl with the abusive woman. The useful phrase "negative fusion with the perpetrator," which comes out of incest recovery groups, was later to take on extra-frightening significance for me; what does the laudatory term "woman-identified woman" mean when the woman one identifies with is a sexual abuser? Would I become my mother if I had children? Does growing up mean turning into a perpetrator?

My mother denied my autonomy in an absorptive violation that tied me to her. At night she surrounded me like an amoeba, dissolving my boundaries, consuming me into herself as if she believed herself to be still and eternally pregnant with me:

> *I am the outer wall of your being;*
> *you have to go through me to get to anyone else, and*
> *I'll stop you in whatever way I can;*
> *you'll never love anyone else:*
> *I'll stop you in whatever way I can.*

That was the contract through which affection, touch, and thus survival itself were secured in my family. Probably an incest survivor herself, Mother used me as cannon fodder in her war against men: she used my presence in her bed as a literal buffer between herself and my father, whose touch she couldn't stand; and she usurped my childish yearning for my father's attention, interposing herself between us— between me and the whole rest of the human world—as the sole and appropriate source of all my affectional needs. Like most perpetrators, she justified her physical intrusions as protection from outside influence and danger.

Though I have considered myself a feminist I have had great difficulty with some of the major tenets of the women's movement— notably, that women are each other's "natural" allies, that we never hurt each other, or if we do, it's not our fault—there's a bunch of white guys in gray suits pulling strings behind a screen over there like so many wizards of Oz. I've silenced myself about conflicts with other women, including strong feminists, for fear of the charge of incorrectness—and this dishonesty appeared to be encouraged in the early days of my feminist hanging-out; it sometimes seemed that the only conflicts admissible between women concerned one's failing to be sufficiently feminist (or, probably more likely, personal disharmony was cast in ideological terms, so that someone or some position she took was "more feminist" than [that of] her opponent). While intellectually I know that my caution about this aspect of feminism paints an unfairly stereotyped and incomplete picture of the movement, viscerally I continue to feel claustrophobic and nauseous when conversation among feminist friends turns to "the patriarchy" (is there only one? what's so great about "the matriarchy"?), "male values" (negatively compared to "female values," as in feminist reception of Carol Gilligan's work, for example), and so on.

When I read Luce Irigaray's celebration of female relationship I feel that I'm drowning in sexually expressed maternal power-lust. Incest survivors have extreme difficulty understanding and respecting their own need for boundaries—if women are victims/survivors of institutional and individual incest, how healthy is it to celebrate a merging of women in primal undifferentiation? Are boundaries, difference and separation really simply oppressive patriarchal constructs, or do we only call it "violation" when those boundaries are challenged or neutralized by a man? I feel these reservations even though many feminist writers presumably celebrate a union of two equals, which is not the case in incest; incest survivors find it hard even to conceive of a sexual relationship between equals.

As a result of my ambivalence, I feel inadequate as a feminist, afraid that my constant need for self-differentiation will be read as contentious, undaughterly and excessively defensive. This mistrust and fear of reprisal for "telling the secret" of my discomfort, commonplace traits of survivors, also means that I have not availed myself of genuine friendships and support offered me in feminist circles; I have projected the figure of my mother onto leaders in my local feminist communities; I have not known how to let in comradely love from other women for fear it would be tainted with sadism, competition, and denial of difference.

And I have not known how to love others—either men or women—with true intimacy, for fear of finding these traits in myself; recently I have found myself saying, in differing contexts, "I would sooner die than have anyone experience me the way I experienced my mother." Terror of being a perpetrator literalizes this statement: when I've felt sexual love for a man I've injured myself physically as an alternative to telling my feelings, because to declare my feelings would have been to perpetrate. I've felt that it would be better to hold all my impulses of affection and attraction in check, to smash my head against a wall, to cut my arms and bite myself, than to have people run from me as I've had to run from my mother in order to save my life. Better to die than to hurt others as my mother hurt me; better to die than to be abandoned by others as I was abandoned by my mother, because, in short, in the name of motherhood, in the name of love, she betrayed me.

I've experienced some echoes of a closed-system, incestuous dynamic in my relationship to feminism. The word "feminism" can be used abusively, not only as a threat by anti-feminists to keep women submissive ("You don't want to be one of those shrill feminists, do you?"), but more insidiously, by feminist women against each other: to silence dissent, to force a particular analysis in proscriptive and prescriptive ways at the expense of felt experience, to tie oneself to a specific identity that inhibits exploration and inquiry, to stifle difference. The fear of displaying internal conflict re-enacts the closed system of the incestuous family: I recall some friends' dismay that Rich's "Some Notes on Women and Honor" was anthologized in a non-feminist reader, because it showed that women betrayed women (as if this were news), a piece of information better kept in the closet lest it fall into the hands of the enemy.

Another problem, more subtle because it involves speech instead of silence, and more an issue of insensitivity to abuse than of abuse *per se*, has to do with disrespect for boundaries. A friend who had been a sexual abuse activist for years recently discovered that her mother was among her incestuous abusers and reminisced on her early days of anti-rape activism in light of this new information. "At Take Back the Night marches we'd have these speak-outs against abusers. Women with very shaky boundaries would be encouraged to get up with microphone in hand and accuse their abusers in front of crowds of strangers, and this was considered to be a breakthrough for them. Now I can also see it as a way that the women's movement exploited survivors' vulnerability for its own purposes. The Rape Crisis Hotline would get calls from women saying they'd just spoken at a speak-out and were feeling depressed and didn't know why."

Some women experienced sharp disappointment and betrayal after their self-revelations, indicating that they had indeed not been ready for the gesture that they felt called upon to make. I say "felt" here because another characteristic of survivors is that they do not perceive choice even when there is one. Although they were by no means coerced into public disclosure of their stories, the implication that they would be good girls if they made such disclosure can be internalized and experienced as an imperative. (While I don't want to necessarily equate the two dynamics, it is worth drawing an analogous point that incestuous obedience isn't always elicited by explicit physical force or threats thereof.) And it is doubtful whether, in those early days of anti-rape enthusiasm, there was much sensitive follow-up for speakers-out to process the backlash of shame and discomfort that often attends such confession.

There is a difference, subtle and not always immediately apparent to people who have not focused specifically on recovery from child-hood abuse, between breaking silence in an empowering way and revictimizing oneself through compulsive or compulsory self-disclosure. "In our Hotline training we were constantly told that the most liberating thing for women was to get them to tell the details of their abuse. That seems really wrong to me now," said my friend. Don't get me wrong; I must qualify my friend's newfound certainty by acknowledging that part of breaking silence is the backlash of shame that follows; this is one legacy of growing up in an environment in which "If you tell anyone I'll kill you" is an everyday implicit or explicit reality. Those early second-wavers were right to maintain that silence must be broken for consciousness to be raised, and survivors must be encouraged to understand that a backlash of shame and terror doesn't necessarily invalidate the importance or the liberating effect of speaking the truth. However, I have had, by trial and error, to cultivate a personal sense of safety, and to honor my personal need for safety above other women's political needs to find spokespeople for their causes; in fact, I have experienced such latter needs as exploitative. Survivors of childhood sexual abuse don't have a sound sense of what's appropriate and what's inappropriate to disclose to strangers, and often expose themselves unnecessarily to others' judgments; earlier in my healing process, when I've been asked, with varying degrees of tact, to "prove" to others that my mother really was a perpetrator rather than simply an over-zealous caretaker (another line one hears from people in denial about mother-daughter incest, as well as from the perpetrators themselves), I've told the graphic details only to feel uncomfortable and ashamed of myself in front of my interlocutor, on whose face I read the silent but dying attempt to come up with rationalizations for what Mother did. Much less often am I called upon to supply details—to "prove" anything—when I mention my male perpetrators.

In my adolescence and early twenties, my future-fantasies had me as a single mother of a single child. Even before I was able to be self-critical about it, I knew that my motive was to create a creature who would have to love me and would not betray or abandon me as I had been abandoned as a child. While from the outside, under camouflage of a crude feminist self-sufficiency, I appeared to be Lady Madonna planning to chart a brave and unconventional course, I would have duplicated the incestuous scenario emotionally if not physically. At the same time, the line of feminist poetry, "I am a woman giving birth to myself," gave me the heebie-jeebies because it evoked my mother's perversion of that concept: because she had given birth to me, I was her and consequently she could do whatever she wanted to me.

Currently I am thankful to be childless and that my one pregnancy—by someone I didn't love whom I, unable to set boundaries as a result of the incest, thought I was supposed to mother through sex—terminated in an abortion over ten years ago. My survivor friends who are mothers tell me that to be a mother is to wonder, a hundred times a day, if they've crossed that boundary, if they've abused their children, and every day, a hundred times, to forgive themselves. This makes me feel hopeful about the possibility of my own future motherhood, and that eventuality will unfold as it will. While I have no great investment in maintaining my childlessness forever, I know now that the child I wanted to have was myself, and I understand that line of poetry as giving me permission to do it over the right way. "Feminist mothering" has to do, precisely, with learning to stick up for myself and speaking my truth, without abandoning or betraying myself.

I have been asked to address the wider redemptive possibilities of feminism; I have recouped myself in the course of this essay, one reader told me, but can I recoup feminism? I see myself participating in current revisions of feminism from the inside, revisions which tear down the edifice of "feminism as monolith," the walls of the convent, the hege-mommy[1]. The anger in this piece identifies me as being *in medias res,* mid-process, undignified, perhaps venting at the wrong people for now. What I want to shed is my own primitive and disingenuous maternally inculcated feminism, in which I reveled in my status as victim and, like my mother, used my own self-victimization as cannon fodder in a war against my male perpetrators. Next to my comrades in incest recovery—both male and female—feminists are the people who have most encouraged my exploring this issue, who have given this text the most sophisticated responses, be they supportively confrontational or uncritically enthusiastic. Not surprising, since they are the only people I dare show it to. Being a feminist obliges one, at least nominally, to be open-minded—and this obligation seems to lead to genuine desire that all people empower themselves. (As the leftist pedagogical slogan has it, "Open the mind and the heart will follow.")

The three Fates on my academic panel would have respected my simultaneous reticence and desire to participate, had I been in a position to take care of myself and articulate my needs. But I wasn't, and if it helps me to live, I get to be mad at them until I can, in contemporary therapeutic terms, "put my anger where it belongs." And it belongs, for the time being, directed not only at some abstract "patriarchy" but also at the specific, scarred, damaged beings who hurt me.

I sense this work to be my true feminist awakening, in that I'm

---

1. I coined the term "hegemommy" in 1988 in informal conversation to describe a particular dynamic in which I found myself expected to act and speak in deferential consensus with a group of feminists; I now use it to invoke a more generalized factional or generational dynamic in which older/cultural/essentialistic feminists invoke maternalistic tropes (I typo'ed it "tripes") to achieve a hegemony through their expectations of loyalty and acknowledgement of the suffering involved in their pioneering efforts. While I do acknowledge their struggles, I see no need to conform to their expectations any more than I would to my own mother's, based on the suffering she underwent to bring me into the world and bring me up in it.

coming back to my body and learning to be on my own side from the inside out, rather than adopting a set of rhetorical positions as protective coloring in order to disarm dangerous mother-figures and to buffer me against dangerous father-figures. I used to want other feminists to do for me what I now know only I can do—to heal me with unconditional love. Other women can support me in this journey, but they can't do it *for* me. As I speak my truth more and more I give less of my power away, and women whose rigidity or charisma or anger frightened and attracted me before are shedding their demonic aura. They're just scarred, damaged beings like me.

Women of color have charged white academic feminism with denying difference, and while white feminists have responded by conceding the difference of the "Other"—thereby reproducing the problem of exoticization (witness the token celebrity status of Gayatri Spivak, for example, among high theorists)—they have not fully succeeded in acknowledging difference among and inside themselves. I am not agitating for new categories of difference based on static identity (the holy trinity of class-race-gender expanding to include age-sexual preference-physical challenge and perhaps the new and improved survivor-of-mother-daughter-incest), but to acknowledge *differentiation* as a dynamic process. People can grow away from an identity, an ideology or a community, come back to it, change their relationship to it, argue with it, watch it melt away and re-form—all processes that challenge the hege-mommic, closed system of the incestuous family.

My own evolving relationship to feminism, my invention of my own feminism, is a case in point. It makes sense that the women's movement bears the scars of the oppressive, incestuous society it rose to protest, and that I would come to the movement with my own scars, expecting it to supply the mothering I never got, and re-enacting my incestuous family dynamics. Ultimately there's nothing unfeminist about acknowledging women's abuse of each other; such a revisionist process must be possible in the resilient membrane that is feminism. Just as the issue of lesbian battering has been able to surface as the result of increasing confidence in the flexibility and stability of the lesbian community (it's no longer of primary importance to present a falsely unified face to enemy outsiders), profound conflicts between women—all people—need to be acknowledged and articulated if we conceive of feminism as a long-term commitment to freedom on all levels. Since the most cogent critiques of feminism typically come from within feminism itself, this is happening.[2]

And Afterwards . . .

It is now five years since I wrote this essay and I come back to it one last time. It represents an older state of mind, and I owe myself and you (gentle, angry, jaded or none-of-the-above readers) a retrospective introspective and theoretical update. On the personal plane, the term "incest survivor" has ceded the floor as a primary element in my public persona; I would never now begin an essay with the in-your-face dramatic words "As an incest survivor." I would use, parenthetically, the term "child sexual abuse" or "inappropriate boundaries"—more euphemistic and less confrontational, less provocative.

This does not mean, of course, that I am "rethinking" my past to the degree that I no longer consider myself an incest survivor, but rather that I don't want to provoke other people's defensive or pained fetishizing of the more charged term. No longer preoccupied with that aspect of my recovery and growth, I'd rather not offer it up to others as my main persona.

Besides which, it has become clear to me that my thinking about my mother is limited by something—I don't know what yet. Since writing the essay, I learned more, and more directly horrifying, instances of sexual abuse that left my mother no longer the "primary perpetrator." While I'm not so invested in the abuse-survivor aspect of my identity, I

---

2. As to the broader aspect of the essay, namely, its potential contribution to feminist thought: Five years later, the general tenets of what I've been saying—the "exportable" aspects of my observations—are no longer news: feminism against itself has taken the form of thoughtful self-assessment (*Conflicts in Feminism,* for example, is an excellent compendium of academic feminist essays), hot debates about Madonna's radical feminism or radical sexism, Katie Roiphe's well-publicized and insightful if somewhat mean-spirited attack on her monolithic invention ("rape crisis feminists"), intense debates about censorship and pornography, and backlashes even in the feminist community, as elsewhere, against the child sexual abuse awareness movement (theorists who are willing to grant the necessity of a pre-existing context—like a community with a developed narrative—for a memory to emerge somehow draw the line at those particular memories, charging that the memories are falsely called into being by anti-sexual victimage-mongers).

realize how much more difficult it is for me to forgive my mother than some of the other people (men) whose sexual mistreatment of me was far more unambiguous.

However, I also don't want to offer my evolution away from that stance as "evidence" of the not-so-serious-after-all nature of child sexual abuse or incest. There's all too much of that in the media now. So I want now both to let the essay stand as I initially wrote it *and* to distance myself from it here, in an afterword. I hope by this strategy to affirm the significance of my pain and trauma, and simultaneously to suggest that there is recovery.

Blood Chant

Linnea Johnson

Stop saying you are a woman whose mother
tells you she does not love you. Your veins thin,

blood inside them wanting out, wet tin, the taste
in your mouth. If my mother gave me away

earlier than yours is doing,
head through vagina the first and last squeeze
between us, why ask what causes love

if not birth between women. Stop saying

you are daughter to a woman whose baby died
when you were two; stop trying to equal his quiet,
quit her, as he did, that she might love you, too.

Where women are not loved, how can we ask
love of them? How have they berthage in their home harbor
to offer the mooring love we beat against them for?

They who gave us life, let them live.

Muscles of wet rope,
blood from our wrists on our hands, let us
give them life among us, as one of us, if not as
mothers, as women bloody as newborns, wet as orphaned ships,

loud as daughters crying *mother,* chanting *mother, love me.*

The Reconstruction

Judy Remington

The music is irresistible. A live band is playing "Let's Dance," "Runaround Sue"—one after another of those high-spirited songs I grew up with. I've not danced so much since . . . well, *never* have I danced so continuously, so joyously or with so many people in one night.

As much as I love the music, it's necessary to sit down for a moment to catch my breath. I'm no longer young. The gynecologist, the dentist and the ophthalmologist have all, during the past year, prefaced their remarks to me with: "Well, *at your age . . . .*"

I may not be young, but neither am I old. Inhabiting this confusing place in the middle, youth and old age both feel close to me, and injuries, rather than healing quickly, settle into permanent conditions to be "managed." My knees are going to hurt for weeks after this night, but I don't care. I'm dancing with my brothers, my sons and my father; with my friend, my lover and my brand new daughter-in-law. I don't dance with my ex-husband, but I'm glad he's here.

Looking around the room, I see all the separate, fragmented pieces

246 / THE RECONSTRUCTION

of my life together in one place. I feel healed, and awed, as though a film projectionist has just played in reverse the demolition of a large apartment building. Before my eyes, the dust has scurried back into the ground, the foundation has re-cemented, the pipes and wires have reconnected, the windows are whole, the bricks are holding again to each other and the roof has plopped itself precisely in place on top of it all.

It is my first-born child's wedding dance. I am happier than I can remember ever being and astounded that I feel this way.

I am a lesbian immersed in women's culture—a teacher and a free-lance writer and editor for a couple of women's organizations. Occasionally, I work at the local women's bookstore, which shelves the blazing pink and purple covers of *Lesbian Sex* and *Lesbian Passion* immediately inside the front door. I can spout lesbian-feminist rhetoric with the best of them and live it almost as fervently as anyone: working on "issues" (although I have come to despise the word); worrying about the environment and being inclusive; reading about goddesses and recovering from all the conditions people used to call life.

I am not inclined to excitement over *anybody's* wedding (including the new church-blessed lesbian commitment ceremonies), nor to wearing dresses. Yet, here I am, at a wedding, having what may be the best time of my life in a rose-flowered dress that drapes, loosely and comfortably, over the spreadings and saggings that have recently become me. Smoothing the dress over my lap, I think it was good my son gave us a year and a half to prepare for the wedding. It took most of that time for me to decide what I'd wear, and it took all of that time for me to sort out who I was and where I stood.

I'd not been sure about my identity or my convictions for ten years, since the edifice that had been me—the rural-dwelling homemaker/wife/mother who grew a large garden, raised purebred dogs and harvested wild rice—exploded into an urban-dwelling lesbian and live-away mother who studied feminist theory and shopped at neighborhood food co-ops. Actually, the problem was not with my self-assurance; it was that there were too many of me to be sure about.

The structure that was me housed many different characters who seldom fit peacefully into one body. For the first several years following my eruption into a new life, I often wrote journal dialogues among my many selves. I wanted to get the respectable wife and mother whose life had revolved around caring for her home and children every day to talk to the woman who was living on the edge of the city slums with several women, some of whom were diabolical in their disregard for order or even cleanliness.

It wasn't easy. The city-dweller was a feminist who believed she'd liberated herself from the patriarchal institutions of marriage and motherhood, but she was also a poverty-stricken displaced person trying desperately to believe she continued to be the mother of her children.

There also lived in me the newly awakened lesbian joyously finding what felt like home, but that home was among women who were inclined to regard all males (including my own sons) as the enemy. The writer-self worked to assure the rest of my inhabitants of the rightness of our course, but the daughter of my quintessentially proper mother knew that every act and decision was wrong, wrong, wrong.

Fortunately, there were some things my many selves agreed upon: they all disliked dresses, dirty houses and winter weather. They all loved their children very much and liked to eat well, to work late into the night and to wake without an alarm clock. Like an active business, they managed to stave off their deeper conflicts by tending to the pressing demands of every day.

But children force you to face many things you might otherwise avoid. Growing older is one of them. Children age you, but it's not only because caring for them wears you down. Children age you simply by growing up themselves. Even though the doctors had begun (not very subtly) hinting that I was getting older, it didn't begin to sink in until I drove through the winter-browned flatness of southern Minnesota and Iowa to visit my eldest son in his first home-away-from-home. My lover and I had packed up Thanksgiving dinner and set off to spend the weekend in a god-forsaken town in southeastern Iowa with him and his sweetheart.

My mother was appalled that I condoned their live-together arrangement, but I considered it a good idea and a great preventer of too-early marriage. Besides, how could I, a lesbian and live-away mother, judge the way anyone lives? At its best, marginality can promote a healthy tolerance.

The problems I had with my son living with a woman were not moral or political; they were personal. If he had grown old enough to be working at a real job and living away from home, with the love of his life, what did that make me? After seven hours of droning wheels and frozen cornfields, my mind turned toward accepting that my son had become an adult and I was older than I felt.

Thus fortified with the idea of his maturity, we arrived at their apartment where I was soon reminded that nothing involving children can ever be simple. In the dining area rested an ancient card table, a piece that seemed fitting for young adults' first venture on their own and which supported my notion that my son and I had both moved up a notch in our age categories. Confirming this was the satin-sheeted queen-sized bed that presided in their bedroom—a sure indication of adulthood, and their only substantial piece of furniture.

The living area contained no furniture at all, but neither was it empty. His workout bench anchored the far end, and filling the rest of the room were his precisely arranged collection of model cars (hundreds of them) and her collection of nearly as many stuffed animals. Seeing this melange of childhood treasures and adult apparatus confused, comforted, dismayed and amused me. My new understandings of his adulthood and my middle age felt solid only if I looked in a particular direction; in the blink of an eye—with one glimpse of car models and teddy bears—we were back to who we'd been.

It was hard to know how to act with one other. I had brought the food (*that* much felt familiar) but *they* set their wobbly old card table with dishes I'd never seen before; *they* heated and served the food, poured the beverages. Our fumbling for new roles felt as awkward as trying to slice turkey on that table without spilling the water.

Just when you think you've found some stability and are relatively in control of your identity, your children upset it. When my son and his sweetheart came for Christmas that year with starry eyes and wedding plans reflected in a diamond engagement ring, I remembered bringing the same announcement to my own parents. They'd looked old—or, at least, definitely grown up—to me then. Now I stood in their shoes, uttering the same wishes that the marriage be delayed and knowing, as they had, that it wouldn't be. With bewildered astonishment, I understood that, to my children, I must look like someone who'd been ensconced in adulthood for a long time. It felt like having cement poured all over me.

Announcement of the wedding reawakened the bickering among my several selves. The lesbian politico felt offended by all the support and hoopla that surrounds heterosexual coupling. The live-away mother worried that she would be relegated to a secondary position in the various rituals to come. The lesbian wondered how her relationship would be handled, especially since her partner, who had been involved with the children's lives all through their adolescence, had no legal or blood right to be involved at all. The ex-wife dreaded the prospect of having to see her ex-husband again. The daughter fussed about what her mother would think if the lesbian and her lover behaved like the partners they were.

These problems, though, seemed minor compared to the ones my son and his fiancée had to work out, most of which were not even of their own making. True children of the 1980s, both came from divorced families, with complicated and convoluted parental relationships. The seating arrangements alone could have kept two negotiators in business for months.

My former husband and I, on neither friendly nor unfriendly terms, spoke civilly, when necessary. At the time of the marriage announcement, he was pursuing a woman fifteen years younger. She had four young children and, unbeknownst to us at the time, was pregnant with their daughter.

The prospective bride's parents had been divorced for several years, but they had periodic reconciliations, routinely followed by door-slamming estrangements. At the time of the Christmas engagement announcement, these two lived separately and the mother was involved with another man. Five months later, when my son was laid off from his job and he and his fiancée moved back into her parents' house, the mother had moved back home with the father. The four of them lived together peacefully until a few months before the wedding when it all fell apart between the parents again, the mother moved out and the father declared he would not come to the wedding because the mother would be there. He never wanted to see her again as long as he lived. Meanwhile, my ex-husband re-married and announced the impending birth of their daughter.

This chaotic, soap opera–like scenario affected each of us differently. In the context of the solid and sordid evidence of the precariousness of marriage provided by their parents, my son and his sweetheart concluded that *their* marriage was going to last forever. They decided that, since they were only going to do it once, they were going to do it up right, in the traditional way. They worked night and day for a year and a half planning and earning money for the best celebration they could imagine, one that all of their guests could enjoy.

My staunchly Catholic mother, buffeted by my divorce, my brother's divorce, another brother's entry into a Baptist congregation, a third brother's marriage to a divorced, non-Catholic mother of two daughters, and my sister's failure to add to the list of grandchildren, was relieved that someone had finally come along with the proper priorities. My lesbian friends, statistically proven to be the virtuosos of serial monogamy, could only shake their heads at my son's innocence.

Surprising even myself, I began acting in proper motherly ways. It was my prerogative to worry, and so I did. Chances are not good that high school sweethearts who marry in their early twenties will wake up to each other ten or twenty years later. I wished they could acknowledge the possibility that it might not be forever and thus spare themselves some of the suffering of surprise and disappointment if they later separated.

And then I began to surprise myself even more. In the face of the two earnest young people standing before me and the obvious love and respect they had for each other, I began to emerge from the haze of my conflicts and concerns. I started to admire their courage to dare a lifelong commitment. My lesbian repugnance toward marriage blew away like a dry leaf in the wind of my desire to support my son and future daughter-in-law's evident happiness. My politically based need to have my lesbian relationship recognized throughout the upcoming events became secondary to my wish to minimize the complications we parents were causing. It seemed to me that *somebody* needed to be grown-up.

Life is endlessly surprising. The day had come when I—the lesbian, the sometimes-radical feminist, the writer who made a precarious living, the mother who had left home and children—I, of all people, was looking like a model of stability. I'd been with the same partner for six years, and she was someone my sons knew well and loved. And she had loved them, even through the years they had struggled through to manhood, strutting their macho stuff and temporarily repudiating me. She had loved them anyway, sometimes with more patience than I.

As the months passed, the cement of adulthood my child had dumped on me settled into a solid base beneath my feet. I scrounged up a writing project that would bring in sufficient income for me to buy shower and wedding presents and appropriate clothes to wear to those events. I asked my ex-husband to go half the cost of a rehearsal dinner for the wedding party. I invited my parents over for Sunday brunch and finally attached the word "lesbian" to myself. Since they'd already come to know and love my partner, they couldn't disapprove nearly as much as they probably felt they should, nor did they reject me as I'd feared they might. In fact, the distance between us brought about by my years of evasions and half-truths began that day to close.

My son started coming back to me, too. It crossed my mind that mothers are often jealous of their sons' lovers, but I just couldn't be. I liked my future daughter-in-law too much and could see she understood and loved my son. Besides, while they were preparing for their marriage, my son began behaving again like the sensitive, fair-minded person he'd been. He started making a fuss about Mother's Day and calling me on the phone just to talk. When I began to think seriously about forgetting my birthdays, he started to remember them.

My soon-to-be daughter-in-law knew me well enough to guess my aversion to showers and so called to ask whether I'd like to be on the invitation lists. Given permission to dislike them, I could, and did, choose to participate. Then, passing the homophobia test with surprising grace, she asked whether my partner would like to be invited, too. She responded happily to that as well as to their request that she, a frequent soloist for her church choir, sing a solo during their wedding ceremony.

For the first shower, my partner and I donned our best slacks and sensible shoes and headed into the polyester world of straight working-class women who lived at the juncture of suburb and country—a place, we found, where the vivid darkness of the night is lit by stars of astounding brilliance. We ate our barbecued meatballs, our toothpicked cheese chunks and our frosted brownies; my partner discussed bowling with honest enthusiasm. After checking us out with a skill rivalling that of lesbians, my son's future mother-in-law and his newly acquired stepmother spoke with us. I was introduced as the mother; my lover as my friend.

My co-workers at the bookstore, audience to my ongoing tale about the wedding preparations, harrumphed at the terminology used for my lover. It was bad enough we should participate in such foolish hetero frivolity but, if we did, we should at least make use of the opportunity to raise a few consciousnesses. My partner didn't object to being introduced as my friend but did think it unfair that my ex-husband's new wife should be the stepmother. On our drive home from the first shower, she archly declared that *she* should be the stepmother because she, after all, had cared about the boys for many years and this new woman had been around barely long enough to learn their names.

At another shower, my mother ended up seated next to the bride's mother. Having previously heard about the bride's mother's romantic exploits, my mother came with strong reservations about her. When the bride opened a present from her mother containing a sheer negligee and satin slippers, an equally sexy outfit for my son and a book on *How to Make Love to a Woman* with a holy card inserted as place marker, my mother's reservations converted to final judgment. Anyone who explicitly acknowledged sex—and then mixed it with religion—was not fit to be spoken to.

Fortunately, that was the last shower. The next event was the wedding rehearsal. Deciding where everyone would sit took up two long hours. The only certainty was that the two mothers were the premier guests of honor and would be awarded front-row seats. This simple statement of protocol ended my ten-year struggle for legitimacy, for acknowledgement that I was, still and always, the mother of my son.

As mother of the groom, I would be escorted to my place with due pomp and circumstance. Not only that, but my escort, the bride's uncle just arrived from Seattle, was a drag queen whose sharp nose, long, curly locks and left earring brought to mind a second incarnation of Captain Hook. We grinned at each other in recognition.

It was decided that my partner, after singing her solo, was to slip in beside me. At the rehearsal, no one objected. By the next day, however, after sitting across from us at the rehearsal dinner and perhaps catching sight of a quick kiss in his rearview mirror as we drove from church to restaurant, the preacher apparently decided to sabotage that arrangement.

After my parents had been seated, he instructed the usher to move them into the row in which I was to sit. I arrived at the back of the church in time to see my mother (mortified by the breach in protocol) scooping her purse onto her arm and stepping out into the aisle. I could not bring myself to have her and my dad returned to their appointed places and so had to satisfy myself by yelling at the preacher—in a whisper. With the smug righteousness of those caught up in their own holiness, he responded by pointing out that the usher was waiting to seat me. My Captain Hook apologized all the way down the aisle, and we were laughing by the time he left me to sit beside my parents. My partner stayed beside the organist throughout the wedding.

There were other imperfections—such as my ex-husband's baby babbling through most of the ceremony—but the spirit of love and reconciliation was so strong at this wedding that nothing could ruin it. Perhaps caught up in the spirit, the bride's father had decided two days before to participate. He accompanied his only child on her walk to the altar, sat meekly beside his ex-wife and cried through the entire ceremony.

Here at the dance, the bride's parents, who sat together at dinner, have been gazing fondly at each other for several hours. It looks like they'll be going home to the same house tonight. The older generation of grandparents has gone home to bed, and soon I will, too. I want to leave while the band is still playing and the young people are still dancing. I want to remember this day as it is now—still bright with light, alive with music and filled with people from all the parts of my life, happily and peacefully together, in one place.

Mother

Jewelle L. Gomez

---

for Toi

a mother has no time to know herself
except in refracted images of the assurance
found in brown paper lunch bags
and clean, pressed sheets.
the humming noise she makes
around the endless utensils
necessary to her craft
is not always a song
often it is a whirring of her engine
trying to keep pace with demands.
when she hides in the downstairs bathroom
behind the kitchen
it is not to read magazines
or admire the wallpaper
but to search the mirror
for a trace of someone behind the title.

on the steps
in the crisp fall air—her hands
cupped against her mouth amplify
the sound of her call
to the dog to the cat
set out for freedom now to end.
inside she hopes they will not come,
that they have boarded a raft
floating in the tiny brook
headed down to Newark Bay
and Shangri-La.
she still has time
to smash the mirrors that line
the walls and continue her search.

Beginning with Gussie

Maxine Kumin

In a way, Tweedie's out-of-wedlock pregnancy—did people still call it that?—was mostly her grandmother's fault. Augusta James, born in the opening year of the twentieth century, an internationally respected botanist in the '40s, was always exhorting her, "Follow your star, Tweedie. 'Extra vagance! It depends how you are yarded'."[1]

There was something in Gussie's past, hinted at. Darkly alluded to. Tweedie could never tell if it was real or imagined. There were so many sides to Grammy James. She was earthy, iconoclastic, politically naive, with an underpinning of good family, old money, and the lingering traces of a private-school accent.

Forcibly retired from the faculty of Smith College at the age of seventy, Gussie had not yet given up field trips to alpine meadows. The year she became *emerita ejecta,* as she called it, she had made a modest find. A species of arctic rhododendron had been named after her.

Gussie and Tweedie had bonded early. Sometimes Rebecca felt that

---

1. Henry David Thoreau, *Walden,* ed. by J. Lyndon Shanley, Princeton Edition © 1971, 324.

her mother had pounced on the baby like some fierce, infertile tabby determined to acquire a kitten of her own. She had carried the child off with her every summer to her unrestored farmhouse in the Berkshires, in spite of Rebecca's protests.

"It's good for a baby to grow up in nature. And besides, it's important for children to have a sense of the generations. Would you deny me my rights as a grandparent?"

"What about my rights as a mother?"

"Sweetydarl, you have her ten months of the year."

"But all summer . . . ."

"You will have her the rest of your life," Gussie pronounced.

Grandmother and grandchild shared the dusty, cluttered space in Becket with an array of creatures. One year it was a bummer lamb, the last-born of triplets, being raised on a bottle, and an orphaned raccoon in his own playpen. A nest of baby rabbits saved from the sickle bar, kittens from an adjoining farm slated to be drowned, were commonplace. Succeeding summers produced comparable rescues.

Tweedie at four, the only child of an only child, explained to her parents' dinner guests, "It isn't fair to a mother cat to let her have so many kittens. Granny James says she should be spaded."

"The word is 'spayed,' darling," Rebecca said. "Do you know what it means?"

"'Spaded' means to have her kitten room taken out. And the daddy cats should be neutraled, they just snip off their pepsicles."

Gussie had been a bluestocking graduate of Barnard in 1922 and took a Ph.D. from Columbia six years later. She taught for several years before marrying an astronomer, who died of pneumonia not long after. Although she never married again, her daughter Rebecca, who could only dimly remember her father's beard and his pervasive aroma of peppermint, noted the ease with which Gussie attracted younger men.

Rebecca James Gruber, a Ph.D. in history, heading into college administration, was fond of calling her mother "a lovable eccentric."

But Tweedie protested. "Ec-centric, out of center, that just means out of the ordinary. If people would behave in ordinary, decent ways, there wouldn't *be* any animals to rescue."

Tweedie was ten the year of that pronouncement. Her father had recently decamped, gone to California to write film scripts. They had always called her Tweedie, a child's pronunciation of "Sweetie," something Joseph had called Rebecca in those first good years. Her real name was Elizabeth.

Tweedie-Elizabeth was born in 1950. Rebecca had married Joseph Gruber, the wildly successful novelist, three months earlier, in the middle of both her sophomore year and his survey of twentieth-century fiction, in which she took an incomplete. It would not have been ethical to compete for an A, she reasoned, even though she deserved one, while carrying his child. Rebecca heard that he now wore an earring. She hoped it was true.

"You didn't have to have me!" Tweedie, age twelve or thirteen, had cried with terrible prescience.

But Rebecca refused the bait. How could she, the woman in the middle, daughter and mother, possibly justify her choice to this furious adolescent? She had been determined to fasten Joseph to her, pin him down, make him serve as father and husband all in one.

What could she have said to Tweedie? *I wasn't pretty. I was almost fat.* Bryn Mawr was a cloister for bright girls like me, all of us fell in love with our professors, made them over into our images of Zeus, Apollo, whatever. I don't know how it happened, I'll never know . . . but he stood there facing the class with that way he had—has—of ramming his hands deep in his pockets, then rocking back and forth on the balls of his feet. He always wore clean tennis sneakers. His lectures were extemporaneous, brilliant, he never spoke from notes. The hour was over almost before it began. He was famous, a giant in that landscape. Of course I didn't know then he was mildly afflicted with satyriasis, I only knew I had been chosen! I was the luckiest girl in the world. And I didn't tell him I was pregnant until it was too late, really, to do anything about it.

"Your father," she called him to Tweedie, who screamed back, eyes screwed tight as if in pain, "Stop saying that! His name is Joseph Gruber."

Now, when Rebecca remembered him, she had to take little tucks and darts in the picture. Once he had been seamless, shining, perfect. Now he toed out like a duck as he walked. Under his lovely cleft chin another chin had formed. He was of only middling height, of only average athletic ability with his slight paunch, his sloping, almost-womanly shoulders. For ten years he had been the center of a universe around which she and Tweedie gladly spun, a parent to both of them, a friend, a conspirator.

Mama hadn't. Couldn't. Was walled off from Rebecca in mysterious ways. Clear, outspoken, competent Gussie, so full of fun and distances.

"I brought you up to be all the things women were not supposed to be," Gussie told her the night before her high-school graduation. "To be strong and bold and full of adventure. To be forceful and innovative."

Rebecca, who was neither valedictorian nor class president, cheerleader nor Most Likely to Succeed, wanted the earth to open and receive her. She was nothing more than Honor Society, she was a signal failure, an experiment that never jelled.

Not even two years later, Rebecca and Joseph drove to the farm for Easter recess. Their marriage certificate, three days old, reposed in a file folder marked Personal.

Joseph went fishing. Rebecca faced Gussie across the big trestle table that had served for dining, mushroom identification, mail-sorting and elbow-on discussions for as far back as she could remember.

"You must have been very angry with me not to have told me at Christmas," Gussie said, gesturing at the mound of Rebecca's belly which Joseph's white shirttails did nothing to diminish. "Were you afraid I would try to talk you out of it?"

"No. I don't know, maybe. It's just what I wanted. Oh Mom, we're *married!* He's so wonderful! We're so happy!" And to her total surprise, Rebecca put her head down on the table and sobbed.

"I suppose I wasn't around enough," Gussie suggested. "I wasn't . . . tender enough . . . long enough."

"It's not in your nature to be tender," Rebecca said blowing her nose. "With people, that is."

"You're right. I don't know what gets in the way. I wish I had held you more, cuddled you."

"Even though I was half an orphan."

"I'm sorry. I thought about your moral education and your intellect. It was all John Dewey and progressive education. I was too sorry for myself, Sweetydarl, long after your father died."

They stumbled awkwardly into each other's arms. Rebecca could still feel that harsh and salty embrace. It was as close as they could ever come to saying *I love you.*

If Gussie had weathered the shock of Rebecca's pregnancy a bit grimly at first, she was weathering this one quite cheerfully. Her letters crossing the ocean to Tweedie contained dissertations on calcium and iron, emollients for the skin, and the magical properties of vitamin E oil.

To Rebecca and Milton, the once-young virologist who lived with her, she only said once or twice, "I *do* wish this baby could have a father. It makes it so hard. I *do* wish, Rebecca, that our Tweedie were a little less . . . headstrong."

Milton made little murmurs of assent.

The ensuing silence acknowledged the way Tweedie was.

In mid-adolescence Tweedie had made the leap from animal to human rights. In the ferment of the '60s, she collated and stapled, joined hands and sang, marched and sat in, and was arrested twice. Both times, because she was a juvenile, her case had been continued with no finding. Once, she had sat in at the Boston Navy Yard with Rebecca and twice she had marched in Washington with Gussie. *Grandmother and Granddaughter Arrested at Pentagon* made headlines in the Springfield *Republican* and merited a feature article in the Washington *Post.*

Ten years later, armed with an advanced degree in international law from Georgetown, Tweedie landed a job with Horn Relief, a world-wide agency based in the Sudan. From headquarters in Khartoum, she lobbied desperately for volunteer doctors and nurses and drug supplies. In Juba she structured food distribution and storage techniques. The Japanese and Australians were bulwarks in the acquisition and husbanding of water resources. Tweedie attended conferences in Sydney and Nagoya dedicated to adapting modern technology for use in desert encampments.

Now she has friends in a dozen different embassies, and a few enemies as well. After several months of witnessing the hunger-bloated bellies of children, Tweedie no longer saw the starved and overloaded beasts of burden in the countryside. She hardly noticed the pariah dogs whipped away from cooking fires, or the gaunt mother cats scavenging in every settlement.

Two years ago she took a post with an intergovernmental agency called Migration Assistance Organization, pronounced "Mayo," as if it were a binder for tuna or chicken salad. Headquartered in the heart of Europe, Mayo is dedicated to finding resettlement places for refugees and stateless persons, especially for the so-called "hopeless cases." Tweedie has shucked the past and been reborn in her humanitarian zeal. She is a gifted administrator in a line of work that requires skillful dealing.

Rebecca remembers Tweedie describing a cocktail party in Islamabad attended by a well-known Ugandan, who in an earlier time supervised the torture of revolutionaries.

"He's a chameleon, he hangs on through every change of government. Now he's a bureaucrat again, he blocked the embarkation of one of our planeloads of refugees from their airport to a transfer point last week. There were 342 people on board, people who had just given up their housing—such as it was—their cooking pots—God! He kept them sitting on the tarmac for eighteen hours in the blazing heat, not knowing whether they would fly out of there or just get stuffed back into the cesspool of the tent city again. Only this time without identities."

"You know each other? I mean, you're personally acquainted?"

"Oh yes. He's very suave, would you believe, he has a degree from the Sorbonne. Anyway, he handled me three or four times ...."

"Brushed against you? How?"

"Stroking my arm, my neck. Then managed to corner me between the hall and the stairway."

"What did you do?"

"Stepped on his instep very hard, with my high heel. Then said, 'O, je m'excuse, j'ai perdu mon equilibre.' Walked away."

This was last Christmas on home leave. Tweedie is extremely loyal to family. Two weeks with Rebecca, two weeks with Gussie, a week in California with her father and his latest new family (Joseph has remarried three times), then she's off to Rome or Athens or Dakar to "visit a colleague." Of course there are lovers. Names are dropped and anecdotes told, but there is something brittle in the telling.

"How would you like to be my birth partner?" Tweedie asked Rebecca in one of their weekly transatlantic phone conversations. Her voice always faded in and out, as though snippets of syllables became detached from it along the underwater cable. "We could write a whole new chapter in the history of mother-daughter relations."

Rebecca, president of a small liberal arts college in northern Michigan, her head spinning from the request, riffled the pages of her calendar to cover her momentary vertigo. "When will this be, exactly? Or inexactly."

"January something. Around the tenth."

The scratch of a pen x-ing out a cluster of days. "Good academic timing! I'd love to. I'm flattered that you asked me."

At the other end she could imagine Tweedie drawing a line through this item on her list. It was probably followed by Request Maternity Leave. Order Bassinet.

To be fair, that wasn't the first word of the impending baby. Tweedie had chosen to convey that news in a letter that contained all the appropriate cliches: "Something I've always wanted ... very excited about ... biological clock [she was thirty-six] ... on the basis of good genes . . . has no wish to be acknowledged as father . . . promised not to divulge."

She had written Gussie at the same time, but far more frankly.

"You know how I feel about betraying a confidence," Gussie said during Rebecca's weekend visit to the farmhouse. Milton brought them both Bloody Marys and then went tactfully off for a jog with the dogs. "But really, Rebecca, I don't like this . . . selectivity of Tweedie's. I think you need all the facts we can muster before you go off midwifing."

She unfolded the letter and passed it over.

"I don't know what you'll think of this piece of *extra vagance*, but I've decided it is now or never. I don't see why I should be cheated out of motherhood for want of a marriageable partner. The man I've chosen is an Indian diplomat, Oxford-educated, gifted in languages. He speaks seven fluently and plays the sitar and the saxophone. Since I was but an impolitic dalliance, he is furious at my refusal to have an abortion. I am hoping for a little girl—I have no idea at all how to bring up a little boy—but whichever it is, I plan to bring it home during my four-month maternity leave for you to admire."

"Poor Tweedie," Rebecca said. "She must have had such high hopes."

"So you see why she couldn't bring herself to tell you."

Rebecca nodded, aware that tears were swimming in her eyes. She hoped they would get reabsorbed, she couldn't bear it if they fell, spattering her drink.

"Don't be hurt, Sweetydarl."

"Hard not to."

"I shouldn't have taken her from you every summer. It was wrong of me. Selfish. But I was lonely."

Rebecca wanted to cry out, But what about me? I was lonely too.

"Sweetydarl. I'm getting close to the end, you know. You're still in the middle."

"Meaning you're handing her back to me?"

"As if I could. As if anybody hands Tweedie."

They both reflected on this. Rebecca waited: was her mother about to say something more? There *was* something more, she was sure of it.

But Gussie, her conscience clear, got up briskly. "Time to pick peas for supper."

After the plane lifted off from Kennedy, Rebecca ordered two vodka martinis. She had already been in transit most of the day, but the fund-raising, morale-building concerns of her job were not easily dispelled. How to keep up enrollments with a broadly-based program aimed at married women in the area—ecology, Eastern philosophies, behavioral psychology, and poetry workshops—still ghosted her thoughts. The second cocktail went so quickly to her head that she gave in to the pleasant, mizzly sensation, cradled her head between the seat-back and the cool window glass and let herself drift.

Of course what came up was Tweedie. Tweedie and Gussie, on either end of a seesaw. Rebecca as the fulcrum. Thirty-six years of this.

One of the ongoing mysteries of this triad was why the pensioned horses, the old foundered donkey, the fledgling birds saved alive with eyedropper and worm of hamburger had never quite seized her conscience in the fierce grip that tightened on Tweedie. They had, after all, been subjected to almost identical proselytizing.

In a kitchen littered with fungi, wild grasses, and bits of birdshell, the child Rebecca had mastered the identification of a hundred specimens. The family cats slept on her bed. She fed the dogs, rode and cared for a retired police horse named King. But she was restless, anxious to break away. There was never a time—after the age of, say, ten—that she did not feel embarrassed by her mother's huge enthusiasms, her excesses. Do children ever understand how fame overtakes their parents? Just last year, during a month-long expedition in Denali, Augusta turned up a new moss of the tundra not yet taxonomized, but sure to be one of her major finds. And crowed unduly.

This woman is eighty-five years old! Rebecca admonished herself. She is a living legend! Why can't you stop . . . blaming her? For loving Tweedie more than me? For taking Tweedie away from me?

Dinner arrived on its little plastic tray, a welcome diversion. She ordered a split of white wine and focused on hoping that Tweedie's baby would appear on schedule. She dreaded the prospect of waiting around for a week, God forbid, for two weeks, in attitudes of forced equanimity. They would cheer each other on, mother and daughter, intimate strangers while every neuron had already begun to jitter and twinge. She would aspire to an orderly calm for Tweedie's sake. Tweedie, fighting off the impulse to retreat into the solipsism of late pregnancy, would exhaust them both with little expeditions, projects and bravados that both of them detested. Deferring to each other across the invisible wire that connected them for life.

≋

Mr. Assounyub, the Afghan with impeccable manners, in detention in Papua–New Guinea has written again. *My dear Madame.* Tweedie reads his jagged script on pale blue paper so thin that the whorls of her own fingertips shine through as she holds the page under the lamp. *Permit me once again to bring to the attention of your esteemed self my wretched circumstance.* But the page unfurls like a scroll in her lap; Mr. Assounyub's complaint grows longer and longer. It will take all morning to decipher this latest saga, and meanwhile his plane! His plane is being posted! She holds his expensive travel documents, his doctored passport in her hands, but they become a sparrow. She can feel its quick heart beating in her palm. Before she can open her fingers to release the bird, she wakes in the chill of January in her own bed.

Each time a jet takes off from the country's major airport less than a kilometer away, the walls of her floor-through apartment in this converted farmhouse tremble. The wine glasses sing in the cupboard. Planes depart every minute and a half, streaking off to Bucharest and Bombay, Dakar, Damascus, New York. Although daylight only creeps onto the rime-coated pastures at eight a.m., the planes begin to rise from the valley floor between two mountain ranges at six. By the time Tweedie leaves for the office, hundreds of people are halfway to Helsinki or Athens.

In this life Tweedie is called Elizabeth. She is a Protection Officer; she knows how to wheedle and bargain and even, from time to time, extort. Mr. Assounyub's hearing will take place today. If not the Dutch, then perhaps the Danes can be persuaded to take in this former student leader, whose English is eloquent and Victorian, and whose chief sin, ten years ago, was to lead a strike against the university administration. In Berkeley he would have been acclaimed a hero.

Fully awake now, getting up awkwardly, she hopes again that the baby will be early. Her mother is arriving this afternoon. If it turns out to be a long wait there will not be enough ways to fill the available time. Subjects are bound to come up, to be flung up heedlessly. Questions will be raised, problems for which there are no solutions. Tweedie remembers something the Deputy says: "There are no lasting solutions. Everything is *pro tem.*"

She and her mother are intimate without being confidential. They have lived together so long in their tandem singularity that they have learned, like yoked oxen, not to pull against each other. In fact, they make a conscious effort not to intrude on one another's private domains. This leaves long corridors of untenanted space between them, something they are both uneasy about. Even though their mutual sympathies bind them together as surely as the braids of a rope, Tweedie feels a little phobic flutter at the prospect of Rebecca's presence.

She stands barefoot in the kitchen, vaguely aware that something is out of plumb. Once again it rained during the night. Because her only windows at this end of the house are skylights as well, she cannot open them without incurring leaks. Now as she empties the buckets and stacks them in the closet against the next rainy night, bending to put them in the corner, she feels the first squeeze of a contraction rise across her belly, harden, then slip away.

Magically, she is already in labor as the plane bearing her mother across the ocean passes Gander and heads out over the water. It is a walking-around labor, possibly a false labor, possibly it is nothing at all. She nibbles on a banana and some *petits beurres* and does a load of laundry, balancing the basket on her hip as she crosses the courtyard to the communal laundry room.

The zeal to start out clean, she thinks. She showers, washes her hair, has two cups of tea. More contractions, mild enough to walk through. She is too restless to write letters, but puts Vivaldi on the record player and tries to plan a strategy for the four Sikhs stranded in a luxury hotel at the Tripoli airport who arrived there via a hijacking in which they were taken hostage. But now it is hard to think clearly; this iron hand across the abdomen is the real thing. By prearrangement she calls her closest friend, a colleague at the office. Indeed, after Jenny arrives with her Jamaican backcountry wild talk, the contractions subside to mere twinges. There is much forced hilarity. Tweedie is surprised to discover that she is on the verge of tears.

Meanwhile, Rebecca's plane is approaching, Rebecca is bringing with her the little hooded towels, the vitamin E oil for the nipples of nursing mothers, and a convertible cradle from Sears Roebuck designed to hang from its own tripod, which has attached to it a crank. A few turns of the handle and the cradle will rock unattended for an hour. It has been an albatross for Rebecca to transport.

Jenny is waiting at the airport when Rebecca gruels through customs and is permitted to enter the public space. Her English is crisply British, though her inflection lends it an exotic quality. The words appear to break open as she enunciates them. Later, reporting the rendezvous to Tweedie, Jenny says "Indeed, we recognized one another at once."

By the time Rebecca enters the apartment, Tweedie's contractions are five minutes apart. She can still walk, talk through them. The doctor is called. He promises to come by within the hour, but that hour and most of the next pass before they hear him, audible a hundred meters away on his Motobécane. He balances his helmet upright on the kitchen table and, still in his leather jacket, pulls on a rubber glove to examine Tweedie casually on the living room sofa. She is already two centimeters dilated. Perhaps they should go. He must pay one more call, he will meet them shortly in hospital. His manner is distant, diffident, reminding Rebecca of an uneasy schoolboy.

A last look around. Rebecca takes a banana and a few cookies for sustenance, drops them in her shoulder bag, picks up Tweedie's overnight case, and they set off.

"Left here, then right at that church," Tweedie directs. "You go three cross streets and take another left, by that little *épicerie*, see?"

It is dusk. Peering down the unfamiliar streets, Rebecca tries to assemble landmarks to come home by. The little Volkswagen jiggles and spurts each time she shifts, she has not mastered the distances between gears yet. "Sorry, Darlie," she murmurs. Receiving no answer, she reaches over to take Tweedie's hand and is surprised—no, unsurprised—by the fierceness of that grip. "You can do it, Tweedie, you're all right," she says, words older than time.

"You all right, though, Mom?" Tweedie manages. "Not such good timing, you must be ... exhausted."

"Terrific timing! We'll have a whole two weeks on the other side of this birth, much the best way," and then mercifully they are there.

Although English is her mother tongue, Tweedie will have this baby in her second or third language. She has gone conscientiously to all the meetings of the childbirth class in her sector, even the final practice ones when each of the other women had a husband for a partner and she had to make do with the instructor, a German-speaking midwife of truly imposing dimensions. Frau Lansdorf's thighs when she squatted to demonstrate an alternate pushing position loomed inside their leotard coverings as massive as old tree trunks. She looked as though she could deliver a baby with the direct dispatch of a hen laying an egg.

Early on, Tweedie took a stand about single parenting. She comported herself as if it were an ordinary happenstance, as if marriage were a quaint custom shortly to fall into disuse, like calling cards or the wearing of white gloves in the evening. And she has played this part so faithfully and with such granitic determination that she can no longer (she tells herself) feel the bitter envy, the savage, corrosive longing to belong, the harsh inveighings of loneliness or the slow clots of unsatisfied lust she had fought her way past six months ago. She will have this baby. She will have it in the prescribed manner and it will be hers in the way nothing else before has ever been so wholly and singly hers. "A son is a son till he takes him a wife, but a daughter's a daughter the rest of your life"; that was something Grammy James used to say approvingly of Rebecca, and of Rebecca and Tweedie, and by extension of women in general. The baby would be a girl.

Now the contractions are three minutes apart, they are serious contractions going somewhere, and she breathes as she has learned to breathe, riding the big wave up to the top on a series of puppy-like pants, then exhaling as it subsides, to coast for a blessed minute in the beautiful blue sky of painlessness.

Chiding herself, I must not think of these as pains! even as the first harsh moan bubbles out of her mouth. O God it was hard, what liars they all were with their bright talk of lollipops and tea, and cries out, O God! meanwhile clutching Rebecca's hand, mashing it into her own as she rises to the top and then ever so gradually slips down the other side.

When Tweedie is in labor, Rebecca becomes her. She too is feeling the balloon of contraction, how it hardens with a crust, like a loaf of round bread, growing and growing. "*Inspirez, inspirez,*" the *sage-femme* urges, her practiced hands measuring the rise and fall. Four centimeters, six . . . . Now Rebecca is lulling her daughter, using the yoga-drift, hypnotically soothing her to rest between the rich, gripping seizures. "Go with it, go with it, lie back, drift as if you are lying on the sand in the sun." And indeed Tweedie closes her eyes, the frown lines ease, vanish, she seems almost to doze, then stiffens with the next big one.

Now she *is* Tweedie, but alone, terrified, taken, racked, and praying to God O God, just let me get through this, I swear I'll never again, no never . . . and then the murdering oblivion of the scopolamine, followed by huge, wet cobwebs pressed over her face so that she fought screaming to get free, *bastards, you bastards,* and came to, afterwards, bruises on her shoulders and the insides of her upper arms from where they had held her down on the table, and two spidery hematomas inside her thighs from where they had forced them apart (she supposed; she was not there) the moment the head crowned.

And here in this room with white curtains and wallpaper flecked with bright dots, this room with its ordinary bed and pillows, a teapot on the table, a chair, a squatting stool, and behind a screen, discreetly, a delivery table, the backache takes hold of Tweedie, pressing, aching, pounding across the vulnerable small of the back, the lifting and holding arc of her body. Rebecca takes out her aloe cream and rubs, pressing down hard where Tweedie, in a passionate groan, directs. The other midwife, the one who speaks English with a rich New York accent (she worked for six years at Columbia Presbyterian), takes turns with her pressing, and the contractions still come and go. The mother enters the daughter and rises and falls with her as she has all her life, but before this, always in secret, at a remove. Now they are one woman in labor, passing the distended belly between them, puffing up the terrible mountain of rock, slipping half-conscious down the other side of it, filling their lungs at the bottom, making ready. *Ready.* Ready to push. *Now.*

"Mahvelous, mahvelous, dahling," croons the midwife. "I think we have this baby in five minutes now. And push! Push to the count of ten! Push not with the face, not with the neck, push from the chest. Push like the *caca*."

"Much! easier!" Tweedie calls out, re-energized. But at the last, with all the bearing down, all the *poussez, poussez!* encouragements, the fetal heart wobbles and slows and the indifferent, silent, long-haired doctor, who arrived thirty minutes ago and has been standing at the window peering out as if awaiting a message, now squats to his work. He inserts the *ventouse* and sucks the baby's head to the mouth of the cave.

At that moment Rebecca re-enters her own body. She sees a creature come out. A large rat is backing out of the birth canal, the wet, matted hair rat-color and sparse. It is all a terrible mistake. Then the whole head emerges and she sees it has indeed a human face, still cowled in a marble-like material, something at once silken but mottled, like stone. The umbilicus, as thick as a grapevine and braided like the cord of a monk's robe, is wrapped tightly around the baby's neck. The baby holds it in one fist. The midwife quickly inserts a finger between the cord and the neck in order to loosen the noose, and the membrane breaks and the baby's face comes alive, gasping. One shoulder slips free, then the other, then the whole length of him—for it is a boy— slips free and howls discomfort into the world. The doctor lifts him, floppy and bloody to his mother's chest and he lies there, almost comforted, while the cord still pulses. Someone dims the lights just as, with a snip, he is set free on his own support system. The other *sage-femme* takes him now, to suction his mouth and nose as he roars protests.

"Would you like to bathe him?" she asks Rebecca, who nods yes, and then he is in her hands, submerged in a warm bath, and he falls silent. This skill comes back unbidden. In minutes he is swaddled and dressed and put to his mother's breast. New as they both are, he manages to take hold and she to accept. He suckles a few minutes at each breast, a midwife on either side of Tweedie, like devout acolytes, and then lies calm and alert under his *duvet* on the lap of the grandmother who has also delivered him.

The midwives bring a feast of custard and tea and champagne and zwieback and they relive the birthing, like a sporting event, phase by phase, each fiercely proud of the other, and proudest of all of the little pale brown boy (they had both wanted a girl) who is neither exceptionally large nor exceptionally small, neither long nor short, who resembles all the other neonates and is their prize, their conspiracy.

Four days later, Tweedie and Rebecca sit on the floor of the living room with a bottle of Beaujolais and a full page of diagrams and instructions. They are assembling the Sears Roebuck cradle, which comes with pointed screw, end nuts, acorn push nuts, carriage bolts, knob, hanger wire, washer, and four rubber leg tips.

Tweedie reads: " 'A. Slide end cover into motor unit by straddling the inside end plate, as shown. B. Insert two top leg sections into motor unit as shown, and then line up the holes in the upper leg section with the holes in the end cover and inside end plate. Secure with two pointed screws'."

An hour later they get to E. Rebecca is now reading: "'Insert seat push rod into rear key hole of motor unit by alining push rod ear with keyhole slot.' Shouldn't that be 'aligning'? and why 'key hole' first, then 'keyhole', one word?"

Finally, a yellow slip in the bottom of the box. Rebecca again: "'Once in a while we are less than perfect and one of our products reaches a customer with a problem or our instructions are not clear. Please use our toll free number 800-et cetera.'" and they rock with laughter.

The baby is eight days old, vigorous, alert, and a poor sleeper. The mechanical cradle is something of a godsend, when all else fails. In the night Rebecca retrieves him once he is truly awake and squeaking. Sometimes she can forestall a feeding and spell Tweedie a little longer by walking the floor with him, a well-wrapped package, high on her shoulder. This too she has not forgotten. She and Tweedie are trying to discover the baby's natural schedule, but he is wildly erratic, sleeping only two hours between some feedings, then going more than six. Occasionally he is happy, a wide-awake little sailor rocking from side to side in the wind-up contraption.

Tweedie and Rebecca talk to Gussie every day, luxuriously long phone conversations. Gussie is failing, having little black-out episodes that she of course does not admit to, but Milton, her faithful companion, has called to report these mini-strokes. The vision in one eye has been affected, but her mind is perfectly clear.

"I meant to tell you this yesterday, Tweedie. The duckbill platypus has no nipples. Milk oozes through the pores of the skin of its abdomen, and the young ones simply suck up the droplets as they appear."

"That's fascinating," Tweedie says.

"Of course it's just garbage-pail information, but I thought you'd appreciate it. How is the vitamin E oil doing?"

"Just fine, Grammy. No problems nursing. The only problem is getting him to sleep."

"Swaddling. Tuck him up tight, he will feel more secure. In a litter the young always lie touching, you remember that? We poor humans are singular. No one should have to sleep alone."

Day ten. Rebecca and Tweedie are reading on opposite sides of the living room, texts on nursing and child care; they are staunch believers in book knowledge. How to make a solar heater, how to build a purple martin birdhouse, six steps to a slimmer you, it's all there. The British books are best, they agree: breezy, informational and non-condescending. The La Leche League is too evangelical.

The majestic baby, whose dark scrotum betrays the fact that he is of mixed blood (so the head nurse, a starchy nun, had announced), for the skin tone darkens only gradually, is sleeping fitfully, sucking the cuff of his sleeve. Sometimes he puts his whole fist in his mouth. He has not been circumcised, although Rebecca had promised Joseph that she would urge their daughter to arrange this little amenity. In this country circumcision is thought to be a barbarism; medieval. Rebecca and Tweedie will conspire to convince Joseph that it was impossible to achieve, the baby's condition was not stable enough to permit it. It is doubtful that this child will grow up to be the chief rabbi of Rome or Vienna, Rebecca reasons.

Tweedie is reading about wet-nursing in the eighteenth century. It was common practice for poor unwed mothers to put their babies out to baby farms, where they frequently sickened and died, and then to hire out as wet nurses to the wealthy. Often such a woman would substitute her own baby for the wealthy woman's. The heir would die at the baby farm and the wet nurse would bring up her own child in comfort. A great many plots in literature revolve around this switch— Gilbert and Sullivan's *Pinafore,* for one, Twain's *Pudd'nhead Wilson* for another.

It is the kind of subject Gussie would love to discuss. Gussie would know that wet-nursing never became deeply established in the United States. She would say, "American women were always too independent to take on *that* job for somebody else," and then add, "except maybe in the South. My own uncles," Gussie would say, "change-of-life babies, were suckled by the descendant of a wet-nurse slave."

But Gussie's life ends this same evening, which is midmorning on the Continent. Milton the virologist calls to say that Augusta James died peacefully in her sleep. She left a will, she left notes and messages to them both. He sounds very composed, but sad.

"I want you to know, Milt, that Tweedie and I are deeply grateful to you," Rebecca tells him, but there is more. Gussie left her animals with explicit instructions as to their disposal. The old horses are to be euthanized, as is the donkey. Milton himself will take the dogs, he has grown quite fond of them and they know him.

Should Rebecca return immediately? It hardly seems necessary. They spend some time commiserating. They agree to hold a public memorial service for Gussie at a later date, when Tweedie comes to the States for her maternity leave. Perhaps they could establish a scholarship fund in her name.

The baby is not so fretful this day. He seems finally to be able to lie awake without making those grating, fussy noises that neither the mother nor the grandmother can bear. The fussiness, say the books, indicates an immature nervous system, a condition he will outgrow.

"I have to tell you something about Grammy James," Tweedie says. "It's something she wrote me a couple of months ago."

"After you told her you were pregnant?"

Tweedie nods. "It's the most astonishing thing, a confession, a document, actually. Wait, let me get it for you."

Rebecca sees it is indeed a document, several single-spaced pages typed on her mother's Smith Corona with the tail-letters—q's and y's—that always printed a little below the line they belonged on.

"When Grammy was seventeen," says Tweedie, shuffling the pages, "she had a mad, wonderful love affair with the guy who was the chief trainer for the Thoroughbred farm across from their property."

"The old Stoddard estate?"

"I guess so. It was in 1917, the year of the first flu epidemic. She had just graduated from high school, a private day school, really." Now Tweedie is reading. " 'There was no question of an abortion, of course. In addition to the disgrace attendant on one, the illegal procedure, usually performed by a failed doctor or a veterinarian, was extremely dangerous. My parents were beside themselves with fury and terror. I had to be removed from the scene at once! So I was sent off to Indiana to live with some distant impecunious cousins, two dry sticks, staunch Methodists, who ran the local hardware emporium. I was alone in the house all day with two cats whom I observed very closely, keeping records of their sleep and awake times, and so on. Also, I studied Greek. After supper, as soon as it was too dark for my condition to be taken note of, I went for my daily long walk . . . . '"

"God," Rebecca says.

"The day the baby was born he was put up for adoption and she never saw him again. Then she got the flu and she hoped she would die of it, romantically. 'Having lost my lover and given away my child,' she said, 'I was ready to lose my life.' She was so sick that all her hair fell out 'ignominiously'."

"I think I always knew about this," Rebecca says slowly. "I mean, not the whole story, but I think I always knew there had been a great love when she was quite young, and that it ended badly. In my mind it had something to do with World War I, the influence of all those stories, I suppose."

"You mean about fiancés being killed at the Marne and the women vowing never to marry?"

"Something like that. They all became high-school English teachers."

"But the way she described it," Tweedie says, "Listen to this: 'I must tell you, Tweedie, this grand passion was the sweetest interlude of my life. Even after almost seventy years, I have perfect recall for our feelings, our gaiety, indeed even our conversations. It was wonderful how he used to lift me up, his hands around my waist—I had a tiny waist, then—and twirl me around in the boxstall. 'Augusta Wadsworth Kensington,' he'd say, 'second cousin twice removed of the poet! Watch her fly through the air'."

Rebecca is crying.

"Don't cry, Mom. Think how happy he made her. 'He taught me how to shake straw on the pitchfork—it's a fine art, to distribute it evenly—and we used to ride out together, galloping the jump course. Even though I was terrified of the drop jumps I followed him over every one with perfect confidence'."

"Can't you just see it, though," Rebecca says. "Packed off to cousins in the Middle West, undoubtedly paid to keep it quiet. Abandoned by those bitchy, upper-class parents with their expensive reputation. The groom was probably bought off, too. Banished to Virginia."

"Trainer," Tweedie corrects. "Actually, he went to Kentucky."

They are both silent a minute. Rebecca blows her nose.

"They gave her chloroform," Tweedie says. "She described how they put a few drops on a handkerchief tied around her wrist and told her to sniff it when the pains got too bad. So she would sort of pass out and her arm would drop and then she'd come to and sniff again and pass out. Primitive but effective. The thing was, it's very bad for the baby."

"She never found out who adopted it?"

"She said she tried to trace him through the minister of the Methodist church in Leedsville. But I guess back then a natural mother had no rights. They could keep the records from you."

"Strange," says Rebecca. "Mom was so . . . indomitable. It seems to me that if she wanted to know badly enough, she'd have found out."

"Want to hear what she wrote at the end?" Tweedie asks. She has not known until just now that she would share this with Rebecca.

"'And thus, Tweedie, while I cannot applaud your reliving my history, I am deeply happy to think that my genes are being handed on. Modified, broadened, no doubt improved upon. I know you will hold fast to your baby and that he will be a credit to us all'."

The baby starts to squeak then and soon works up to full scale. Rebecca diapering him, Tweedie nursing him, separately and silently think how it all comes down to this moment. That the baby begins with Gussie.

On Weaning in America

Genny Lim

At 13 months
May Ching's tender skin has erupted into
flaming rash from neck to ankle
Blotchy red patches—
wild strawberries proliferating under moonlight

Give her ginseng
Rub the sores with ointments, lotions
Bathe in rind of winter melon
Powder of oatmeal
Paw-Paw's[1] herbs

She sleeps fitfully
Surrounded by shadow puppets, stuffed animals
In a while she will awaken and
I will go to her

---

1. Matriarchal grandmother

When I think of Ma-Ma
Walking down the dock
Third sister in hand
Following a thousand men and women
Down a dirt path
I not yet even born for eight years
You disappear into a wooden building
Never to emerge again
Never to speak English

When I think of you
Sitting before the white interrogation officer
Speaking a foreign tongue
Answering back in *thlee-yip*[2]
I am tongue-tied

When I think of who you might have been
A young Kwantung woman
So lucky, yes, so lucky, they said
To have married a handsome *gum-san hock*
And go to *Gum-San*[3]
Leaving two daughters behind who never forgot
Who never forgot because
They were reported sons
They were left behind

When I think of who you might have been besides
A seamstress
Besides a mother of seven
Besides a green card holder
I imagine you escaping
Smoke from a burning bush
Your life like ashes about your feet

---

2. A Toisan dialect (Lit. 4th district)
3. Gold Mountain (U.S.A.)

Yellow woman
Moon chanter
Spinner of Truth
Weaver of dynasties
Wisdom and magic
Silent sorceress
Herb healer
Mother of Pearl
Stone of Heaven
Wings of Dragon
Claws of Tiger
Ocean Goddess

Ah-Paw
Ah-Goo[4]
Ah-Ma

Bending over ricefields
Stirring supper over coals
Sewing blouses, scrubbing floors

Your days burned soon as they were lit
Like firecrackers, *pop-pop!*
Leaving only little shreds of memory
Paper-wrapped money for *mui-mui*
Red ribbons, pomegranate cheeks,
Bright oranges, good-luck scrolls
Thousand-year-old eggs
Waiting to be scraped

When I think of you in that boat
Third sister in hand
Alone among the seaweed, fish and anemone
Eating salt cabbage and gruel
I am ashamed of my wastefulness

---

4. Great Aunt

Before me, bits of poems
Fragments of dreams
scattered strawberries
unripe

Ma
I have dreamed of you
Head bent, staring out of open windows
Burning incense with ivory fingers
Boiling herbs in a dark kitchen
Where demons were cursed

Ma
I have dreamed of you
You are the face I have seen
Illuminated in the water
You are the slave-girl
Riding Pacific waves

Ma-Ma
You are the wisdom
Between reason and truth
You are the ancestral lamb
You are the ritual that
I must repeat

Ah-Ma
You tell me to take May Ching off my breast
But when I feel her reaching for me, looking up at me
Eye full of innocence and wonder
Tugging at my blouse
When I hear the rhythm of her gentle sucking
and the river of sighs

I think of long journeys
Sisters left behind
And I think
How can I deny my daughter
The breast I never got?

Mother Underground

Molly Hite

My mother called last night. I record this fact noting that it
sounds reassuringly normal, as if telephone conversations
between my mother and me were as habitual and unreflective as swal-
lowing, as if my mother were anybody's mother and I were anybody's
daughter, as if our relations adhered to the model of female bonding
enjoined first by the sitcoms of my adolescence and then by the feminist psychoanalytic studies of my adulthood, as if my mother had been
calling regularly throughout the twenty-five years since I was purged
from the family. In point of fact, my mother has been actively engaged
in not speaking to me during about half this period—about half my
adult life, although the silences are as sporadic and intermittent as the
bursts of speech. The call last night is one of a number of calls over the
last few years leading me to the guarded conclusion that this period is
finally over. I tend to think we have both outgrown it. But the conclusion remains guarded: tentative on both sides, I imagine. We are both
protective of these conversations. We collude in the fiction that we have
always had them.

This means there are still things we don't say to each other. Most things, I suppose. There are times when the unsaid is the whole basis of the conversation, a tacit obbligato over which we intone our prescribed phrases, formulary as monks. For instance, my mother gives me advice about my son, currently in the enraged flowering of adolescence. "I've learned that your children are what they are," she tells me. "There is very little you can take credit for. On the other hand, there is very little you need to blame yourself for." *What are we talking about?* I think, still at some bone-deep level the enraged adolescent to whom my mother once refused to speak for an entire week although we were stuffed with my father and my two younger sisters into a tract house so small that we could not avoid each other unless we refrained entirely from using the bathroom. She would *hum* as she passed me on the stairs, I recall, cold blue eyes sliding over me like water. For whom do we take neither credit nor blame? I ask myself. I don't ask her. It may be that my mother acknowledges the double application. Perhaps she intends it. I am not ready to find out. But I do know she is a very intelligent woman.

Only recently, from the pitch of a midlife that slides me back into that same adolescence—or a parodic version of it—at unanticipated moments and from odd directions, have I come to see what it might mean that my mother is a very intelligent woman. Up until recently I was aware of the intelligence but unwilling to attach it to specific manifestations: to her speech and silences; to her unheralded and alarming explosions of activity, at first in service of an ideal of housewifery that seemed compulsive to the point of insanity, later in reaction to the executive careers she attempted and then, cataclysmically, abandoned. I was aware of intelligence as a property attaching to my mother like her ability to make bread or her long chestnut hair, which she wore wound up in a bobby pin-filled mound on top of her head. I saw it as only an aspect of her, so limited as to be virtually detachable. I knew she was very intelligent because she had skipped four grades in school, because her vocabulary was vast and polyglot, because she read constantly, and because her friends periodically remarked on the fact, usually by way of excuse. When I look back on our tract house neighborhood in the small college town of my youth, I realize that my mother's bridge club and book club and coffee-klatch friends, none of them slouches by prevailing university-wife standards of cultural literacy, treated my mother as if she were a chess prodigy or infant math whiz, congenitally overdeveloped in a capacity that had little practical application.

All of which is only to say that she was very intelligent. I suppose she was too intelligent for her own good. That phrase actually meant something in those tidy postwar years when everything was clipped back: lawn, hair, aspirations. I came to consciousness in an environment permeated with concern over being safe, with staying inside houses and norms. Certainly the mothers in our neighborhood, women who had been swept into the home in droves after the war, spent most of their time in the home and *on* the home, sweeping and dusting and scouring and disinfecting and waxing and buffing their meager dwellings as if they were in danger of being hauled before the House Un-American Activities Committee if their vigilance lapsed. Looking back on that period, I find the mania for good housekeeping irrevocably mixed up with our small-town experience of the Cold War. Both germs and Communists were insidious presences you had to take great pains to keep at bay, and both had secret and shameful associations with my parents, former socialists turned liberal Democrats in John Birch country and so by implication potential slobs, latent harborers of disease-bearing dust and grease and ambiguous odors.

I became aware of my family's precarious status the way I became aware of almost everything when I was growing up, through my mother, who brought me up on stories of Norman Thomas and Paul Robeson and how a commodity goes through the stages of production to make exorbitant profits for the capitalist, but who also warned me never to say *Commie* out loud and stood over me while I washed window sashes with an old toothbrush and scraped the inside of the toilet bowl with a razor blade. I ascertained fairly early that the toothbrush and the razor blade were my mother's own inventions, not instruments of the craft that other girls used in their own apprenticeships with their own mothers. "A razor blade?" these girls would ask me. "What for?" To scrape the feces out of the toilet bowl, my mother told me, her lips tight with disapproval at my unsanctioned question and at the word *feces,* which seemed to have been wrenched by force out of her own embattled interior. I inferred that these arcane means of cleaning were intended to humiliate and hamper me as I struggled like a bad-tempered Cinderella through a burgeoning list of chores to buy my Saturday night freedom. The conclusion was not unreasonable—housework was the inevitable site of our clashes over issues of obedience, identity, destiny, and betrayal—but I see now that I was dead wrong. My mother had originally come up with the toothbrush and the razor blade not for me but for herself, as adjuncts to the enterprise of making housework so arduous, risky, and intellectually challenging that you might conceivably justify devoting all your time to it.

I also have come to see that I was necessary to this enterprise, both as ally and as enemy. As the oldest daughter, I was the elected bearer of simultaneous and contradictory responsibilities: first, to emulate my mother and so vindicate the choices she had in fact made; second, to oppose her and so realize the choices she might have made if she had been given the chance. I was far better at opposing than at emulating, but her messages were so conflicted that I'm still not sure it was possible for me to conform to the model she presented. I suspect that at the deepest level she didn't want her choices vindicated. On one hand, she would be censorious when I came home with a good report card or one of the fatuous school literary awards. "Your father and I don't want you to be a *grind*, dear," she would say, looking somewhere other than at me. "It's more important for you to be well-liked. We'd like people to think of you as a good kid." My father was often invoked for such purposes but rarely present. I gathered that they conferred about my case late at night, while I simmered in my bedroom with my books and my opera records, the latter turned up just loud enough to annoy them. On the other hand, she encouraged me to make fun of other girls my age, the more successful girls, good kids in the toils of the feminine mystique. "I don't *get* it, kid," I'd whine in imitation of the authorized female response to class work of any kind. "Do *you* get it, kid? Oh, me *either*, kid, it's ha-ard." "My God!" she would gasp, almost speechless with a hilarity she clearly regarded as seditious. "No, they don't *say* that, do they? What else do they say?" These scenes were the only occasions when my mother and I were close, and then we were suddenly very close, co-conspirators against a force that threatened both of us and that neither of us could put a name to. The role-playing was cathartic, of course. I was acting out a primary source of terror in my own life, the phenomenon of dumbing-down that appeared to have struck almost all my female classmates between sixth and seventh grade. Always suspicious of mass movements that excluded me, I intuited a plot rather than some biologically-cued regression. They weren't really dumb, those girls, erstwhile friends of mine. In a peculiar way that I couldn't quite follow, they were smarter, in that they had figured out it was smart to be dumb while my hand was still shooting up in a Pavlovian spasm every time some teacher asked a question. I could tell I wasn't catching on by their reproving murmurs and giggles and by the satisfaction they derived from the assertion that *they* weren't catching on. They were, moreover, catching boys, who were all of a sudden the makers of dates, the answerers of classroom questions, and not my friends either. It was all very confusing.

For this reason, the little drama sessions with my mother were an enormous relief. But they were rare, and complicated by the fact that most of the time my mother sided with the other girls, who were after all committed to a future inside a house provided by one of the question-answering boys and, presumably, a career of keeping it extremely clean. So that while she was sometimes disposed to ridicule the vapidity and banality I was acting out for her edification, at other times she would intervene sternly. "It wouldn't hurt you to try getting along a little," she would say. "It's important what people think of you." I received this news with sensations of terror and manifestations of scorn. I knew what people thought of me. They thought I wasn't fitting in. My only hope was that they wouldn't find out I minded.

We settled into a routine in which she laid down rules of conduct and I disobeyed them and was punished, both of us reflexively enacting extreme versions of our articulated positions. The rest of the family fled from these scenes, which absorbed us almost completely even though much of the time they kept us from acknowledging that the other even existed. I'm quite sure now that our behavior was—in descriptive rather than merely pejorative terms—sick, and that we were complicit to the point of interdependency in this sickness, which served for both of us as a locus of consuming interest. I'm not sure we were all that unusual. I still don't know what either of us could have done differently, except perhaps been different people. Heredity and environment had combined to make us sources of exquisite irritation to each other.

Yet the great pivotal event of my teenage years was a catastrophic moment when my mother, against all expectation, took my side. It occurred during my sophomore year when I began arguing with the teacher of a course in Twentieth-Century History over the conclusions he was drawing from purported facts. "History has proved" was how he closed off argument, and as the semester wore on it became clear that history had proved any number of things inimical to the values I had grown up with. Not coincidentally, history had, it seemed, come out solidly in favor of the values that he and most of the other members of our deeply conservative community had grown up with. History endorsed strong leaders, elites of various stripes, large and well-funded armies, and enterprise somewhat freer than anything the original John D. Rockefeller had enjoyed. I fought all these assertions, which showed up regularly on examinations, without much skill but with a great deal of conviction that too much was being taken for granted. The day everything blew up, however, I was fighting not for an inherited ideal of political liberalism but for my own continued existence on terms I could accept. History had proved, we learned that day, that women were not creative; their role was to inspire men to create works of art.

It is important to note that I was not precisely kicked out of school for my feminism: there was no such thing back then, or rather, there had been something called feminism, which had expired upon securing the vote for women. (The vote for women was a mixed blessing according to my teacher and of course history, which had proved women really weren't much interested in voting. The girl at the desk alongside mine had been writing *mixed blessing* in round, loopy script when my hand shot up that time.) Nor was my argument really made for the sake of all women, although I didn't mind if it had side benefits. I had simply proceeded syllogistically. If women were not creative and if I was a woman, then I was not creative and had to be content with inspiring the various Bobs and Bills of my acquaintance to create works of art, a dubious career goal even if I hadn't thought I could write things by myself.

"Charlotte Brontë," I said promptly, not even bothering to wait until he had called on me.

"Minor," he shot back.

"*Emily* Brontë."

He glowered at me, punchy with history. "The brother was the genius."

"Virginia Woolf," I said.

He regarded me with pity. "Virginia Woolf," he said, "was not really a woman." That shut me up, although I had no idea what he meant. It sounded like the sort of thing he might say about me next. But it was already too late and I was thrown out of class, an inconceivable humiliation at our well-behaved school. I went snuffling home at an hour when no one my age was in sight, anticipating further body blows from my mother, who had already told me frostily that if I couldn't learn to keep my mouth shut there were people who would eventually do the job for me.

Incredibly, she puffed up like a cobra as soon as I'd sobbed and hiccupped my way through my account of what had happened. "Why that stupid man," she murmured in a voice that I had only heard turned on me. "That stupid *little* man." Then she did another amazing thing. She took me out shopping for clothes, at ten-thirty in the morning on a school day. Furthermore, she bought me several tight and short dresses, which eventually got me in further trouble with the administration of the high school. By that time, however, I had settled into my new and recognizable identity as a troublemaker and was dyeing my hair unnatural colors and investing in dancers' tights, and my mother was once again not speaking to me, in part for wearing the things she bought me. I suspect now that she was jealous. She would have been a great troublemaker. But that was later. First she called the Superintendent of Schools who called the principal and got us all cozily together to chat about what history had proved and what you really ought to refrain from doing in the classroom. I sat amazed and perfectly quiet, for once. For all my sense of outraged justice, I had never really believed there could be a situation where I confronted adult authority and turned out to be right. Actually, I don't think this was a case of right prevailing. I think this was just another power play. But for once in my life I had more power. For once in my life I had my mother on my side.

After that incident, however, we went back to our old positions and spent a great deal of time acting out our mutual repugnance until I left high school and figured out how to leave home for good. At that point, things got very bad for my mother. Ten years later, in therapy for the first time in my life, I read some of R.D. Laing's work on the family and began to see how my rebellions and rages had deflected attention and onus from my mother's own deep conflicts. I had conveniently turned bad so that my mother would not be perceived as mad—or that was Laing's succinct formulation. Indeed, my abrupt departure from the family left her exposed in her own peculiar preoccupations. If she was not crazy, she was certainly unhappy, and she began expressing that unhappiness in noticeably odd ways.

Through the good offices of one of her friends and because of a gradual change in the prevailing attitude toward women and careers, she began working at fairly high-level jobs, administrative positions, first at the university, later with other institutions. She invariably loved these jobs, talked adoringly of her cohorts, related in ecstatic detail every business trip she took. But eventually something happened. There would be a bitter argument with one of the adored cohorts or she would make a mistake that she regarded as intolerable or irreparable. Then she would quit and go back into the home, reenacting the mass movement of the late Forties that drove her to toothbrushes and razor blades in the first place. But in these reenactments she went somewhat further. She went down, into the cellar, locked the door, and stayed there for weeks.

The first time this happened I learned about it by chance from my father, whom I had called from the faraway coast where I had finally washed up. "Your mother's in the basement," he said carefully.

"Oh," I said, curiously unsurprised. "What's she doing there?"

"I think she needs a rest," he told me that first time. "We're kind of a rowdy bunch, you know." They were a very timid bunch when I was around, but I said I knew. "She's got a little air mattress down there," my father continued. "And we've got that half-bathroom. So she's fine there. She'll be up any day now."

"What's she *eat?*" I asked.

"Oh," he said, palpably relieved at such a practical question, "the freezer's down there. We still keep a lot of ice cream on hand. She took a spoon."

My first therapist welcomed all this as evidence of my mother's looniness and my own consequent victimization. We pay therapists to be on our side when our mothers won't be. For a while I felt vindicated, if uncharacteristically martyred. Now I'm not so sure it was that clear-cut. Laing stopped his analysis at the borders of the family. I keep remembering the very intelligent woman forced into an obsession with the home by history, which had turned on her, proclaiming it had proved her essential dependence in an economy newly glutted with employable men. Like many of her contemporaries, she was made agoraphobic by her ostensible vocation, pressed into little service in a little space and encouraged to shrink away from an outside world represented to her as vast and alien. I think of her as one of those fish that live in underground caves, white and blinded, all those splendid capacities atrophied or redirected to feed on constriction and darkness.

In this context there is something admirably satiric about her voluntary descent into the region of cold storage. But there is more, or I think there is more, although I never saw her take leave, vanish into that underworld without a backward glance, the latch sliding shut at the top of the stairs.

I picture her going slowly down those stairs with the spoon upraised, her olive branch or golden bough or maybe some device for dealing with pomegranates.

I wonder if I am to go after her or if in some way she has gone after me, to fetch me back to light and health and a boundless earth ready for spring planting. I wonder which of us is the daughter and which is the mother, who is the victim and who is the savior. On occasion I wonder which way is up.

I also wonder if she thinks of me at all and am sometimes comforted by the idea that she crosses her own particular Lethe as a condition of the journey, leaving me completely behind. In many ways I want to be forgotten. Or rather, I want to be misremembered, able to receive advice as if it came from nobody's mother in particular, a generic daughter rubbed smooth by water over the dam.

Anti-Demeter

(The More I Give the More You Steal / The More You Give the More I Need)

Carolee Schneemann

———————

She stood framed: open closet, shadowed textures a backdrop, clothes filled with her body's sensual shape. Cylinders filled and moving or hanging, lateral fabric edges press into each other. On their wide blue bed, my child hands shift piles of clean socks. Dad's—largest rolls of brown, black, or green. Hers—white rough cotton for gardening and snaky brown nylons draped in separate layers. Brother's—mud-stained, big white ones for football. Sister's—multicolored, small thin cotton ones. The matched balls accumulate while her terror unhinged my concentration, my placement as witness. She stood framed by the closet doors—undressed, pink bra, pink panties with lacy sides, hand raised over her left breast (to salute the school flag. . . no!). Her startled face turned to my face. "There is a lump in my breast. Feel this!" As if I were her sister or a friend. My fingers pull away from cotton, wool, to touch her skin. A small little lump . . . there, where I touch my mother's breast.

(. . . sucking cock—envy of suckling infant maternal body . . . sorry
boys, you can't feed these infants with your own body . . . take penis in
mouth . . . suckle there . . .)

That year my brother began sleepwalking. Somehow she would
know . . . alert in sleep, *hearing* the hushed tread no one else could hear.
To rush down the stairs in a fluttering robe to find the front door open.
. . . golden ruff of hair a moon moving slowly down the silent road.

Those long solid ruddy legs running ahead of me. I scrub at his pink
skin, he closes his blue eyes. One Christmas when he was four, he was
given a miniature carpentry set. I found the face of my antique porce-
lain doll smashed in, the "real" eyelashes buried in ceramic dust. Later,
the ivory piano keys—her pride and dreams for music—were
hammered off at the edges, hostile biting broken teeth.

Her few solitary pleasures: to be bent over the clattering sewing
machine, domestic alchemy, aromas of starch mildew springtime, a
dense shifting clutter of fabrics, threads, pins, buttons. There were
lengths of rayon, flannel, silk, cotton to become curtains, flowered
dresses for my sister or me, or something envisioned from swaths of
silky fabric cut on the bias if they planned a trip to the city—dancing, a
concert. Companionably at her side on its metal leg stood a bronze-
colored fiberboard replica of her own exact shape but headless,
armless, almost sexless. The month *before* she discovered the lump in
her left breast, she had found the left breast of the sewing model
smashed in, its idealized bronze-colored breast indented, broken.
Small hammer blows. No one ever spoke of this assaultive prediction,
his guilt, the destructive impulse foretelling an invitation to Cancer, the
point of invasion marked in advance.

A dream reiterates the search for my/our mother. Both books are missing! The diary and the flower-covered notebook . . . phone calls . . .
messages left that she *had* been seen . . . was at a certain hotel, but my
father and brother told inquiring friends that she was definitely
"missing."

You are not invited into my body. I did not invite an alien being, a "child," into my future. I had a mountainside to climb, my back pushing against a heavy rucksack filled with paints, turpentine, oils, brushes, the roll of canvas. There were sharp rocks to climb, to see over the horizon into a crashing ocean storm. And lovers to mesh with unencumbered. I did not accept swelling tender breasts, rounding belly, the constant need to leave what I was looking at in its transformative swift tonalities under passing clouds, to drop wet brushes, to piss again in shrubs. Pregnancy was constant pissing and terror, not nausea but terror. I was taken over. I was no longer an "I." Someone unchosen was inhabiting me, would claim love, attention, care, would use me to become itself, would live in my thoughts and intentions. The umbilicus unfurled years of eternal distractions, demands: needs to be fed, washed, dried, clothed, walked, spoken to, taught everything! There was a lump growing in my body.

To see, to make images was to be alive. Not possessed, inhabited, co-opted, distracted, and at the mercy of male pride. But each pregnancy posited a "higher value" than making work; the explorations I choose to follow—total concentration, the bliss of coherence and unexpected discrepancies, rhythms within one rectangle. Painting into the night and, on waking, to go immediately to the studio to engage with history—personal, ancient. Pregnancy meant a social usurpation of the private products and processes of my body—even the ecstatic fucking.

> *I'm not your dog bone your hearth and cupboard your steaming kettle on the stove your stack of pancakes I'm not your socks folded and matched . . .*

(In sixth grade I had a crush on Bert, a farmer's son. His yellow hair stood up like straw. One morning he squeezed onto the seat beside me, mixing his soapy smell with the pungent gasoline aroma of the orange school bus rumbling along. He put his hand on the edge of my skirt—red and green plaid—looked into my eyes and said, "You're so pretty. When we grow up, would you breed my children?" It was indelibly clear that no matter my dreams and wishes there was a cow-like destiny in store. I never let him kiss me again during spin-the-bottle. . . .)

By going public with my body I de-privatized it.

Every time she got pregnant it was more work for me, more problems. I caught on after the first one, but it was already too late. I became a wise insightful helping little mother. . . .

Tell me: what is more forbidden a positive conscious association than the comingling of Artist/Mother? Mother-as-Artist . . . Mother-and-Artist . . . female . . . muse . . . blank canvas . . . un-named . . . unexplored territory . . . daunting . . . unknown. Western male aesthetic myths strike a bargain with the displaced femaleness of their own unconscious as space to be penetrated, defined, brought to life. If women artists already occupy the space of the once devoted/eroticized but bloodless muse, then his high heroic stakes are contaminated and diminished! (Mad woman in his attic . . .)

Now I see: our father stole us from her arms, from her escape from death back into his arms where she would be filled again with another baby from him—just as Jesus stole Mary from the fertile Goddess pantheon. Daddy runs toward us in a flapping apron—huge feet in laced-up boots, his arms are full, ecstatic smile. He has stolen another baby from a woman's wide-opened legs . . . son adored among sisters becomes doctor deliverer. He charmed the children's hearts away— loving blue eyes, candy in pockets, forgiving our crimes which she had punished with systematic slaps and screams. Her weary artificial cheer at meals, the plates burned into her extended hands. Daddy is dancing around the cozy fire-lit room, Christmas tree lights flicker between his raised arms, feet poked into the center of her narrow navy sling-back pumps. Daddy is dancing and singing. She is abashed charmed fearful . . . a little zany hat, a long wavering feather perched on his head. We scream *Daddy Daddy Daddy* . . . throw us in the air! Our wild hearts explode with joy and wonder—our handsome laughing Daddy. When *she* sings, I crawl under the dining room table and weep, my brother sleepwalks and smashes things with his toy hammer, my sister twitches under her hands. "Don't touch me Mom!"

Missing

Rita Dove

———————

I am the daughter who went out with the girls,
never checked back in and nothing marked my "last
known whereabouts," not a single lavender petal.

Horror is partial; it keeps you going. A lost
child is a fact hardening around its absence,
a knot in the breast purring *Touch, and I will*

come true. I was "returned," I watched her
watch as I babbled *It could have been worse...*
Who can tell
what penetrates? Pity's the brutal
discipline. Now I understand she can never
die, just as nothing can bring me back—
I am the one who comes and goes;
I am the footfall that hovers.

Persephone, Falling

Rita Dove

One narcissus among the ordinary beautiful
flowers, one unlike all the others! She pulled,
stooped to pull harder—
when, sprung out of the earth
on his glittering terrible
carriage, he claimed his due.
It is finished. No one heard her.
No one! She had strayed from the herd.

(Remember: go straight to school.
This is important, stop fooling around!
Don't answer to strangers. Stick
with your playmates. Keep your eyes down.)
This is how easily the pit
is waiting. This is how one foot sinks into the ground.

Persephone Underground

Rita Dove

If I could just touch your ankle, he whispers, *there*
on the inside, above the bone—leans closer,
breath of lime and peppers—*I know I could*
make love to you. She considers
this, secretly thrilled, though she wasn't quite
sure what he meant. He was good
with words, words that went straight to the liver.
Was she falling for him out of sheer boredom—
cooped up in this anything-but-humble dive, stone
gargoyles leering and brocade drapes licked with fire?
Her ankle burns where he described it. She sighs
just as her mother aboveground stumbles, is caught
by the fetlock—bereft in an instant—
while the Great Man drives home his desire.

The Mother Journey

Molly Collins Layton

When I was a dreamy little Texas girl roaming the soft hills beside my home, I never thought "too awful long" of becoming a mother. My friend Puddin and I played fashion design and put on elaborate shows—the Months of the Year was a favorite theme—but we avoided dolls. I was a terrible babysitter, well-meaning but inept. I preferred reading.

Nonetheless, when I was a twenty-three-year-old graduate student and finishing up notes for an oral report on the *Philosophical Investigations* of Wittgenstein, I went into labor. My husband Charles and I dropped the paper off at a friend's house so he could present it in my stead at a philosophy seminar. Then we drove through Austin's balmy November twilight to the local hospital where David, six pounds and so-many ounces, was born early the next morning.

It was the ordinariness of becoming a mother that first struck me with a hot blast of wonder. Women had babies all the time, and yet in the great novels I had read, no one ever talked about the experience of becoming a mother, nor about the sticky details of birthing and nursing. As a person accustomed to research, I found even the most practical information hard to come by. This was in 1966, and I had to send off to France for a book about the new Lamaze method of childbirth. Because of the popularity of bottles, even the informal lore of breastfeeding, handed down from older to younger women, had been lost. It seemed I had landed at the center of human life and, surprisingly, found myself alone, engulfed in an inchoate and banal silence. How bewildering that a process as grand and scary and tedious as becoming a mother should be so *unremarkable*, literally not worthy of remark.

I myself was adrift in immaturity, about as unformed and malleable as my own small baby who, I was now genuinely startled to discover, needed my intense concentration. Before he was born, the fetal David was a rosy abstraction in a blithely comfortable pregnancy. I glowed, I thrived, I brushed aside the cautionary tales. Not until I saw *Rosemary's Baby* much later did I consciously recognize the dark side there all along—the baby as parasite, the sinister "other" placed within the soul-self by strange and alien powers, the invasive fetus vanquishing the helpless mother. This is not merely the baby of horror stories and psychotic nightmares: this is the shadow side of symbiosis.

Truly the infant David overwhelmed me. Even now in recalling the early days of motherhood, I feel again that first shock of my own responsibility for this tiny, fragile person, the clear and compelling demand that I harden into a self, a definite persona, that I come out of the mists of graduate study. But captured by his presence, I found I could neither read nor write. Eventually I abandoned my training in philosophy to study instead this small, willful, and physically beautiful person. I had to push away my books and my thoughts so that I could hear his tiny demands. So David was the person who made me pay attention to the world outside myself, to boiled eggs and washed sheets and flirty babies.

Because we stubbornly identify always with the helpless infants, we human beings find it hard to accept the frail and tenuous humanity of the mother. We easily and sentimentally resonate to the emotional nurturance that we as infants need from mothers. Our infant-selves are masters of longing, and masters too in imagining the mother's unlimited strength and unlimited supply of love. And the mother goes along with this demand. The mother soon learns what is required to support the life of the child. She just does it. Whatever she thinks the child needs, that's what she does.

But the mother's motivation arises from her discovery of a terrible truth: she must keep and hold someone who is perilously fragile in a world now suddenly filled with danger. This demand—the demand to preserve—is so clear and so penetrating that it forces even the most philosophical among us to abandon our relativism and shuck off our existential blues.

It was the bald inescapability of my new identity that shocked me the most, sometimes making me proud of myself, sometimes guilty and confused, sometimes just exhausted. But of course I had to stay in role: my baby held me as I held him. Until then, I had never been so located in time and space.

The relationship with the baby is startlingly intimate, beginning with the privacy of the nursing relationship and continuing *ad nauseum* into all the untidy details of baby bodies. There is, of course, excrement in an amazing variety of textures, colors, and odors, all necessarily subject to the intense scrutiny of the mother, a sort of high-priestess of fecal matter. But there is also drool, milky spit, vomit, nose runs, boogers, ear wax, blood, urine—every drop and smear of which someone must wipe away, clean up, wash off, or launder. The mother must develop a kind of hardiness to face this flow of human juices, and a forgiveness too. She learns to say, "It's all right," and comes to accept the body, its impolite realness, its frailty, its pleasures. Indeed, the baby is such a sensualist that the mother must quickly learn the language of holding and stroking. The sly and secret delight of mothers, if I may speak for all of us, is baby buns—smooth, lusciously curved, actually tauter and tinier than the diaper would have you believe.

By the time Rebecca was born, over three years later, David had slowly trained me into a fairly sociable, level-headed citizen, less likely to drift airily around our tiny apartment like a balloon losing its helium. Consequently, Rebecca and I recognized each other as soon as the nurse handed her to me. Thanks to David, I knew then how to dampen my anxiety in the face of her howls of indignation and I knew too the companionate pleasures of rocking idly with a soft baby in the empty spaces of the night.

In *Maternal Thinking*, Sara Ruddick has written of the disorienting experience of caring for a growing baby "whose acts are irregular, unpredictable, often mysterious. A mother, in order to understand her child, must assume the existence of a conscious continuing person whose acts make sense in terms of perceptions and responses to a meaning-filled world." A mother "assumes the priority of personhood over action." The foundation of the special mode of perception Ruddick calls maternal thinking is an unquestioning belief in the continuity of the child-self despite enormous changes and even contradictory phenomena.

The illusion of a constant self is great: one long, loopy afternoon, when David was three years old and Rebecca still growing inside me, I tended my own and my sister's children. Suddenly I was torn open with grief merely watching my young nephew toddle down the hallway stalking the voices of his older cousins and siblings. He wore David's recently cast-off blue suit, one that I had made, and viewed from the back, with the sailor hat on his head, he was for me the two-year-old David come again. The surprise was that I had not known that that person was gone until he magically reappeared.

So there is a bittersweet paradox at the heart of maternal thinking. The mother aches for her child's growth, but the growth is double-stranded with her joy and grief. In the baby's cupholding, the mother thrills at growing skills—at the intelligence, at this demonstration of the capacity to survive without her. At the same time, she must prepare to leave behind the cosy and intimate warmth of the baby at her breast. The mother's rockbottom interest in fostering the child's growth sets her up for the continual experience of separation.

But the most extraordinary demand that infant David made of me was the demand for a resolute good humor. It somehow went without saying that anything negative about myself would be bad for my child—if I threw dishes or sank inconsolably depressed on the couch or growled and cursed at the vacuum cleaner, not to mention growling and cursing at David himself. As a child, I had always been a shy, mild sort of person, but as a mother I experienced for the first time my own capacity to be a difficult, even toxic, and possibly destructive force. I managed daily to be of good cheer but did not like the feelings that threatened to surface when I was tired or confused. The first scary hint I ever had of real rage in myself was one long, hot, exhausting summer afternoon when the toddler David would not go down for a nap; after I had tiptoed out of his room for the fourth or fifth time, he cried awake again and to my eternal dismay I found myself struggling with the evil impulse to shake him really hard. To protect David, I did not return at once to his room, and so the two of us cried in frustration, David in his crib and me in the kitchen. Once, years later, I lost my temper with

David, and my outrage escalated so rapidly that again I found myself perilously close to harming him, and at the last minute kicked the door instead. The door was cracked forever after, and I never repaired it so that I would never forget. If we lived there still, I would repair the door now, as a ritual of the mending between the two of us.

But mostly I found myself cheerily, patiently, doggedly pursuing the tedious details of the day, at my worst like some unctuous master of ceremonies for my tiny and captive audience. "Okay," I would announce to a rapt but two-month-old David, as we strolled down the supermarket aisle, "let's look for the tomatoes!" At my best I was sweet and low-keyed and optimistic—the kind of sunny outlook that reflected David's demand for someone to instill a fundamental trust and interest in life itself. Strangely, I felt it my duty to point out things: "There's a cow!" "See Daddy?" and even, "Where's David? There he is!" I would talk seductively or pretend to gobble up his foot or I would cover my face with his blanket and peek out at him, until to my amazement he slowly organized his responses, first arching his back, later squirming in delight, finally singing back at me.

This is the sort of stuff people love to hear about mothers, their delight in their children, their boundless energy, their unending fascination with the simple details of little bodies and daily routines. I like to hear it too. But like all simplifications, it has its costs. What is the mother to do with her cynicism, her irony, her urge to throw the dinner plates against the fence?

Instead, the mother constructs a world that is benign and uncomplicated, as bland and digestible as baby food itself. And as she does, she finds herself perforce tuning in to the simple shapes and rhythms of living: coming and going, big and little, time for this and time for that, a space for everything. It's a Richard Scarry world, where the happy baker waves hello to the happy mailman, the postal truck is marked "U.S. Mail," the bakery window announces "Bakery" and flowers bloom in the window box. Everything is labeled. I love this world, its industry, its relentless sunshine, its illusory security. Turning the pages of our book, sometimes I needed to believe its truth as much as the toddler on my lap did, feeling always my own longing for a world in which my child could grow up safely. I was saving the stories about automobile accidents and war and horrible diseases for later.

For both the mother and the infant, the tension between growing and keeping safe was sometimes complementary, sometimes opposing. The toddler comes and goes, tumbling back into the lap of the comforting mother when he has stretched his fears too far. The mother fears as well, sometimes experiencing the child's own curiosity as the enemy to a safe life. In preserving and holding, it seemed I sat forever on shady lawns, watching David in the sandbox and Rebecca on the blanket, the first of our line of cats stalking the fence of trumpet vines. The effort to be watchful was at times overwhelming for me, my eyes glazing over, my own stuporous emptiness such a bald experience that it seemed to constitute a kind of neglect. I could become a parody of caretaking, or worse, a sort of ghost-mother, out of whose bones the children arose, like mushrooms on a soft rotting log. When we at last bought our first television set, I found myself pausing beside David as, legs out, mouth open, he watched the gray screen. Both of us were nodding our heads to Mr. Rogers' comforting balm: You are special. How much I needed to hear that myself.

Our family did most of its growing up in a little house on an ivied street right outside Philadelphia, where we shared the peculiarly inter-locking lives of four busy people and one lone bathroom. As the children's range now took in front porches and sidewalks, then whole blocks, and at last the corner store and the elementary school a short walk away, we evolved a different kind of symbiosis. I could not hold them or pat bottoms so cavalierly, and they no longer fell asleep on my shoulder in the dark drive home from movies. As they launched themselves out, we learned to keep each other in our hearts, the kids down the block, me crosstown at the university. Sometimes I did not even know what they were eating.

When school days came, it seemed we were always madly prepar-ing for the next day, a fictitious time when we would be "caught up," in contrast to the uncontained hysteria of today. To sit on a lawn now seemed the rarest of luxuries. In its breathless busyness, the family was then like some gangly machine, a relentless contraption with cycles and epicycles set long ago and now lurching along according to its predeter-mined plan. Then again, in the maw of the machine, I struggled with fears of engulfment and contrariwise, fears of an unknown name, the anger of someone cast into the role of Prime Mover, without whose energy the universe would grind to a halt. I knew it must all make sense, but who had the space on the kitchen table to sit down and figure it out? Often it seemed to me I risked confusing my kids with their laundry, that I spent most of my "quality" time corraling t-shirts and socks, driving them downstairs toward the laundry room, herding the stock from one machine to another, culling the dried clothes into baskets that sat around until our naked desperation made me sort and fold the contents.

In some ways it got easier as the kids grew older: we were lucky, there were no big disasters. But it got more complicated too, because the very helplessness of the infant makes the mother's job clear. But an eight year old! Messy hair—who combs it? Mosquitoes—who sprays the Cutter's? Since when did I become the nag representing order and civilization? It seemed that without me they would have eaten standing in the kitchen, wandering through the house, and most disastrously, plopped in front of the TV set. When did I become the vigilante for such trivia—grease on the sofa, shoes in the living room, wet towels on the rug? In the school years, the issues about discipline and doing things right mounted and mounted, and what I saw demanded of me was even more strength and indefatigable practicality.

Often I felt dumber than dirt. Could Rebecca spend TWO nights in a row sleeping over at friends'? "Duh, I dunno, gee, I have to think about that, duh." How could a person who wrote about Wittgenstein have a brain that just folded in on itself like that, pummeled by an eight-year-old's torturous pleas? My guts say, keep her home, but why? Isn't this just a tad over-involved? Why not give in? Indeed, why not just let her drift from house to house on the block, eating white bread, wearing dirty borrowed clothes, while I . . . I . . . get a massage! Wade in the surf, high-heeled shoes tossed on beach! Not brave or selfish enough to head for the beach, instead, pestered and squinty-eyed, I was forced to think about our rules, think about reasons, make decisions, revise decisions, change my mind, hold fast, explain, insist, give up, clamp down.

Because of this persistent centrality, the mother is the object, the bull's eye, of her children's feelings, some of which could stun an ox. She is intensely loved, hated, seized, ignored. I was thunderstruck by the blunt distortions my children made of my motives, and then at other times struck by their keen accuracy. In writing this, it occurs to me that they might say the same of me.

The children grew like kudzu, changing so fast that I struggled always with mothering by hindsight, barely sizing up one situation as the child metamorphosed into another. I could not shake the anxiety that my faults were magnified in my children's character. As I watched them grow it seemed inescapable to me that their own struggles were the fruit of my inadequacies as a human being. At my worst, I found myself growing more anxious as a mother, my heart so helplessly tied to my children's growth that their blooming became what I demanded for my own survival as well. *Be happy or I grieve.* What a strange demand.

A teacher spoke to me with disgust curling off her lip about how angry and helpless she felt with David, whose work then did not match his brightness. I was so numb with guilt and hurt that I stumbled away from the school, leaving behind another meeting I was to attend, forgot my car and walked distractedly home. How hopelessly and fluently connected we were.

I can actually remember the first time I felt my anxiety melt, felt it lift a little and drift to one side, and I took a good breath. Charles had brought us out to Rose River in the Shenandoah Valley to backpack for the first time. Unimpressed, I had trudged along for the hike up, had dutifully organized our site, had worried about animals, had risen with Charles in the night's drizzle to string tarps over our bare sleeping bags. The next day I sat by a rocky creek watching David and Rebecca and Charles make great, Errol Flynn leaps across the boulders above. I should have been afraid for them, but instead I munched a chocolate bar and admired my childrens' easy grace, their springy legs, their banter with their father. The rains came again, harder, and we left early, hiking down the mountain in a downpour, only my feet dry in new boots, but the kids chirped along like hearty crickets, and my heart was luminously happy at the vision of the family I had seen.

I learned from this and other moments that my own pleasure in the children was vital, that my capacity to treasure them should not be taken for granted but had to be cultivated and treasured itself. I later learned a Yiddish word, *nachas,* the swelling heart a parent has for a child's accomplishments, an experience we did not label so well in my Anglo-Saxon family. I worried less and made more soup and lived for those moments when we were hanging around the dining room table running through our impressive recall of 101 Hamburger Jokes. To place a vase of feverfew gathered from the backyard in the center of this table was for me a way to celebrate our own gracious capacity to enjoy each other.

In taking on more celebration, I also put more limits on housework, not always with a clear conscience. The sacrifice of the mother is not only the guilty joke of psychiatry, but also the heart of the family system. The siren call of the mother is *Never Enough:* she can never do enough, plan enough, love enough, make enough cookies. Whatever she does, it is not soft enough, not tough enough. When I taught my children to use the washing machines themselves, some observers thought this move was smart, and others, no doubt seeing the wrinkled products, thought it an act of callous neglect. Eventually I had the wondrous privilege of giving up housework altogether. When I took the woman from the cleaning service around the house, to show her what had to be done, I noticed on my bedside table an empty glass with a comb and a walnut in it, just one of the little vignettes of inexplicable chaos that I was handing over to her, thankfully and with only a little embarrassment.

My transformation into the mother of adolescents was far more dramatic and demanding than I had anticipated: it seemed one day Rebecca was sunny and open and the next day she was dashing through the living room with a face preternaturally bright from rouge and slamming the door on her way out. The tiresome question was whether to let it go, confront her later, or get up to follow her out the door. On these dreary occasions, I hated many of the feelings I had: I hated it when someone was not home when they agreed to be home, I hated worrying about accidents and city psychopaths, I hated seeing college applications languishing under piles of records, I hated the worries about drugs and alcohol. So I learned to follow Rebecca out the door.

My worry for the adolescent David befitted his position as first child and fit too his growing differences from me, his lengthening and hardening into someone tall, utterly hip, mysteriously masculine. If Gary Cooper were a witty seventeen years old and read Walker Percy and delivered pizzas, that would be David then. I had a secret grief about David, a worry about his school work and a worry too that we were like two boats caught in a squall. Any fights I had with David came to no good, more moods, more misunderstanding. But I watched in amazement as he and Charles fought: stormy scenes with a fine sun coming out afterwards, the two of them closer than before. My identification with David was so complete I rejoiced to see him happy with his father, with only the barest whiff of jealously that he did not respond that way with me. When the Phillies headed toward the World Series, we all waxed rapturous in our family, but it was clear that the two tickets for the big game should go to David and Charles. It was for me the purest pleasure to stay home that afternoon, imagining the two of them making their way on the subway, swarming in with the happy crowds, sitting in the stands watching larger-than-life baseball.

The intensity in a home with adolescents is startling, and I am not speaking here merely of the jacked-up emotionality of adolescents or their ballyhooed rebellion, but of the kind of intensity that the parents themselves must bring to the experience: the capacity to be angry, to confront sexual issues—including one's own—and the capacity to fight for trust and respect. So when Rebecca asked me not to observe in her classroom on Parents' Day, at first I said weakly, "Well, if that's what you want," a little miffed, and then something clicked and I said, "Hell, no. I'm your mother! I'm interested in your classes." Not only was I coming but when I came in, *I would appreciate a gracious greeting from you*—which on that day she smilingly gave me, and I smiled back, and we had a fine time.

I wanted to be as powerful a mother as possible, vivid and stubborn and feisty if necessary, an opinionated debater, a force, a serious woman. In struggling to leave behind the Madonna-mother role, I was motivated not only by my own inner needs, but also by a longing that my children see me as a real person, and a belief that their development as well as mine depended on it. How else could they trust me with their confusion, unless I were strong?

It seemed to me that the person in my family to whom my own development mattered most was the teenaged Rebecca. I had always admired Rebecca with a mother's ready admiration for sweet youth itself: her peachy skin, her demure smile, her tender sympathies. But when Rebecca became convinced that her body was ugly, I found that it did no good to reassure her sweetly that she was attractive. Instead, I learned to fight with her, sometimes on the soapbox, ranting about Twiggy and Jane Fonda and Kim Chernin, sometimes yelling at her when she complained that a perfectly molded thigh was somehow "too big." Finally whenever she had doubts she would come to me, serious and trusting: "How do I look? Truthfully!" "You look wonderful. The truth." She took me in through fighting.

So the shift for me was from the accommodating, observing mother of infants to the kind of lively, interesting, kick-ass parenting that adolescents needed. The marriage became lively and interesting as well: in helping each child to resolve ambivalence about the other parent, we were forced to settle our own massive ambivalence as well. Charles and I never played half-court basketball with our children, but it seems that for both of us it was more like that: good tracking, swift darts and changes, sweat and worry, great jokes, heart-breaking misses, angry discussions about the rules.

Of course, you'd have to imagine that after a while the bleachers started to fill up with observers, people commenting on the players, speculating who was good stuff or not. Teachers, admissions officers, neighbors, owners of businesses, *your own friends!* Tillie Olsen's brilliant and raspy monologue, "I Stand Here Ironing," always touches my sympathy and my anger. It is a mother's sharp reaction to a telephone call to come for a meeting about her school child: *"I stand here ironing, and what you asked me moved tormented back and forth with the iron."* That's the kind of raw emotion a person feels before the world court of opinion, which every mother feels. The worry of the mother is not just that she feels judged too, although that happens inevitably, nor that she is disappointed in her children. The real worry of the mother is that the world court is so often wrong, so often smug, naming and sizing a child's soul so that the name itself is taken for the thing. Olsen's mother's plea to the school teacher is to help her daughter believe she is *"more than this dress on the ironing board, helpless before the iron."*

I knew I had matured as a mother when I could listen to other people's questioning opinions of my children without crumpling inside with guilt and helplessness. As the kids revealed more and more of who they were deciding to be—making decisions about politics and clothes and friends—it dawned on me that my own children were becoming some of the most interesting people that I knew.

I had my first out-of-body experience when sixteen-year-old Rebecca flew to Cyprus for a month. She was by all appearances a solo traveler, but the physical distance she traveled was so palpable that I leapt the space anyway, staying awake all that night arcing across the black Atlantic, getting a little fuzzy for the London stop-over, but reconstituting my presence well enough to make the final leg into Larnaca, my mother's intensity paralyzing any terrorists that might have been on board. When we got the call that she was safely in Nicosia, I was content that I had done my job well and settled down happily to my reading—Durrell's *Bitter Lemons,* histories of the Mediterranean, whatever would help me experience the new worlds of a faraway daughter.

This process has not been easy, this launching of my children into space. In the middle-class family, the infants enter the family as if coming into a room, which they then leave years later, by another door. It is this entering and exiting which has most vividly helped me measure the experience of mothering. I entered too, but do not exit. My fear in watching the last kid leave was that a door would close, and I did not know then, although I do know now, whether our lives would continue to carry such rich meaning for each other.

In May, 1987, I flew down to Austin to launch David off to Brazil for three months, as far into exotica as his earnings would take him. We had lunch with his Portuguese professor and wife, a Brazilian couple whose excitement about David's journey made my own anxiety at last tolerable. We ran errands and made his tiny apartment shipshape; inevitably I had to reorganize the furniture. I came across a lifesize cardboard figure of Indiana Jones in the grocery store, and the manager let me take it after I explained that my son was leaving for the Amazon. We propped it up amid the rearranged furniture, Indy giving a farewell wave of the whip. We talked a lot. I thought, as I often have, how kind, how funny, how artfully wise he is, how much I love his ironic dash and verve, his Thomas Jefferson poster falling off the wall, his cheap and tasteful cotton shirts. I made him promise to call us often in the beginning, knowing by now that all I need are some reports from the scene, some details of that particular reality, even if it is words about theft and diseases and political unrest, no matter, its incantation of a real place holds me securely.

Spring 1988 was Rebecca's last time at home before she too went off to college. That May, during my daily walks along the Wissahickon Creek I found myself admiring the dogs accompanying their walkers. How nice it would be, I imagined, to get a dog someday. Maybe in the next year. The dog and I would exercise together up and back Forbidden Drive to Valley Green. She would bound along enthusiastically the way young dogs do. I would be the conscientious owner, careful to train the dog thoroughly and consistently—a reader of dog books, a builder of dog runs, a groomer of dog coats.

It was with a sad shock that I realized the true source of these fancies. One day while reading a short story, I heard one fictional character argue with her fictional lover, "Pets are only child substitutes." At that moment I understood that my happy dog fantasy was a cover for the decidedly bittersweet departure of Rebecca at the end of the month.

Part of the fantasy was clearly to do a better job with the dog than I was sometimes able to do with Rebecca, who as the young daughter of an overworked doctoral student had too often bounded off to school with hair that needed cutting and socks that needed matching. But the truth is, I had to admit, I could never focus on haircuts and socks for long. They were not all that interesting. I groomed Rebecca in other ways. When she had a headache, I tranquilized her with hypnosis and together we made the pain shrink and disappear. I taught her how to write with good, blunt Anglo-Saxon words instead of long dopey Latin ones. Driving the long route across the river to her new school, we talked of Carol Gilligan. I fought the dark angel in her that would convince her to hate her own body. And always, I insisted that she take herself seriously.

I walked along Forbidden Drive thinking of all the wise and memorable things I still wanted to teach Rebecca: Travel abroad whenever you can. Learn the names of wildflowers. Watch out for the big trucks and tanks. Talk to your teachers. Did I tell her well enough how afraid I am of nuclear war? My neglect was so vast it made my teeth ache. But I did not remember to say it all, and we were caught in time's implacable grind. Our life together was measured then in weeks, and before us was a certain slant of light, an open door. *There was no shutting it.* My formal grief was bound only by the thrill of watching my last child step into the glare of a vast and uneasy world.

Epilogue

No one is born a mother. Women become mothers through the irrevocable physical and emotional changes of pregnancy, birth, and childrearing, as well as through the social, economic, and psychological changes that accompany motherhood. *Mother Journeys* has given readers an opportunity to glimpse into many feminist women's lives as they tell in words and images about the process, craft, poetry, pain, and wisdom of their mothering experiences. This book does what women have been doing since the world began: women tell each other stories, making it clear that each one finds her own meaning in this journey.

Mother Journeys also makes clear that motherhood is about the hard work of doing mothering, and that it has a constantly shifting set of meanings in women's lives. The meanings of motherhood are dynamic, changing with age and life stage, and women try to understand them as long as they live. Much mothering work is mental, not visible from the outside, and the strength for it comes from women's feeling, memory, judgment, and faith.

Part of mothering work is an effort to make sense out of a social ideal that women have engaged with since childhood, when girls play at being mommies. Feminist mothering involves coming up against social expectations for how to be a mother that lack appropriateness, truth, or even meaning for women. Each woman is left with the potentially creative task of resisting and transforming the socially dominant ideas of motherhood in order to fashion her own truth of the experience. We hope readers will draw inspiration from these stories and images, especially those who are engaged in the process.

No anthology covers everything, of course, and although this one is broad, feminist mothering is still broader. Five years in the making, this collection predates some of the current debates about mothering, although their seeds can be found here. We, the editors, would be pleased to have this book open up all kinds of debates—about cross-cultural adoption, for example, or class, or infertility, or interracial familial relations. We hope readers will examine their lives and find stories not told here, and tell them. We hope you will use *Mother Journeys* to begin your own exploration of the territory.

About the Contributors

About the Contributors

Linda P. Aaker is the mother of three children, Elizabeth, Sarah, and Michael. Sarah died 15^1/$_2$ days after birth. The anguish of Sarah's birth has brought its own gifts to Linda. In addition to her role as mother, Linda is an attorney who strives to find more time for writing.

Judith Arcana teaches literature and interdisciplinary Women's Studies in The Union Institute Graduate School, and writes both poems and prose. Her most recent book is *Grace Paley's Life Stories, A Literary Biography*. She wants very much to publish *Celebrating Nelly*, her book about a young girl starting to menstruate.

Martha Boesing, the founder of At the Foot of the Mountain, a professional women's theater in Minneapolis, began her forty-year theater career as an apprentice in summer stock when she was sixteen. Two college degrees and three children later, Martha has authored more than thirty scripts and librettos. Over the years she has given lectures, taught classes and workshops in playwriting and acting, and has been the subject of essays, articles, and books relating to her work as a leading feminist theater artist in the U.S. She has spent her career creating and directing plays which have a radical voice and an iconoclastic aesthetic.

Sheila Fay Braithwaite lives in Dallas, Texas, with her two children. She holds a B.A. in history and an M.Ed. as a reading specialist. She teaches English as a second language and writes for children and young adults. She has been in recovery for nine years.

Sarah Bruckner is the pseudonym of a writer who teaches English and Comparative Literature in a small Quaker college. She has published books and articles in the fields of eighteenth-century literature, gender studies, and the history of medicine.

Judith Lermer Crawley, born in Canada in 1945 to Jewish-Polish Holocaust survivors, is a teacher and self-taught photographer. Her work, which has been exhibited and published for more than a decade, focuses on personal experience within a social context. Her most recent exhibition, "One in five . . . ," concerns single parenting. She is also the Photography Coordinator of the Montreal Health Press.

Rita Dove is currently the Poet Laureate of the United States. A Pulitzer Prize-winning author, she has published five poetry collections, most recently *Grace Notes* (1989) and *Selected Poems* (1993), as well as a volume of short stories, the novel *Through the Ivory Gate* (1992), and the verse drama *The Darker Face of the Earth* (1994). Among her many honors are grants from the Guggenheim Foundation and the National Endowment for the Arts, a Mellon Fellowship at the National Humanities Center and the 1993 NAACP Award. Ms. Dove lives with her husband and daughter in Charlottesville, where she is Commonwealth Professor of English at the University of Virginia.

Shirley Nelson Garner is Professor of English and Director of the Center for Advanced Feminist Studies at the University of Minnesota, Twin Cities. She has written articles on Shakespeare and women writers and is a co-editor of *The (M)other Tongue: Essays in Feminist Psychoanalytic Interpretation* and of *Interpreting Women's Lives: Personal Narratives and Feminist Theory.*

Jewelle L. Gomez, originally from Boston, lived in New York City for twenty-two years before moving to San Francisco in 1993. She is the author of *Forty-Three Septembers,* a collection of essays, and *The Gilda Stories,* a novel (both from Firebrand Books), as well as two collections of poetry, *Flamingoes and Bears* and *The Lipstick Papers* (Grace Publications).

Marilyn Hacker is the author of eight books of poetry, including Lambda Literary Award-winning *Going Back to the River* (1990) and the verse novel *Love, Death and the Changing of the Seasons.* A new collection, *Winter Numbers,* as well as a *Selected Poems,* are forthcoming from Norton in the fall. The poems in this anthology are from *Taking Notice* (1980).

Kimiko Hahn was born in 1955 just outside New York City to a Japanese American mother and German American father. Her influences primarily come from her Asian background, including the study of classical Japanese literature, as well as American poetry, rock 'n' roll, political work and feminism. Poetry collections: *We Stand Our Ground* (IKON, 1988, with Sherman and Jackson), *Air Pocket* (Hanging Loose Press, 1989), *Earshot* (Hanging Loose Press, 1992), and *The Unbearable Heart* (forthcoming Kaya Press, 1995). Currently Assistant Professor of English at Queens College (CUNY), Hahn lives in New York City with her husband and their two daughters and is working on her fourth book of poetry, a collection of short fiction, and a series of children's stories.

Molly Hite is Professor of English at Cornell University. She is the author of *Ideas of Order in the Novels of Thomas Pynchon; The Other Side of the Story: Structures and Strategies of Contemporary Feminist Narrative;* and the novels *Class Porn* and *Breach of Immunity.* She is working on a study of Virginia Woolf and a new novel.

Linda Hogan is a Chickasaw poet, novelist, and essayist. She is the author of several books of poetry and a collection of short fiction. Her novel, *Mean Spirit,* published by Atheneum, received the Oklahoma Book Award for fiction in 1990, and the Mountains and Plains Booksellers Award. It was also one of three finalists for the Pulitzer in 1991. Her book, *Seeing Through the Sun,* received an American Book Award from the Before Columbus Foundation. *The Book of Medicines* (Coffee House Press, 1993) has received much critical attention. Hogan is the recipient of an NEA grant, a Guggenheim fellowship, Minnesota Arts Board Grant, Colorado Writers Fellowship, and the Five Civilized Tribes Museum Playwriting Award. She is a professor at the University of Colorado.

Nicole Hollander syndicates her cartoon strip *Sylvia,* which appears daily and weekly in over fifty newspapers. Thirteen collections of Sylvia cartoons have been published thus far, including *Tales from the Planet Sylvia* and *You Can't Take it with You, So Eat it Now.* Hollander has also illustrated children's books and co-authored a musical comedy, *Sylvia's Real Good Advice.*

Akasha (Gloria T.) Hull is Professor of Women's Studies and Literature at the University of California, Santa Cruz. Her numerous publications include *Color, Sex, and Poetry: Three Women Writers of the Harlem Renaissance* (1987) and *Healing Heart: Poems* (1989). She was selected as a summer 1994 Artist-in-Residence at the Djerassi program, Woodside, California.

Linnea Johnson is a poet, fiction writer, essayist, photographer, and papermaker; much of her written work concerns the politics of poetry, pedagogy, and abortion, and of the political construction of women, motherhood, and marriage. Off-springing from her too are a daughter, Morgan, and son, Jason, and her volume of poetry, *The Chicago Home.*

Maxine Kumin was born in 1925 in Philadelphia, and educated at Radcliffe College. She is the author of ten collections of poetry, most notably *Up Country,* which won the Pulitzer Prize in 1973, and *Looking for Luck,* which was awarded The Poet's Prize in 1993. She and her husband raise horses in central New Hampshire.

Molly Collins Layton, Ph.D., is a psychologist in private practice in Philadelphia. A contributing editor for *The Family Therapy Networker,* she is a member of the editorial board of *The Journal of Feminist Family Therapy.*

Jane Lazarre's books include *The Mother Knot, On Loving Men, Some Kind of Innocence, The Powers of Charlotte,* and *Worlds Beyond My Control.* Her short fiction and essays have been widely published and anthologized. She is an award-winning writer who also directs the

Writing Program at the Eugene Lang College of the New School for Social Research. She is currently working on a memoir about being a white mother of black sons to be published in 1995.

Sherry Lee graduated from the University of Minnesota with an individualized B.A. degree in creative writing, and feminist and multicultural studies. February 1994, Lee quit her University job and cashed in her small retirement fund so she could spend more time writing; she has been accepted for graduate school. Recently published articles include: "A Little Mixed Up," *COLORS,* July/August 1993; "Interview with Nikki Giovanni," *COLORS,* September/October 1993; "Poetic Justice, Giovanni Revisited," *Minnesota Daily,* February 1994; and a poem, "Civil War," *A Woman's Place,* June 1994.

Genny Lim is a Chinese-American native San Franciscan poet, performer, and playwright. She is a recipient of a Goldie from the *Bay Guardian* and an ImprovisAsians! Award from Asian ImprovArts for her performance poetry. Her performance pieces *XX, Winter Place,* and *La China Poblana* have incorporated Butoh, sculpture, live jazz music, and video. She is co-author of the American Book Award-winning *Island: Poetry and History of Chinese Immigrants on Angel Island, 1910-1940.*

Kathryn S. March earned a Ph.D. in Anthropology, Women's Studies, and Asian Studies at Cornell University after work with Sherpa and Tamang peoples in Nepal. She has been teaching those same subjects at Cornell ever since and shares both work and home with the same extraordinary partner and their two children.

Lynda Marín is the mother of Alexander, age eight, and Nina, age three. She has been teaching writing and literature a long time, most recently in the Women's Studies Program at the University of California, Santa Cruz, where she is also pursuing a Ph.D. in literature. Her dissertation is entitled "Remaking Mother: Maternal Discourse in Resistance Literatures of the Americas." She hopes that seeing this title in print will help to call forth the rest of the dissertation.

Diane McPherson was born and brought up in Maine, the eldest of eleven children. She decided early in childhood to be a writer, since above all else she loved reading and words. She went to college, majored in something completely impractical, married, divorced, married again, and had one child (a son). After a second divorce, McPherson entered Cornell's MFA program. She emerged eight years later with an MFA and a Ph.D. in Women's Literature. A lesbian, McPherson lives with her life partner and son in Ithaca, where she teaches and writes fiction. The story excerpt in "Making Do" is part of a book in progress, a collection of family stories called *Starting from Endwell*.

Greta Hofmann Nemiroff, mother to three adult children, holds the Joint Chair of Women's Studies at Carleton University and the University of Ottawa in Ottawa, Canada. She has given talks and workshops throughout North America as well as written and edited several books on feminism and education. She has been active in the women's movements of Quebec and Canada since 1968.

Sharon Olds was born in San Francisco and educated at Stanford University and Columbia University. Her books are *The Father, Satan Says, The Gold Cell,* and *The Dead and the Living,* which was the Lamont Poetry Selection and was awarded the National Book Critics Circle Award. Olds has received grants and fellowships from the National Endowment for the Arts and the Guggenheim Foundation. She lives in New York City, where she teaches in the Graduate Creative Writing Program at New York University and at the NYU writing workshop at Goldwater Hospital, a public hospital for the severely disabled. The workshop is now in its seventh year, and will be the community aspect of her Lila Acheson Wallace—Readers Digest Writers Award (1993–1996).

Alicia Ostriker has published seven volumes of poetry, most recently *Green Age*. She is also the author of *Stealing the Language: The Emergence of Women's Poetry in America,* and *Feminist Revision and the Bible*. Her newest book, *The Nakedness of the Fathers: Biblical Visions and Revisions,* combines poetry and prose.

Minnie Bruce Pratt is the author of *Crime Against Nature,* the 1989 Lamont Poetry Selection by the Academy of American Poets, and of two other volumes of poetry, *The Sound of One Fork* and *We Say We Love Each Other.* With Elly Bulkin and Barbara Smith, she co-edited *Yours in Struggle: Three Feminist Perspectives on Anti-Semitism and Racism.* Her most recent book is *Rebellion: Essays 1980–1991.*

Judy Remington, a Minneapolis writer, editor, and educator, is getting used to being middle-aged. She finds it has advantages (she feels freer) and disadvantages (her body is reluctant to take her where she now feels free to go), but she's secretly pleased that her grand-daughter calls her "Judy" rather than "Grandma."

Barbara Schapiro is an associate professor of English at Rhode Island College. She is the author of *The Romantic Mother: Narcissistic Patterns in Romantic Poetry* and, most recently, *Literature and the Rela- tional Self* (New York University Press, 1994). She is also co-editor with Lynne Layton of *Narcissism and the Text: Studies in Literature and the Psychology of the Self.*

Carolee Schneemann has exhibited her paintings and kinetic sculptures since the 1960s, while extending the boundaries of perfor- mance, video, and film. A 1993 recipient of a Guggenheim Fellowship, her work has been included in recent exhibitions in the U.S., France, and Italy. In 1992, *Cycladic Imprints (1988–1991),* a major kinetic project installation, was exhibited at the San Francisco Museum of Modern Art and the Contemporary Art Center in Cincinnati. Her books include *Parts of A Body House Book* (1972), *Cezanne, She Was a Great Painter* (1976), *ABC—We Print Anything in the Cards* (1977), *More Than Meat Joy: Complete Performance Works and Selected Writ- ings* (1979), and *Early & Recent Work* (1983).

Nancy Spero is an artist living and working in New York City.

Madelon Sprengnether teaches English and American litera- ture at the University of Minnesota. She has published a collection of poems, *The Normal Heart* (1981), and a book of personal essays, *Rivers, Stories, Houses, Dreams* (1983). Most recently she has co-edited a collection of women's travel writing, *The House on Via Gombito: Writing by North American Women Abroad* (1990), all New Rivers Press. She also writes on Freud and feminist theory. Her daughter Jessica is a smart, funny, generous, and beautiful age twenty-five.

Rose Stone is a writer who lives in Minneapolis.

Vera B. Williams is an educator and political activist as well as an award-winning writer and graphic artist. She is a graduate of Black Mountain College in North Carolina, where she studied with artists from the Bauhaus, and she helped to found an intentional community at Stony Point, New York. Her books for children include: *Three Days on a River in a Red Canoe; A Chair for My Mother; Something Special for Me; Music, Music for Everyone;* and *More, More, More Said the Baby.* She lives in New York City where she is an active participant in the work of the War Resisters League, and she is a frequent visiting writer/ artist at schools and at librarians' and teachers' conferences.

About the Editors

Angell Photography

Maureen T. Reddy is an associate professor of English and director of the Women's Studies Program at Rhode Island College. Her most recent book, *Crossing the Color Line: Race, Parenting, and Culture* (Rutgers University Press, 1994), blends memoir, literary analysis, and theory. She is now working on a collection of essays about learning and teaching anti-racism.

Photo by Donna Kelly

Martha Roth, a founding editor of *Hurricane Alice: A Feminist Quarterly,* is an essayist and fiction writer as well as co-editor (with Emilie Buchwald and Pamela R. Fletcher) of *Transforming a Rape Culture* (Milkweed Editions, 1993). She has also written the meditationals *A New Life* (Bantam, 1990); (with Karen Casey) *The Promise of a New Day* (Hazelden, 1983); and (with her late mother, Sylvia Silverman) *Family Feelings* (Bantam, 1989).

Photo by Donna Kelly

Amy Sheldon is a professor of linguistics and feminist studies at the University of Minnesota. She has published numerous articles on child and adult language acquisition. As a fellow at the Society for the Humanities at Cornell University, she engaged her linguistic research on children's conversations with feminist scholarship and she continues to write, teach, and lecture about language and gender. After the birth of her first child, she helped create the University of Minnesota's maternity and family leave policy.